Vasu Daryanani was educated as a Mechanical Engineer in Mumbai, India. He started his career working with Otis Elevator, Mumbai. He came to the UK and worked with ICI in their Petro-Chemical Industry in North East England. Thirty years ago he changed his profession and became an Independent Financial Adviser. He made a success of it and qualified as a Life Member of Million Dollar Round Table, an elite International Assurance Association. In twilight of his life he decided to tell all about his enjoyable life. It is quite an interesting and educational reading.

OH! WHAT A LOVELY LIFE

Vasu Daryanani

OH!
WHAT A LOVELY LIFE

Copyright © Vasu Daryanani

The right of Vasu Daryanani to be identified as author of this work has been asserted by his in accordance with section 77 and 78 of the Copyright, Designs and Patents Act 1988.

All rights reserved. No part of this publication may be reproduced, stored in a retrieval system, or transmitted in any form or by any means, electronic, mechanical, photocopying, recording, or otherwise, without the prior permission of the publishers.

Any person who commits any unauthorized act in relation to this publication may be liable to criminal prosecution and civil claims for damages.

A CIP catalogue record for this title is
available from the British Library.

ISBN 978 1 905609 73 4

www.austinmacauley.com

First Published (2009)
Austin & Macauley Publishers Ltd.
25 Canada Square
Canary Wharf
London
E14 5LB

Printed & Bound in Great Britain

DEDICATION

To

Jaik

My brother and a very good friend

ACKNOWLEDGEMENTS

During the year and a half while I have been busy with writing, I have been very moody. I sincerely thank my loving and lovely wife Sujatha who has been patient and has put up with swings in my moods.

I also thank my editor Annette Longman and co-ordinator Frances Moldschol. They have been very helpful and accommodating with my weakness in computing. My special thanks goes to David Calvert. He was my first contact with the publishers. I had a strong feeling during my first contact with him that he would help me get my manuscript to the right persons for publishing. My inner voice was right.

Finally my sincere and special thanks to my ramblers and long distance walker friends, with whom I have been walking every Sunday. They have been supportive and have given me moral support. I couldn't have carried on and finished my book without their genuine friendship.

Contents

	Preface by David Burrowes M.P	15
	Prologue	17
1.	Death of a Good and Honest Man	21
2.	Early Years	29
3.	Partition of India	41
4.	Life in India	51
5.	My Journey into the Unknown	87
6.	Lyke Wake Walk	105
7.	How I Located my Friend in a Foreign Land	117
8.	How I met the Pope and Shook Hands with Him	127
9.	Life in ICI	134
10.	Start of Married Life	154
11.	Troubled Waters	162
12.	How I Helped my Children to do Well in School Also how we Lost and Found our Children	173
13.	How I Raised Myself from Failure to Success	185
14.	Start of the New Life	197
15.	From North London to North India	206
16.	How I Became a Volunteer for Charity Shops	214
17.	How I Located Long Lost Friends	222
18.	Walking with Ramblers and Long Distance Walkers	232
19.	Discrimination? What Discrimination?	247
20.	Sickness/Illness/Accidents/Hospitalisation/ Homeopathy	262
	Epilogue	285
	Index	287

PREFACE

David Burrowes MP October 2008

Vasu Daryanani's *Oh! What A Lovely Life* is a tale of two countries. It is a tale of which we are all aware and which is becoming increasingly relevant in our globalised world. It is the story of a young Indian immigrant of the 1960s who discovers a new country and a new culture and seeks, unwittingly at first, to make it his own. Mr Daryanani does not lay claim to any particular distinction, but the very typicality of his situation will resonate with those who shared his experience in those early years of Commonwealth immigration and indeed with those who for the most part charitably received them.

Mr Daryanani's life is a successful example of distinctive integration. By that I mean the process whereby a person becomes fully British while maintaining all that is best of their culture of origin. In his own words he sought 'to integrate with British society and continue being an ambassador'. Modern Britain is immeasurably enriched by the fusion and interaction of the multitude of cultures which have arrived on our shores since the Second World War. Who is now surprised that the nation's favourite dish (and indeed mine too!) is curry? In this day and age we must all be 'cultural ambassadors'.

This story is also a testament to the generosity and acceptance of British society and to the opportunities which this country continues to provide for those willing to work hard. Mr Daryanani is very positive about the welcome he received and we can be justifiably proud that concurrently with the civil rights struggle in the United States our nation was at the forefront of encouraging and welcoming immigration from the West Indies and the Indian subcontinent. There were not many countries in the world at that time that would have provided a young Indian graduate with the opportunities to pursue successful life assurance and restauranteur businesses, buy several properties, and provide his family with a sound education and upbringing. Mr Daryanani does not gloss over the instances of discrimination he did encounter, but by countering them with that most British of characteristics – self-deprecating humour – he quickly won the respect and affection of the people he adopted.

However there is no room for complacency. Out society is faced with a fundamentalist threat which denies the possibility of peaceful co-operation of cultures and worldviews. We are confronted with the danger of the 'ghettoisation' of our cities. In the current climate more stories like this one need to be told, and I for one am glad that Mr Daryanani has taken it upon himself to share his illuminating life experiences with us.

In conclusion I can only echo Mr Daryanani's heartfelt plea: 'We in this world are brothers and sisters. Then why is there so much friction and dispute between brothers and sisters?' I warmly commend this book as a testimony to what tolerance, generosity of spirit, and love for one's brothers and sisters can achieve in the life of individuals and of the nation they collectively constitute.

Prologue

June 2007

I opened my eyes and looked around. I asked myself, 'where am I?' I was very confused. The surroundings were very unfamiliar to me. I had never seen them before. Suddenly it dawned on me. I was suspended in the air and was very near to the ceiling of a building. I couldn't understand it. I looked down. I found myself very high above the ground. I got scared and I shrieked but no voice came from my throat. I was trying to figure out what predicament I was in. Suddenly a figure stood beside me. The figure was also floating in the mid air. He was in dark attire. I couldn't see his face. The only feeling I got was that he had a smiling face.

"Hello." The figure wished me. He had a very pleasant voice as well. I liked him and his manners.

"Hello," I replied. "Who are you?"

"Don't you know me?"

"I can't see your face so I can't recognise you."

"You are not supposed to see my face."

"I wouldn't know who you are if I can't see your face."

He did not reply. He remained silent.

My brain was going 'clickety click'. I wanted answers to all kinds of questions I had in mind. 'Where am I? Why am I suspended in the air without any visible support? Who is he? Suddenly I had an idea. If he is not telling me who he is, at least he can help me in my thinking. He sounded very confident.

"Can you help me?"

"It depends."

"I want answers to a few questions. I am very confused."

"I can help you in any way I am allowed to."

"Where are we?"

"In a hospital."

"Why are we suspended in the air?"

"I am always suspended. In your case you are in the middle state."

"Middle state of what?"

"You are neither dead nor alive."

"Are you dead or alive?"

"Please don't be personal," he replied sharply. He was a bit upset.

"Sorry." Then I added, "I am still very confused. Can you remove my confusion?"

When I said sorry he realised that he was not being fair with me.

"OK. I shall help you to clarify your thinking. You look down."

I looked down. I noticed that there were six beds in a large hall.

"Can you see those six beds?"

"Yes."

"Do you notice that there are a few hospital staff doing something to the person on one of the beds?"

"Yes. They are very busy attaching some kind of gadgets and wires on him."

"That is you lying on the bed."

"What?" I shouted.

"Calm down, calm down." He pacified me. "If you get agitated that way, then I can't help you."

"What do you suggest I do? You say I am over there, when I know I am over here with you?"

He looked at me. I could feel that he was smiling.

Suddenly there was a whining noise coming from his person. He said, "You have to excuse me for a moment. I have an urgent call from my boss. I shall see you shortly, please don't go away." He was gone. I was very amused. Where can I go, if I don't know where I am?

He vanished. I had no choice but to wait for him and find out what actually was going on. While he was away, I looked down in the hospital hall. I noticed that the few hospital staff who were attaching gadgets to me on the bed, hurriedly left. They were called away urgently. After a while, I don't know how long, they came back, and so did the figure in black.

"I hope it went alright for you."

He was silent and became broody. I didn't ask him any more questions. I just waited for him to continue where he left off.

"Now I shall tell you everything and clear your mind. For your information I am Death. I had a message from my boss that you are to be collected. I came running to the hospital, I was watching the hospital staff to see if they were able to revive you or not. It seems they have been successful. They don't need me now. I shall go away and report to my boss. After a while you will also go and join your body lying on the bed in the hospital. I shall see you again sometime in the future. Hope it is not too soon. In the meantime please look after yourself."

"I always look after myself."

"I know. Few times I have been called to collect you, but it seems there is an invisible force which is protecting you from me."

"What kind of force are you talking about?"

"I don't know. I can only guess. I guess that blessings from your parents may have been the force."

"Thank you for your kind and wise words. Will I remember this meeting when I join my body?"

"If you concentrate hard enough, you will. Otherwise you will forget."

He vanished very quickly before I could ask him any more questions.

A nurse woke me up. I opened my eyes. I found myself on the hospital bed.

"Where am I?" I asked.

"You are in Wittington Hospital, London." The nurse replied.

"Were you dreaming, Mr Vasu?" The nurse enquired anxiously.

"Yes," I replied hesitantly. I didn't know what else to say.

"Why did you wake me up?"

"You kept repeating, 'Thank you my friend, thank you my friend'." The nurse replied.

Slowly I recollected the floating experience and the conversation with the figure in black. I realised that the figure in black was not nasty at all. He had told me, 'You should treat me like a friend. That way the life is much easier. I am just obeying orders from my boss'.

Chapter One

Death of a Good and Honest Man

I was born in the early morning of the first Friday of November 1934. I was told that it was a very cold morning and it was very foggy as well. At that time people used to burn coal for heating and cooking. People in Kolkata would get up very early and start the fire in the hearth. In India we had and still have a joint life concept. Three generations of a family would live in the same family house. You can well imagine that needs for hot water as well as for cooked food would be immense. The hearth would be used non-stop throughout the day. Due to cold mornings smoke from the coal fire wouldn't rise up, it just remained on the ground. That was the one which created fog and smog. Once the sun came, smoke and fog would disperse. The day would be beautiful. During British rule in India, Kolkata was the capital of India. The British built very good and durable buildings. Many of them are still standing. There is also a very grand building called Victoria memorial. Victoria memorial has a vast garden and quite a few statues of important persons in British Raj.

I was born premature, so I was told. There were a lot of activities around the house. At that time the birth of a child was generally held in the house. Hospitals were quite expensive. The family would need only the midwife. There would be so much help around the house. Joint family concept was very useful for these occasions. The Midwife would be called just before the child was due. Midwife would charge the family on an hourly basis. Family would therefore use the minimum of the midwife's services.

I came to know why I was born premature when I was in my secondary school. My parents used to live in Hyderabad in the province of Sind. Now the province of Sind is no more in India. The whole province of Sind went to Pakistan when during August

1947, India was partitioned into Pakistan and India.

Employment in Hyderabad was not very good. It is a small town. People from Sind are called Sindhi. Sindhi are generally businessmen. Many Sindhi businessmen had gone to bigger cities like Mumbai, Kolkata, Delhi, Chennai. Some businessmen had even ventured to other parts of the World. Initially they would carry on their shoulders general goods and go around houses. They would knock on house doors, show the housewife what they had to sell, and sale the articles. At that time housewives would be on their own, possibly with small children. It would be nice and interesting interlude for the housewife. She would view the household goods, do a bit of bargaining and then buy. These businessmen became very successful in their businesses. They became so successful that they had opened their shops in the high street of that city. These shops would grow bigger as the businessmen became more successful. Some of them would be so successful that they would have chains of shops. Chains of shops are to be supplied constantly with goods to sell. They would open a huge warehouse. The warehouse would supply the required goods to these shops. Businessmen would now need an office from where he could do the banking, import, export and of course control the running of the chains of stores.

These few successful businessmen would need staff to help them carry on running shops, offices and warehouses. They would prefer employees from their own family and friends. They would prefer Sindhi employees. Before they hire any person they would have a written contract with details of employment. Two very important points would be mentioned. One, that the employee has a contract of at least three years. The other point would be that employees would not be allowed to open similar business in the same area. The businessmen would give a very good salary and bonus to employees. The employee had to travel quite far. Of course employer would pay the travelling expenses. The employee had to be away from their family for at least three years. The high salary would attract people to work for these businesses which would be far away from their hometown. Many businesses were established in Africa, mainly in

West Africa. Generally the salary and bonus would be so much that the employee could afford to not only buy their own property in their hometown but also may start their own shop and business after finishing their three year contract. Hyderabad in Sind province was a very thriving town. Either these successful employers had their huge house or employees who had finished their three year contracts and had their own house and businesses. Many times three year contract would be extended. The common reason would be that the employer had not found a replacement yet. Or replacement may be on the way and would be due in a month or two.

My father Sitaldas got a similar job in Kolkata. His boss had a jewellery shop in New Market in Kolkata. New Market was very famous for shopping. The British community in India would shop only in New Market. Any businessman who had a shop in New Market was doing extremely well. My father finished his three year contract and returned back to Hyderabad. He had a good position in the shop. He got not only a good salary but a very good bonus. He had considerably increased the sales in the shop. He had brought lots of gifts for the family. His step-brothers and sisters were very surprised and glad that my father had brought gifts for them as well. The whole family was delighted not only to meet their dad but also getting so many presents and gifts.

Mother Jamna **Father Sitaldas**

Eldest Brother (Motiram) with our joint family

From right to left: we four brothers: Hiranand, Ramchand,: Jaik and Self

It so happened that his co-worker also came back about a month after my dad came back. After another month, another of his co-workers arrived. Three of them would regularly meet and discuss their future. It came out that three of them decided to start their own business. Individually none of them could start on their own. They decided that they should form a partnership and start a jewellery business in Kolkata. They felt that they knew how to run the business. They also knew many good customers. One of them had a contact with King of Nepal. These three so-called partners were spending so much time among themselves that they were ignoring their families. Once they had finalised and discussed the main points of the partnership, they thought that the sooner they start the better it would be. They went to the Railway station and bought three tickets for Kolkata. At that time train journey would take about 48 hours. They would have to change trains at Lahore and stay overnight in a hotel in Lahore.

They came back home after purchasing tickets and dropped a bombshell. My dad told my mother, "We three have formed a partnership and decided to open a jewellery shop in Kolkata. We have booked our tickets for Kolkata. We three will go to Kolkata next Monday." You could imagine how unhappy those three families would have been. I can only perceive, as I was not born yet.

Three of them went to Kolkata and started their new venture. They made contact with bankers, selected a shop, contacted their contacts to make them aware about their new venture. They worked very hard. They got a good order from King of Nepal. They contacted local factory owners. Factory owners would spend a lot of money on their children's weddings. Initially they had made beautiful jewellery set as a sample. This they would show to would be customers. Customers would give confirmed orders. With confirmed orders they would go to the jewellery maker and get them made. This they would then deliver to the customer. Of course they always used to have an initial deposit from the customer. All three decided that now they were established in the business, it was time to have a break and go and visit their families.

It was nearly three years they had been away. They decided to have a break in rotation. In this way at least two partners are on the spot. My dad was the first one to have a break. Our family was very pleased that my dad came first.

Now my dad was a businessman and had earned a good amount of money. The future looked very rosy indeed. He brought lots of gifts for the family as well as for his cousins and step-brothers and sisters. The break was only for a month. Every day he would hire a Victoria carriage and take the family for an outing. The family was very happy. They couldn't ask for more. It was now time for him to go back to Kolkata and relieve one of his partners.

He arrived in Kolkata and was surprised that none of the partners had come to receive him at the station. He hired a Victoria carriage and came to his room in Kolkata. Next morning he went to the shop. He got a shock of a lifetime. He was not allowed in the shop. He also noticed that the shop had a new board which did not mention his name at all. He saw his two partners in the shop. He tried to go in the shop. His partners asked him, "Who are you? We don't know you." They talked very rudely to him and even told their employees in the shop, "Don't let this person in the shop, he is a troublemaker." He went to his bank. He found that his name was not included in the bank account either. He realised that the business had only two partners, his name was not in the partnership. It suddenly dawned on him that he had lost everything. It happened so sudden that he had an attack of angina. At that time angina attack was known to be a killer. My mother in Hyderabad, Sind, came to know that my dad was not feeling well at all. At that time she was pregnant. I was in her tummy.

Immediately she decided to go to Kolkata. I am the youngest in the family. My mother had four sons and four daughters, all of them young. One can't imagine how she managed to start on the journey of 48 hours. She would change at Lahore, she was pregnant and she had eight young children. My mother told me that until she arrived in Kolkata and met my dad, she was praying all the time. She couldn't eat, drink or sleep throughout the journey.

One of my dad's loyal employees came to the station to receive my mother. He helped her and brought my mother and the children to the room where my dad was lying on the bed. The loyal employee told my mother what had happened and how it had happened. Apart from that he couldn't do anything. He wouldn't do much as he was scared of those two partners. My mother was in a new city, she did not know the language which was Bengali. She did not know anybody either. With a lot of difficulty she contacted the local doctor. With his help she contacted the hospital. The doctor from the hospital came and tried to relieve my dad's agony and get rid of the angina. There was no medicine for angina during 1934. Everyone would say, "We can't do anything." Indirectly saying, "He is as good as dead."

While writing this episode, I can't imagine and perceive how difficult the whole situation would have been for my mother. Her husband is on his death bed, eight young children are all over the place, doctors wanting their fees and she not having any money as my dad's bank account was siphoned away by those two partners. I felt like crying.

The year was 1934 when my dad died in Kolkata. My mother during that time suffered quite a lot. Immediately after that in the month of November 1934, I was born. It was a premature birth. My mother was very upset and under terrible stress. She didn't get a chance to call the midwife or anyone. I just came out of her womb without much difficulty.

My mother told me that she was in such a bad state that she couldn't care less if she lived or died. Also she couldn't care less if I lived or died. She would not look at me. Doctors said to her, 'The child is not going to live, he is very weak'. My mother just ignored me. She had believed what the doctors said, 'The child is very weak, he will not survive'. She just went into a trance. When she came out of the trance, she suddenly realised that she had lost her husband and she was going to lose the new born baby. A realisation came to her, 'Perhaps the soul of my dad had gone into my body'. Once she realised it she prayed to God, 'You have snatched away my husband, please don't take this child away from me, I beg of you'. Again she went into a trance. When she came out of the trance, I don't know after how long, family said to her, "He is alive – he is crying for milk." She immediately gave me milk. I stopped crying. After that she kissed and cuddled me. I don't remember it as I was too young to remember. While I am writing this I can imagine and feel the cuddle and kisses.

The following is my family tree. I have given only male members. They retain the same surname. All of them are Daryanani. If I give female members as well the family tree would be huge and very complicated. My uncle Mr Kishinchand very kindly had given me the information. He also mentioned which I never knew. He said that after Daryanomal, the family started calling them the Daryanani family. It seems in our society we have surnames generally ending with 'ani'. They would add 'ani' after their father/grandfather's name. That was how surnames were formed in our society who came from Sind province. It was a pity that during the 1947 partition of India the whole of Sind province was given to Pakistan. I have also ignored other male members related to other brothers of our grandfather. I have just mentioned the direct line.

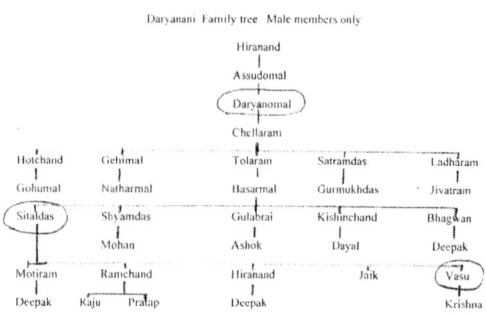

Daryanani Family Tree – Male Members Only

Chapter Two

Early Years

I was the youngest member in the family. Due to my premature birth I was very weak in health. Whatever virus or germs were in the atmosphere, I would get them. I would then be down with various kinds of illnesses. My mother told everyone not to give me a hard time. They would therefore look after me and made sure that I was having an easy life. I had a very sheltered life. In a way I was a spoiled child. At the drop of a hat I would go to elders and complain against whoever had given me some kind of trouble. I sort of felt that I had a power and a hold on the whole family. Many times no one in the family would play with me. They knew what would be the result. The result would be a complaint by me against them.

One day when I was four years old, a few school girls visited my three sisters. My mother was not at home. After a while my sisters and the school girls started playing with skipping rope. I wanted to play as well. My sisters said, "Vasu, you are too young to play with it."

"No, I want to play." But they wouldn't allow me to play.

"I shall tell mother when she comes," I replied.

"Okay. Skip with this rope." I started skipping. I didn't know how. I tripped and banged my head against kerb of the patio. The blood started pouring out. My sisters got very scared thinking that mother would be very angry with them. All three of them pacified me, gave me sweets and made me keep quiet. At that time people would use turmeric powder for that kind of wound. When my mother came, she saw turmeric powder on my forehead and asked, "What have you been doing with my little boy?" My sisters very timidly said, "Vasu wanted to skip, we told him that he is too young, but he was adamant. We allowed him to play. He tripped over and banged his forehead on the kerb." My mother said, "He is only a child. You are big enough to understand that it is dangerous for a child to play with a skipping rope." My mother asked me, "Does it hurt?" By that time the swelling had gone and possibly the turmeric powder had worked. I replied, "I am better now." I looked at my sisters. They were very pleased with my reply and smiled. My mother gave me a cuddle and said, "My poor baby." She loved me more than anyone else in the family. She felt that my father's soul was in me.

The time came when I had to join a school. My brother Jaik who was two years elder to me, had joined a nearby school. It was decided that I should join the same school. Jaik would be there to look after me. Jaik gave my name to the school for admission. The big day came. Jaik was ready to go to school. But I protested saying, "I don't want to go to school."

"Why not?"

"I am scared."

"I will be there in the school," Jaik said.

"You will be in your class, far away from me."

"I shall tell your teacher to look after you."

But still I was not convinced. I cried, "I don't want to go to school."

Possibly I had such a sheltered and easy life that I didn't want to let go of my easy life.

Jaik went to the school and told my would be teacher, "My brother Vasu is not coming to school. He is frightened."

"You bring your brother Vasu tomorrow. Tell him that if he doesn't come I shall send four boys who will carry him from home to school. They will carry him through the high street for everyone to see that he is being carried away. All the people will laugh at him."

Jaik came home and told me what my teacher had said. He and family members thought that I would go with him from that next day onwards. I didn't go with Jaik the next day. I thought that was the end of it. Suddenly four strong boys arrived at our house and called for me. My mother told them where I was. They came to me and grabbed me. Each one of them grabbed either arm or leg and carried me to the school. They had to pass through the high street, as school was in the High Street. I cried and kicked but no one paid any attention to me. At the end of the day teacher asked me, "Do you want to go home on your own or shall they carry you back to your house?" In the meantime Jaik also came to our class. He held my hand very lovingly. We then came back home. My teacher was very considerate with me. I liked him. I liked the school as well. I was quite regular after that. Once I remember that I was not feeling too good. I had over eaten the day before. I thought that I could miss the school. I had a very valid reason. Jaik threatened me, "If you don't come with me, I shall tell your teacher. He will send four boys. They will carry you through the High Street. People will laugh at you." I very meekly went with him. I felt fine as soon as I saw my school friends. I was glad that I went to school. At home I wouldn't have anyone to play with. After that I did not miss a single day of the schooling.

It was the time when all the children would play in the streets. The play would be disorganised. We would do whatever we fancied. One organisation was formed to guide children and adults to play in an organised way and regularly. It was called Rashtriya Swamsevak Sangh, (R.S.S.). Its translation in English is the National Voluntary Organisation. Parents were very happy that children and adults were learning new skills and discipline and not making so much noise in the streets. Every evening for one hour we would go to an appointed place. We used to go to an old fort and play games under the guidance of our leaders. We would be there for one hour. The first half an hour we would play various Indian games. The next fifteen minutes we would listen to a talk by an elder. Generally the talk would be stories about our old culture, about our past history and its main characters who had shaped our India. Finally the last fifteen minutes we would pray to our sacred flag. I really liked that organisation. It taught me discipline and also gave so much information about our country, culture and people who shaped our history.

It was 1942. There was talk going on between the British Government and the Indian leaders. The Indian leaders were demanding independence from the British Government. They had innumerable meetings either in India or London. They couldn't decide on any agreement. In the meantime the tension between two religious groups was increasing. Hindus were in the majority. Muslims were in majority in certain regions. The main stumbling block was, 'Hindus are in the majority. Muslim are in the minority. If the British handed over the power to Hindu leaders, Muslims would be at a very big disadvantage'. Hindus and Muslim leaders tried to get together, but they would not agree to any solution. It was then talked about 'Two Nation Theory'. Religious tension increased substantially all over India. The province of Sind was very peaceful before. It had Muslims majority. But Hindus and Muslim had lived side by side without any problem at all. Now we had undercurrents between the two groups. Over a small point both groups would fight each other. During weddings there would be a wedding procession passing through the High Street. The procession would have groups of musicians playing various kinds of musical instruments. It would be a noisy affair. In protest the other party would throw stones and missiles at them. Then there would be riots. These riots became very frequent affairs. The situation was getting tense and getting worse day by day.

One evening as usual, we went to the fort to play our games. It was quite a windy evening. After about fifteen minutes we saw a large group approaching towards us and shouting, "Allah O Akbar." We realised they were Muslim. All of them had sticks, baseball bats, cricket bats, etc. We didn't know what to do. Our leader was also confused. Suddenly it became very windy, perhaps a gale force. Wind started churning the dirt and sand. It got very dark as well. We couldn't see the approaching group, neither could they see us. But they kept on getting nearer. We ran wherever we could. I found a shelter against the fort wall. There I was standing very frightened and expecting one of the Muslims would find me and beat me up. I was lucky. It was very dark indeed. I could now hear children crying.

They were being beaten up. The Muslim group kept on shouting 'Allah O Akbar'. Many of the children had been lucky like me. It was the most frightening time I had. Suddenly the Muslim group left. We all came out of hiding. The wind had subsided. We could see that many children had been badly hurt. Our leader was in a very bad state. In the fort there were three other groups playing. One group had my brother Hiranand as their leader. The Muslim group after attacking us had gone ahead and attacked the group who had my brother Hiranand as their leader. During that attack the Muslim group did the maximum damage. The reason was that my brother's group did not run away, they faced them. It was an unfair fight. They didn't have anything to fight with. My brother was badly hurt. There was no 999 service then. They hired a few Victorian carriages and took the injured to the local hospital.

My leader was very badly beaten. He couldn't survive. He died in the hospital on the third day. My brother Hiranand was also badly beaten. He was in a coma for six days. Doctors couldn't find any medicines which could help my brother. Doctor said, "He has an internal haemorrhage. The blood is flooding his brain. We haven't got any medicine for it." Doctors consulted their chief. The chief, after examining my brother said, "He will not survive. The only way he may survive is if we can get the wonder drug which has been recently discovered."

"What is it and where do we get it?"

"It is called Penicillin. But I am afraid it is impossible to get it. It is not available to Indian civilians. Only to British people."

The local chief of RSS came and had a meeting with the Chief Surgeon in the hospital.

"Please arrange to get the medicine so that our man can survive."

"In Karachi there is a British Army centre. They keep the supply of it, they have used it very successfully. They will not give it to you. I suggest that you go to the Collector and convince him. He will then give you a letter to release the medicine for Indian civilian use." That evening the local leader of RSS approached the Collector.

He convinced him and got a letter for the Chief of Army Staff in Karachi. With the letter in his hand he and his two assistants caught the night train to Karachi. Karachi is about 120 miles away from Hyderabad. It was a life and death situation. "Don't delay," warned the Chief Surgeon, "or he could die." The local chief of RSS went to Karachi, met the Chief of Staff of the British Army and rushed back to hospital with the drug. At that time they used to call it the Wonder Drug.

The Chief Surgeon used the medicine. My mother prayed day and night while my brother was in the coma. It was definitely a wonder drug. My brother came out of the coma on the third day after they injected him. He very faintly called, "Mama." My mother was near his bed and replied, "Yes, son, I am here." After that slowly and gradually he came out of the coma and recovered. We brought him home. The Chief Surgeon said,

"Do not let him be angry, and avoid all kinds of excitement for him. His brain is very weak. It will not withstand any kind of excitement at all." I am very happy to write that he survived that ordeal. He is still alive and kicking. He is now eighty years old. There doesn't seem to be any bad effect of the bashing on his head he had. I remember during those days, sometime he would say something which may not make any sense to my mother, my mother would say, "You are not cured yet, you still have the effect of the beating you had on your head." My brother would laugh and would drop the subject he was talking about.

My brother Hiranand was very health conscious. He would go to a gym and do some physical exercise. Also he would have a bout or two of boxing. He had brought a sandbag home which he used as a punching bag. He thought that it would be a good idea that his brother Jaik and I should also punch the sandbag. We three of us would punch the bag and make our fists strong. Every day a boy used to deliver milk to our house. One day my brother Hiranand asked this boy, "Would you like to box with my brother? He is younger than you are, but he will beat you." It seemed that my brother thought that by punching the sandbag I had made my fists stronger and could fight with this older boy. The milk boy said, "Yes, I will box with him." My brother was the referee. The fight started. I gave him quite a few hard blows. It seemed the milk boy was losing. My brother had full faith in me, that had given me confidence. Suddenly the boy head butted me. Blood started coming out of my lower lip. My brother Hiranand got very angry and hit the milk boy and said, "I told you to box, not head butt."

The poor boy cried and said, "I shall tell my dad about it, you should fight with him and not with me. I am just a small boy." The next day his dad came and complained about it. My brother Hiranand narrated the whole episode and then apologised to the milkman.

My brother had a good rest at home and got much better. The Chief Surgeon allowed him to go to work. At that time there was a great demand from businessmen who had established businesses in big cities. These businessmen had an office in Hyderabad, Sind. My brother went to their office for a job. My brother said, "I have heard that you have business in Kolkata. My elder brother Ramchand is also in Kolkata. I would like to work in your company in Kolkata." After discussing the salary and various employment issues they hired him. He is quite close to Jaik and I. He said, "Let me establish myself. During your next school holidays you both could visit Kolkata." Jaik and I were very excited at the prospect of going on a holiday to a big city like Kolkata. As you know Kolkata used to be the capital of India during British Raj.

It was 1945. Summer was very hot. We were lucky that Hyderabad Sind was built on a hill. Due to that, evenings and nights were very pleasant. School holidays always used to fall during summer. Out of the blue we got a letter from Hiranand in Kolkata which said, 'My boss' son is joining the business in Kolkata. He is coming next month. I have requested my boss to arrange for his son to bring you safely here with him'. Jaik and I were delighted, or should I say very excited. Immediately my mother contacted the son of the boss and wanted to know if he could take Jaik and I to Kolkata. He had also received a letter from his dad about the same.

When he booked his train tickets, he booked ours as well. Luckily it was school holidays. We didn't have to miss any of our classes.

The big day of our departure came. We were anxiously waiting for it. Our mother had bought new attire for us. Our shoes would make squeaking noises to indicate that they were new. We were very proud of our squeaking shoes. Mother also packed lots of home made sweets and savouries so that we were well fed during our train journey. It was a very long train journey. The train would take us from Hyderabad to Lahore. It seemed we had to stay overnight in Lahore and catch a morning train for Kolkata. The following morning when we went to the railway station to catch the train, we found out that the train was delayed by six hours. The boss' son had been there before, he knew the city. He took us to the High Street for something to eat. He knew that the buttermilk of Lahore is very famous. We went to a restaurant. He ordered three glasses of buttermilk. It was delicious, before this we had never tasted anything so good. We had our food and it was time to go to the station to catch our train. We travelled in real luxury, we travelled in first class. That was equally exciting. Jaik and I were very pleased with all the arrangements.

At Kolkata station we were met by one of the employees. The station was very busy, the train terminated there. Everyone was rushing around. Without much mishap we arrived. It was Sunday. The shop was closed so all employees had a holiday. Our brother Hiranand was waiting for us. He is a strong man. He picked both of us up and cuddled us. He was so happy to see his two kid brothers.

Next morning Hiranand took us to our other brother Ramchand. Ramchand used to work with another firm and was staying in another house. He had been in Kolkata for the last two and a half years. Hiranand briefed us and told us, "Both of you go and explore the city. You can come to this shop whenever you want. But make sure you come back by 1.00pm. At 1.00 we three of us can go for lunch." It was scary being in such a big city. We felt like *Alice In Wonderland*. The city was not as crowded and populated as it is nowadays. Now people live on the pavement, and have a bath getting the water from a nearby broken hydrant. There is too much poverty now. Mother Theresa couldn't bear to see the hardship of the people. She opened her centre and tried to help as many people as she could. About 10 years ago Hollywood made a movie called, *City Of Joy*. It showed how people live in slums, how they are exploited and how bad their health was in the slum. In spite of poverty all the slum dwellers had stuck together and helped each other and made it *City Of Joy*. That was the only positive point in the movie, the rest was very sad and morbid.

Our two brothers Hiranand and Ramchand gave us a really good time. As soon as Sunday came they would take us to various places of interest. Also they would take us to movies. Both of them were fond of Hollywood movies. I remember that they took us to see a movie called *Johnny Angel*. Both of them liked an actor called George Raft. He was in this film. We did not understand the film at all. I only remember the name of the film and the actor. I had a chance to see that film again when they recently showed it on British TV. Then I understood what the film was about.

Our school holidays were ending shortly. It seemed we had to come back on our own. It was not that bad. We had done the journey, so we knew exactly what to expect. Looking back I would confidently say that our two brothers really looked after us, gave us a very good time. We arrived back safely to our hometown. I remember for weeks I would talk quite a lot about our fabulous trip to Kolkata. My school mates were very impressed and jealous of my long and enjoyable holiday.

The long trip to Kolkata did a lot of good to my ego as well as to my self confidence. Suddenly I felt that I had grown up. I was only 11 years old then. Before this long holiday, I was not keeping in good health. I would feel faint as soon as I did a bit of running around while playing games in school. I would sweat and feel faint. I would then sit for a while till I felt better. Perhaps the change of weather did some good to my health. Now I wouldn't feel faint as I used to. Self confidence gave me a boost whereby I wanted to help my mother in whatever way I could. She suggested that I could go shopping early morning and bring back meat, fruit, vegetables, etc. The main market was about a mile away. My morning routine used to be to get up early, go for shopping, come back, have a breakfast and walk to school. The school was also about a mile away but in the opposite direction. I felt really great that now I had become a useful member of the family. It had a downside. The family members would tease me and jokingly blame me for smelly fish and rotten fruit and vegetables. Initially I used to feel hurt. After some time I realised that they were teasing me, and I learned how to handle the criticism.

As I mentioned before every evening I used to play games under the guidance of the National Voluntary Organisation. We had a boy called Lakhi. He was never regular. My leader suggested that every evening before I arrive at the ground to play, I should call on Lakhi and bring him with me. He used to live on the way to the ground. It was better than walking alone. Lakhi also liked the company. We became quite good friends. I shall narrate later in Chapter 17, how and where I met him again, after nearly sixty years.

One evening I went to his house and knocked on the door. The family knew me. As soon as they saw my face they called Lakhi to come down. It so happened that while I was waiting for him at his doorstep, I felt some kind of tug at my left leg. I thought that a child was tugging to attract my attention. I looked down. I was horrified! A street dog had just bitten me and was running away. Lakhi came and I told him what had happened. He said, "That dog keeps biting people. It should be caught and destroyed. You go to a hospital and get some medicines." I went to the hospital. The doctor asked me, "Was the dog foaming at his mouth?"

"I didn't see it, he was running away."

"Tell your friend to keep an eye on the dog. If it is foaming or has died, you come very quickly and we will give you fourteen injections." Lakhi never saw the dog again. We assumed that he had died. The Doctor did not want to wait longer and said, "Today I shall give you one injection in your tummy. Everyday you come so that you finish the fourteen injection course." These injections were making my life very miserable. I couldn't walk straight. I had to walk a bit bent due to pain in my stomach. Finally I finished the course of fourteen injections. These injections gave me a very high temperature. I was in bed for a week, but I was glad that I survived without much bad effect from the dog bite.

Our school holidays and Sundays used to be good fun. We had quite a few cousins who would visit us or we would visit them. It so happened that in the family, schoolbooks were bought only once. They would be handed down to either our cousins or to us. I being the youngest, would get the books in a torn condition, after everybody else had used them. I didn't mind it. On the contrary, I had so many people to get help with in understanding the subjects. All of them had finished with books and passed their examinations. Our family members loved reading history. History had so many stories to tell. Mathematics was another subject which we all liked. At the end of the school year, books would be handed over to the younger members. We would then start reading these books and trying to do mathematics. We would get a lot of guidance from the elder members of the family. It would so happen that before the next year started we would know quite a lot about the subjects. Most of us did very well in studies.

My mother had full faith in home made tonic. Anyone in the family whose health had run down, would get a home made tonic made by my mother. What was the healthy drink? Strange enough I still drink it as and when I feel run down. The drink consisted of egg yolk and a spoonful of honey which is mixed with a cup of hot milk. She would even add a tablespoonful of brandy. It used to do wonders. Winter in Hyderabad was very cold as it was built on a hill. We all used to love the drink, it is so tasty. Come to think of it perhaps I have been drinking brandy from such a young age that I do not get so drunk as to lose sense, if I drink brandy. I found this out when I had quite a few shots of brandy during my visit to the Royal Festival Hall in 1964. I shall give full information later.

I remember that winter was very severe, there was no central heating as we have here now. There would be a fire in the middle of the huge dining room. We all would sit around it. In the middle my mother would be cooking an evening meal. The fire would serve both purposes. It would be used for cooking as well as heating. After the meal, we would go to our huge sitting room. There would be another fire burning. Again we would sit around it and listen to a book read by our eldest brother Motiram. If it was a book in Sindhi, we would all understand. Motiram loved cowboy books by Max Brand and Clarence E Mulford, who wrote *Hopalong Cassidy* books. He would read in English, then translate into Sindhi to tell us what it meant.

My mother used to have a hammock in the sitting room. Her relaxation was just sitting in the hammock and swinging it. This hammock was very popular with her women friends. Many of them would come and meet my mother. All of them would sit in the hammock. They would be talking and gossiping together for hours. I can definitely say I have very happy memories of my childhood.

CHAPTER THREE

Partition of India

The word 'partition' doesn't indicate sadness. Office rooms are partitioned to make two or more rooms out of one big room. But when a partition is constructed in a house to make sure certain people in the family do not enter the room, then it could be a sad situation. Suddenly one large joint family living in a big house have decided to live separately. Then they have no choice but to use partitions to make sure that they are living separately. Any time anyone crosses the partitioned area, there could be very strong arguments. Some times strong arguments can turn into a blood bath. This is what happens when there is a huge gulf between a family. The whole family suffers. But when a country is partitioned and two countries are formed side by side, there is a lot of unhappiness among both countries. Even though borders of countries are discussed and agreed, there are always border disputes. People in the two neighbouring countries harbour a grudge against each other. Constantly they are at each other's throats. Lots of innocent people get caught up in various disputes. Innocent people die, especially helpless ones like children, women and old people.

When India was partitioned I was 13 years old. I didn't know much about politics and did not understand why it had happened. On asking elders about why it had happened I got a reply that the country is being divided. The part of the country with Muslim majority was given to Muslims. That country would be called Pakistan. I did not feel that was bad. I thought that it was a good idea that it was arranged on that basis. Constantly Muslims used to attack Hindu area of our city. There used to be so much disturbance of peace in the city and I felt that these attacks would stop, once Pakistan was agreed and formed. Once a Muslim group attacked school children while the children were playing games. I was among those school children. This is described in the previous chapter. A few years after that incident I came to know why Muslims attacked school children. The RSS was trying to infuse unity among Hindu society. The RSS became so successful that members would resist these Muslim attacks. Local Muslims did not like it. All these years Muslims had a field day. They could do anything to Hindu society. Hindu society would accept it meekly. Muslims would even attack Hindu families: rob them, and carry away the family's women and children. Women and children would be forcibly converted to Islam. Due to resistance from the RSS members these attacks and atrocities were reduced considerably.

15th August 1947 was the day India was partitioned. Before that date, our leaders did not agree to the partition of India. Finally our leaders agreed to the partition. Our leaders realised that the public would not agree to the partition. The famous Mahatma Gandhi had said, 'the partition will be formed over my dead body'. We all believed him. But now it was a problem for leaders on how to approach the public 'on partition of India'. They found a very good solution. They told the public, "We Hindus and Muslims are brothers. We are agreeing to the partition just to get rid of the British. When they go we will join and make it one country again. So you leave your home and property now. Hindus go to India and Muslims to Pakistan. After a short while you can come back to your own houses." We, the public, believed them and left everything we owned and went to India.

We had lots of possessions. We had a five bedroom house. My mother had just refurbished and renovated the property. We had plenty of rooms. I remember we had a huge dining table with a marble top. The family would have a meal together. My mother's name is Jamna, named the house as 'Jamna Nivas' (House of Jamna). We believed our leaders and were planning to leave all our possessions and the house behind. The possessions were too many. We could not accommodate all of them into cupboards and lock the cupboards. We decided that articles which could not be accommodated in cupboards should be sold. Jaik and I had an idea.

Why not go to the High Street, display articles on the footpath and sell them cheap. Cash earned in that way would be useful for the family.

The idea was good. But it didn't work the way we expected. Initially we earned some money by getting rid of articles cheaply. Hindus would not buy our articles, they were in the same situation. We would get Muslim customers only. One morning one big person came and took away a few articles. When Jaik asked him for money, he produced a knife and said, "I will not give you any money, do whatever you want. If you make a scene, I shall cut you up." We both got very frightened. When we told this to mother, she said, "You both are more precious than money, don't go out, we shall just leave articles in the house."

All the time we were hoping that we would come back after a few months and claim our possessions. But it didn't happen that way. Suddenly there was an ugly turn in the situation. We heard that a train had arrived at the railway station and it was full of dead bodies. Not a single person was alive. That was the time our elders wanted to go to leaders and find out what was actually happening. These leaders made themselves so scarce that no one could find them. The whole Hindu society then realised that they had been left in the lurch. Every day we would hear horrible and frightening news about the killing and murdering of Hindus. Hindus had no choice but to leave the country as quick as possible. So many people wanted to leave the city that it was impossible to get any train tickets. Many families had no adult members. Most of the adult male members had gone away on three year contract jobs. The turn in the situation happened so quick that they had no time to come back and help their families. My mother was very worried and kept on praying to God.

The King of Jodhpur had his private railway line. He announced, "Any Hindu who wants to leave for India can use the train free of charge." It was very good news for all of us. We found out that you had to have a ticket before you could board the train. The ticket was to be issued free, on a first come first served basis.

There were so many people leaving the city, it was impossible to get tickets. There was a panic in the city. Our family was lucky that my brother Hiranand had just returned from Kolkata after he finished his three year contract. He tried his best and contacted the right people to get train tickets. My mother was very happy and relieved that he got tickets for all of us. There was a rumour that having a ticket was no guarantee to travel on the train. Muslim groups were waiting at the station and making sure that no one used the train. Luckily the rumour was false. But there was a chance that it could happen. We were therefore advised that the train would leave in the middle of the night. No one should make any noise. Otherwise a Muslim group may come and attack passengers. We were told to take with us not more than 10 pounds luggage per person and no more. The idea was that less the possessions you had the more passengers could use the train. Everyone understood and stuck to that rule.

The day came. My mother carefully filled all the cupboards in the house. My mother had arranged lots of fitted cupboards around the house when the house was refurbished and renovated. She locked all the cupboards. Whatever we couldn't fit into cupboards were left on the beds. Only a very few very important articles we carried with us. Very quietly we came to the station. There were thousands of passengers. My mother was disheartened. She asked my brother Hiranand, "How can we fight through this crowd to grab a seat in the train?" Hiranand tried his best to acquire seats in the train. It seemed seats were impossible to get. The only choice was to get just a space where you could sit or stand. Organisers first allowed women and children inside the carriage. The problem was where would men sit? Suddenly men started climbing the train and sat on the roof of the train. Hiranand, Jaik and I thought that perhaps we three should sit on the roof of the train. My mother and three sisters were inside the carriage. They gently pushed other passengers so that we three also could come in the carriage. The carriage was full of luggage. There was very little space to sit. But very silently and quietly everyone co-operated and obliged. The luggage was nearly touching the ceiling of the carriage. I decided that instead of standing around I could climb the luggage heap and sit on top of it. There was no space for sitting. The only way I could stay on top of the heap was lie spread-eagled on the heap.

Everyone was very quiet but very anxious to know when the train was going to start. As long as we were in Hyderabad, Sind, we were in Pakistan. The whole province of Sind was now part of Pakistan. We all were holding our breath. Finally the train moved very silently and slowly. They again told everyone not to make any sound till the train crossed the border of Pakistan. Frequently women and children would whisper, "Have we crossed the border yet?"

"Not yet." Would be the answer. I don't remember how long it took. The time was passing very slowly. Everyone was on edge. All the women were praying silently. Finally someone said, "We have crossed the border. Now we are in India." Everyone talked and laughed at the same time. Everyone shouted. It was more of a roar than a shout. Everyone congratulated each other. The train also gathered speed and the driver made his engine whistle a few times.

The King of Jodhpur had arranged his officials to receive the train. In a very organised way they brought us to a huge marquee. There were four huge marquees. We were in the marquee where only families with young children could stay. My brother Hiranand was nineteen years old then. He had to stay in another marquee where adult men could stay. Every now and then he would come and meet us to see if we needed any help in any way. We were still hoping that after a while we would go back to our town and to our house.

Time went on and on and there was no sign of any government official who could tell us when we could go back to our own house. We stayed in the marquee for nearly a month. The situation was getting worse. In our house and in our town, we had everything we needed. But here in camp, we had nothing at all. Luckily my brother Ramchand used to work in Kolkata. My mother wrote a letter to him to take us away from the camp and establish us in a proper house. Kolkata was a very expensive city. It was very difficult to get rented accommodation in a short time. He arranged our accommodation in Banaras. There was an old-fashioned palace in Banaras. The King of Darbhanga had died, leaving the palace unoccupied. Our family, with other three families, shared the accommodation. It was a very spacious palace. The construction was of large slabs of stone. Due to that it was always cold. It was very pleasant in summer, nice and cold. It was a pleasure coming back home from the heat outside. But in winter it used to be very cold.

The province where we used to live was called Sind. The whole province went to Pakistan. Due to that we Sindhis had no place or province of our own. We were strangers in India. All other Indians would treat us like strangers. They would tell us to go back where we came from. They never realised that we could not go back. Muslims had killed lots of Hindus in Sind. It was a real 'ethnic cleansing'. In Sind not many Hindus are left now. They had either ran away like we did, or were converted to Islam or butchered.

In Banaras we were treated like outsiders. Locals would be very aggressive towards us. We couldn't identify with them, neither they with us. Local government was told to make provision for Hindus from Pakistan. They put a label on us. They called us 'displaced persons'. It was a very trying time for all of us who had come from Sind. There was no organisation which could help in any way, either with living accommodation or with financially. People from Sind generally form a business community. They started their own businesses. Local people didn't like it. They said, "These outsiders are encroaching on our businesses'. Hindu women generally have gold ornaments. A few families sold their ornaments. With that money they went into business in a small way. Some of them started businesses on footpaths selling small general items like toiletries etc. It so happened that the tension was increasing among locals. Some places locals attacked our businesses and robbed us. Looking back I would say that the situation was very grim. In addition, we had lost everything. We didn't have much money to lean on. There was no organisation who could help us. Of course there were lots of meetings and discussions being held. It looked like they were being held to show that something was being done.

Now I can realise how huge the problem was for the Indian government. To cater for millions and millions of people is not a joke. All these people needed lots of help in all aspects. As the time went on, many adult men who had gone for three year contract jobs arranged to be released so that they could come and join their families and help them.

It was the last day of January 1948. Early morning there was a commotion outside in the street. We didn't understand what they were saying and why they were crying. There was so much noise and crying that Jaik and I came down into the street. Then we knew what were they saying. "Oh! Our Bapu is dead." Generally Bapu is a father. We were puzzled why so many people had lost their father at the same time. Newspapers were selling like hot cakes. The headline in the paper said, 'Mahatma Gandhi is murdered'. It was shocking news for the whole country. At that time I was only fourteen years old. I hadn't known and realised that it was a great tragedy that Bapu was dead. As days passed it came out that a Brahmin man had shot Bapu dead. In Hindus we have four castes, Brahmin, Kshityra, Vaish and Shuder. Brahmin is the highest caste and Shuder is the lowest caste. When people found out that a Brahmin had shot Bapu, around the country many Brahmin's houses were set on fire and families murdered in cold blood. Other news was released saying that the killer was from an organisation called the RSS. Even though the suspect denied that he had anything to do with the RSS, and that he was a lone hand, the Government put many RSS volunteers behind bars. The general public also went on a warpath. They attacked and killed many volunteers of the RSS. The atmosphere was very tense throughout India. During that time bad elements in the country had a field day. There was looting and lots of revenge killings everywhere.

I joined the local school. Due to a problem during partition, I lost quite a lot of schooling time. I joined school when nearly three-quarters of the academic year had passed. I was very poor in school studies. Other school children would bully me. I had a few fights with them. I remember once three boys pounced on me. I freed myself and told them, "Fight like a man. Only one person at a time." They thought that it was a good idea. The leader came and fought with me. I have mentioned that I used to go to the Fort playground and play with other boys. One of our play themes were mock fights with each other. I had learned and had been very successful in catching an opponent's neck in the crook of my arm. So when this leader came to fight with me, I used the fight tactics I had learned playing with other boys. I tried it a few times but I was not successful. In the meantime he gave me a few blows on my face. My lip started bleeding. Finally I got hold of his neck in crook of my arm and twisted it. He cried. I asked him, "Do you give up or shall I twist it a bit more?" He did not reply. I twisted it a bit more. He shouted, "I give up, I give up." The other two boys got scared. After that incident all three of them became my good friends. I had no trouble from any other children either.

I shall refer to this incident again when I refer to coming to the UK and winning a writing competition in 1964.

It is said that Banaras is the oldest living city in the World. At that time I didn't know it. I just learned it recently. It is built on the banks of the Holy river Ganges. According to Hindu beliefs the Ganges is a very Holy river. At least once in their lifetime, every Hindu should visit Banaras and have a dip in the Ganges. In addition to this, the ashes of Hindu dead bodies should be scattered in the Holy river.

Dharbanga Palace, where we lived, was not very far from the river Ganges. The palace was in a narrow street which started at Lord Shiva's temple and ended near the river. Early morning many people would go to the river and have a dip. They would take some water from the Holy river and go to the Lord Shiva's temple and pour water over Shiva's symbol called Lingam. While people passed through the street, they would recite Bhagwat Gita's stanzas. There would be so many people reciting them that one couldn't sleep after 4am. They would start very early. Slowly we got used to it.

Not only local people would go down to the river, but many Hindus would come from all over India, visit Banaras for a while and perform the ritual of going to the river, meanwhile passing through our street on their way to Lord Shiva's temple to pour the holy water on Shiva's Lingam. Due to that, the city had constructed eighty places from where one could go down to the banks of the Ganges. These were called eighty Ghats. Ghats were nothing but a stair which goes down to the river bank. Halfway there would be a large platform where one could sit and pray. Or do Yoga exercises. You would see lots of people busy performing 'Surya Namaskar'. It is a yoga exercise it, in English is called 'Salutation to Sun', sometimes you would see a Yogi sitting on those platforms giving a discourse on 'Bhagwat Gita' to the gathering. My brother Jaik and I, would go and listen to these discourses. We visited a few platforms and found out that one certain Yogi used to come every Thursday around 6.30pm and give the discourse. His discourse was not only effective but his method of communicating to the gathering was very interesting and sometimes funny. My brother and I would attend it every Thursday without fail.

Life in Banaras was interesting and different, but it was hard. We were not used to that kind of hard life. Locals didn't like us at all. At that time, city transport was not very good. We would walk wherever we went. One monsoon was very heavy. The river flooded the city. I remember I had to walk in the waist deep water to reach my home.

Sindhi communities are business communities. Slowly and gradually Sindhis have struggled and started new businesses. They went to other cities and established themselves. They even went to other countries like Africa, Middle East, USA and Europe and established their own businesses. Some of them have become multinational businesses. The wealth they created slowly seeped into Sindhi society and Sindhis again became a well to do community. In the UK there are lots of Sindhis. They have now formed a Sindhi Association of UK. Who hasn't heard of the Hinduja Brothers in the UK? They are Sindhis. There was another Sindhi, Mr R Gidoomal, who stood in the London Mayoral election.

I don't know if it is true or not, but it is said that before Banks introduced a 'Letter of Credit system', Sindhi business communities introduced it into their businesses. The system would work as follows: there would be, say, two brothers in a business. As an example one brother managed an office in Hyderabad, Sind. The other brother would go to Lagos, Nigeria, and open an office there. If any other smaller businessman wanted to start a business in Lagos, he would need money. He would give money to the brother in Hyderabad, Sind. This brother would write a letter to his brother in Lagos to hand over the agreed amount of money to this smaller businessman's brother in Lagos. These big businessmen had many employees. Every now and then new employees would join the organisation. This letter would be given to a new employee to hand over to the brother who would act according to the instructions mentioned in the letter. Of course the big businessman would deduct his commission. These Sindhi businessmen had been operating that way since 1865.

2007 was the year when India celebrated sixty years of Independence. Now we call it Independence. But early on we used to call it 'Partition of India'. On BBC2 TV channel they showed quite a lot of programmes on India. I am glad to say that they have shown India in a very favourable light. They showed how India which is an ancient civilisation and was a very prosperous country three thousand years ago, is again going towards prosperity. There was even a three part programme on the River Ganges. I feel that the wounds created by the partition of India have been healed. It is said, 'time is a great healer'.

Chapter Four

Life in India

There were two more families who were sharing the Dharbhanga Mahal (Dharbanga Palace) in Banaras. Life for all of us was not settled yet. We Sindhis were dispersed and displaced. Initially no one knew where the other family members were. All Sindhis were sailing in the same boat. Families were trying to go wherever they saw a chance of a better and safer life. Many families had young children and no male member to support and guide them. Most of the male members were on three year contracts with their employers. As the time passed, contact with male members were being made. We were lucky that we had two brothers working in Indian city. They were not as far away as West Africa. Many other male family members were serving their contracts in Africa.

Two families who were sharing the palace with us, located their uncle in Lucknow. Luckily the uncle had a business in Lucknow. He came to Banaras and met these two families. These two families were his cousin's families. He took these families to Lucknow, obviously for a better life. Now we were the only ones occupying the whole palace. It sounded great but actually it was too big and very cold due to the construction of the palace. The construction was of huge stone slabs. Even the rent was quite high for only one family to pay. My mother decided that we should move to a smaller house. Not only would we pay less rent, but also would have a comfortable living. My brother Jaik and I had joined a nearby school. We looked for a house just a short walking distance away from the school. Luckily we got a house which was recently constructed.

My elder brother Hiranand was the only earning member in the family. My other two brothers used to send sufficient money so that we could live a comfortable life. Our expenses were quite high. Our family consisted of three sisters, we three brothers and our mother and only one earning member. Hiranand decided that he should start a small general store. When he investigated he found out that shop landlords not only wanted a regular rent but an initial goodwill fee for the shop. In the meantime Jaik and I came across a wholesale market. We found out that there was a price difference of about 25% between the wholesale price and the retail price. Jaik and I had an idea, "Why not buy at the wholesale price and sell to shops keeping our margin?" We went to a few shops and asked them what item they would need and at what price. Then we went to the wholesale market. We could see that profit could be made. Immediately we went to a shopkeeper and got a confirmed offer and price. We went to the wholesale market bought items and sold them items to the shopkeeper. We walked everywhere, so it was a clear profit, no overheads at all. Our elder brother Hiranand was very happy. He gave us a bigger amount to do the buying and selling. It was hard work though.

One day a shopkeeper said, "I want Pepsodant toothpaste." We bought the item and went to him. He said, "I have changed my mind, I want Colgate toothpaste." When we went to the wholesale market, he refused to take back the Pepsodant and would not give us Colgate in return. When we went to other shopkeepers to sell the toothpaste, no one would buy Pepsodant. They said, "It doesn't move." Now we were lumbered with it. I remember that after that our family started using Pepsodant and it took us a very long time to get rid of it. The whole family was sick and tired of that toothpaste. 'Pepsodant' was a revolting word to us.

Life was hard. The money we used to get from our two brothers was not sufficient. My mother therefore persuaded Hiranand to earn some money. He tried but it was impossible to get any job, even though he had completed his matriculation. There was an undercurrent in the atmosphere. Local people were hostile to us and would not give any job to Sindhis. They would say, "You are taking our jobs, why don't you go back where you came from?" Hiranand was in a fix. He couldn't get a job and there was not sufficient money to start a business. He didn't want to leave us saying that we needed a male member in the family to face life in a strange country. He didn't know what to do. He got very depressed. I still remember very clearly one evening he came back home. He had a pound of guava fruit in his hand. He face was very distorted in agony. He was walking in a trance. He was so engrossed in his depressed thoughts that he didn't say anything. He came into the house and just sat down in a chair.

"What is the matter, son?" My mother asked him.

"I don't know how I came here. I think it must be a miracle."

"What do you mean?" My mother asked him. We brothers and sisters were very confused. He didn't look himself at all.

He blurted out. "I was very sick and tired of life. I didn't know what to do. I just wanted to end it all. I went to the river Ganges to just jump in and finish the misery. Then I realised that I had just bought a pound of gauva fruit for you. You like them, so I bought them, they were so nice and fresh, I thought that I should give you the fruit which I had just bought specially for you. Then end it all, next time." He put his face in his two hands and sobbed.

My mother put her arm around him and cuddled him and said, "Son, don't worry about us. We are all alright, you look after yourself. I shall write a letter to Ramchand in Kolkata. He will get a job for you from his employers. Do not worry, everything will be all right. Just trust in God." She immediately sent a telegram to Ramchand, 'Hiranand is feeling very depressed without a job. I am sending him to you. Please look after him and get a job for him'.

"It was 1948, sixty years ago, while I am writing this I can vividly visualise the scene in our house and his distorted face. My eyes get misty and I realise that it was touch and go. Guava fruit saved him and saved the situation. Otherwise my mother would have been in such a state, I was fourteen then, but now I could imagine that it would have been a disaster for the family.

My brother's employer in Kolkata was very considerate and gave Hiranand a job in one of his shops in New Market in Kolkata. His salary helped the family quite a lot. The money problem was now not as bad as it was before. In the meantime we located our mother's sister and her family in Mumbai. Jaik and I had a school holiday. Our aunties suggested that Jaik and I should visit them in Mumbai. My mother wrote to Hiranand in Kolkata. 'Jaik and Vasu are visiting my sister in Mumbai during school holdays'. Hiranand wrote back, 'Jaik and Vasu used to do 'buy and sell' business. If they want to start, they should buy those items in Mumbai's wholesale market. They will get them much cheaper than they would in Banaras'. Jaik and I were very excited about it. We wanted to earn money and help the family. We were in Mumbai for about a month. During that time we found out where the wholesale market was. We found that prices really were cheaper than we used to pay in Banaras wholesale market. We had an idea which items would move. We stayed clear of Pepsodant toothpaste and bought only Colgate paste.

Our auntie's family was quite rich. Her husband Mr Dayaram had a good business in Beira, Mozambique. He and his four brothers had amassed a huge wealth. During partition, their whole family was in Beira. They were not 'Displaced Persons'. Their lifestyle and attitude was very different from our family. They had servants and a car. But the whole family was very nice to us. They did not look down upon us. They really looked after us. One day Mr Dayaram was drinking beer. He offered us and encouraged us to drink. It was the first time I had a taste of beer. I didn't like it at all. It was so bitter. I was wondering, 'What has he seen in the drink. It is so bitter, doesn't taste good at all'.

We bought quite a lot of items for our 'Buy and Sell' business. Our huge steel trunk was full to the brim. It was very heavy. Mr Dayaram brought us in his car to the station to catch a train for Banaras. After that we wouldn't hire a porter. It would have eaten away our profit margin. Jaik and I dragged it around. Looking back, I don't know how we managed to carry it around. Aunties had given us a few articles for my mother and sisters. We also had bought a few articles for the family. Jaik and I had few days left in our school holiday. The next day we visited a few shops and tried to sell articles we had bought in Mumbai wholesale market. We were very pleased that we made a very good profit. It was much more than we had spent for our trip to Mumbai.

Jaik and I had joined a nearby secondary school. The education was in Hindi. We did not know anything about Hindi. We knew only Sindhi, our regional language. It was really very hard for both of us to study in a strange city. Classmates hated us because we had come from a foreign land and we had to learn a new language, called Hindi. At the same time we had to study in that different language. We did not want to lose a year. We both studied hard, in a way burning candles at both ends. Luckily we passed, but just.

We knew that we were not that bad. In Hyderabad, Sind, we both used to come either first or second in our class.

No one in our family wanted to stay in Banaras. The undercurrent and general atmosphere was not congenial at all. We wanted to go to Kolkata where now we had two brothers living. Kolkata was very expensive city. Our brothers did not have that much salary to support us. Our mother decided that we should stay one more year till Jaik and I had finished another year. By this way we wouldn't lose a year of studies. In the meantime our mother wrote a letter to our eldest brother, Motiram who was in Mumbai. He had also been working on a three year service contract with his employer. He had been there before the partition. Initially his reply was that 'Mumbai is very expensive'. My mother wrote back, 'We have nowhere to go. Either we go to Kolkata, or to Mumbai. I don't want to go to Kolkata and stay there. It would bring back very bad old memories. As you know your dad was ill treated by his partners and died in Kolkata. You must find a cheap accommodation in Mumbai for us. The school year finishes in June. We would like to come June/July'. She wrote in such a way that it was an order. Our eldest brother had no choice but to find cheap accommodation. Luckily he found a cheap one quite far away from Mumbai city centre. In the meantime Jaik and I had results of our school examination. The results were not as bad as the previous ones. But we knew that we could do better once we were settled in one place. There were empty army barracks in an area called 'Machhlimar'. Motiram got a room for us in those barracks. It was just a room. The bathroom and toilets were common to all residents and away from our room. There was an outside water tap. All families residing in those army barracks would use it. There was always a queue for use of that single tap.

I was the youngest in the family. So it was up to me to keep an eye on the tap, stand there in the queue and make sure that we had sufficient water for cooking and drinking. It was a tiring job. Sometimes I would protest and suggest that someone else should stand in the queue. Everyone in the family would kiss me, cuddle me and bribe me with nice things and say, "You are a good boy, aren't you? We will give you more pocket money." I was very obedient and would continue with my duty of a 'water supplier' for the family. The life here was much harder than we had in Banaras. But we were happy because our eldest brother was in the same city. He had accommodation with his employer in the city centre. Jaik and I very frequently would go and visit him in his shop in the city centre. He would visit us during weekends. Life was much better than before. But we were still struggling. The beach was not very far, just 200 yards away from our room. Jaik and I would go for a swim. We found out that young boys from other rooms also used to come. We made a few good friends and swam and played together. These families were all from our own communities. We didn't feel any hostile atmosphere. The nearby village was a fishing village. Fishermen were very simple, honest and hard working people. They were very happy that we had come. All the families from the barracks would go to the village and buy fresh fish as soon as the boat landed. Again it was down to me to go early in the morning and buy fish for our family. Initially I was upset because everyone else in the family was just sitting around and I was the only person doing all the work. They convinced me and I also realised that I was better off than they were. I was getting fresh air. Also I had learned bargaining with fishermen. I felt that I was a very important member of our family. I was facing two extremes. I was the youngest in the family and I was being ordered by everyone in the family. On the other hand, everyone loved me and cared for me as much as they could.

That was 1948. In 1988 I had a chance to visit that area again during my visit to India from London. I could not recognise the area. The barracks were gone: there were many new buildings which had been built and it had become a very expensive residential area. Even a few Indian Bollywood film actors had moved into the newly built houses. All thee houses had a sea view and huge front gardens with gardeners working in them. It has become a very expensive area.

Again the question of our education came. We couldn't find any good schools in that area. After searching for a long time, we heard that one philanthropist from our community had just opened a school specially for people from Sind. Mother, Jaik and I went to visit the school. We found out all the information. While we were looking around to see what kind of facilities were in that area, we came across a building being built. It was just 200 yards away from the school. We went and met the owner. His name was Mr Hinduja. He said, "There will be six flats, but they are all booked. We only give these to our own family members." We were very desperate to have better accommodation. My mother said, "I have three young daughters. The area we live in is not very nice. It is very difficult to live in the one room. Please help us."

"Okay. My elder brother's office is at this address, go and meet him and tell him that I have sent you. Have a word with him, if he agrees to give you a flat, you can have it. I can't agree this on my own." He gave us his brother's name and office address. Next morning my mother and I went to the office. After gentle persuasion he agreed to give us a flat. He said, "I have built the building for my son Amar's security. I thought that he should stay in one flat and collect rent from the other five. That would be his income. That is why I am naming the building as 'Amar Cottage'. But lately my son told me that he wanted to live in a bigger flat near to our office. You are lucky you have come at the right time. I shall give you the flat which he would have occupied. It is first floor facing the sea."

We were so delighted and my mother was very thankful to him

and said, "God will give you fame and fortune." In the UK, everyone knows that we have two Hinduja brothers living in the UK. Both are on the rich list of the UK. I came to know that the Mr Hinduja we had met in India in 1948 was the uncle of these two Hinduja brothers. Possibly my mother's blessing had worked.

As soon as the building was completed, we moved into our beautiful new flat. The view from our window was fantastic. You could see a full view of the sea. Every morning we would view the beautiful sunrise. The school was just a short walk from the flat. It seemed that better days had come.

Shortly Jaik finished his matriculation. He wanted to be a pilot. He went for an interview with the Indian Air Force. He failed their medical examination. The Air Force Medical Officer said, "You are wearing glasses, your eyesight is not normal without glasses, sorry we can't take you for a pilot's job." Jaik asked him, "I want to join Air Force, what job can I do in the Air Force?"

"You can be a ground Aircraft Engineer."

A few days after the meeting with the Air Force office, Jaik got a letter and a contract to sign. We were all upset when Jaik told us that the contract was for nine years service. He also mentioned that the nine year contract cannot be broken. If not honoured, the candidate could be imprisoned. My mother was the most upset. She said, "He is only eighteen years old. How can he survive among strangers for so many years. He may not get good food to eat." When Jaik read the contract papers closely he found out that he would be initially stationed in Barrackpur. On the map he noticed that Barrackpur was only 20 miles away from Kolkata. He wrote a letter to his elder brother Hiranand in Kolkata. 'I have just received an offer of working with the Indian Air Force. Initially I shall be stationed at Barrackpur, which I believe is only 20 miles away from Kolkata. Do you think I should join the Air Force?'

'Yes you should. For the last few years you have been very keen on joining the Air Force. Do not lose this opportunity. During weekends either you could visit me or I could visit you'. That reply made everyone very happy. Mother was happy that Jaik would not be far away from his brother, Jaik was happy that he was going to join the Air Force. We were all glad that Jaik was going to be a big man in the government.

Initially we used to get very happy letters from him saying how much he was enjoying himself. Training was tough but he had made a few friends and life according to him was a big holiday. We also would get feedback from Hiranand saying that Jaik was happy and was enjoying himself. Few weekends Jaik visited Hiranand in Kolkata a few times Hiranand visited him in his Air Force base. After training his job started. He liked his job and everything was going fine for him. After a year, he was promoted. Jaik was delighted with the promotion.

From the day of his promotion, Jaik had a problem with his immediate superior. Jaik found out after some time that his superior was from south India. He wanted another south Indian person who was working with Jaik to be promoted instead of Jaik. Jaik was promoted on his merits. Life became very difficult for Jaik. There would be unnecessary arguments between the two. Twice his superior filed papers to authorities that Jaik was not obedient at all. It so happened that Jaik was stubborn as well. He felt that he was being maltreated without any valid reason by his superior. Higher authorities had no choice but to put him in solitary confinement. The first time Jaik accepted it and passed the difficult time in the solitary cell. When he was put again into the cell, he rebelled. There was no one who would listen to him. Possibly he was being treated that way because he was from a different land and possibly because his superior was from the south. The officer wanted the other south Indian to be promoted. It was sheer discrimination.

At it was mentioned earlier we were being discriminated against by locals in Banaras. Now it was happening to Jaik again. With difficulty he survived the solitary confinement and decided that the Air Force was not the place for him. In the meantime he had made friends with another person. He also was Sindhi. Jaik had been there for about three years. There were another six years to finish the contract. It was a long time – Jaik and his friend called Kanal decided that they must do something to escape their hell. Jointly they read the contract of service to see in what way they could get out. They noticed that there were two ways. First, to buy their way out by paying a huge amount of money to the Air Force authorities, or get discharged on medical grounds. Once Jaik faked 'terrible tummy pain'. Medical Office could see it was a fake. Finally they came across a clause which said, 'If an ill and old parent of the candidate needed someone to look after them due to ill health, discharge may be sanctioned'.

Jaik filed papers for discharge on the grounds 'My mother is old, there is no male family member to look after her. She suffers from terrible asthma and arthritis'. My mother's illnesses were genuine, but my three sisters and I were with her. Jaik found out that my three sisters did not count as they were girls. I was the only obstacle for him getting discharged. My mother sent her medical certificate showing her illnesses. Jaik also mentioned that there were three sisters and no male family member with my mother. Jaik wrote to us: 'Before they give me a discharge, an official will visit our house'. We had to make sure that whatever Jaik had written in his discharge papers was seen to be correct.

From then on, we were very careful about any stranger visiting us, in case he was from the Air Force authorities. Any knock on the door would make me jump and either hide, or run away from the balcony. Twice it was a false alarm. I used to be out after breakfast and come back in the evening. For a long time no one visited us. We were a bit relaxed. Still, we had decided that I should not be in the house from 9.00am to 6pm.

One Friday morning I had my breakfast. I didn't want to go out, as I was not feeling good at all. I felt lethargic. But I had to go away as per my routine. I went to the city centre and just pointlessly looked around. After that I went to the beach and walked for a while. But I wasn't myself. I sat down on a bench. My mother had given me a packed lunch. It was nearly lunch time and I was feeling peckish. I thoughtfully ate my lunch. There wasn't any good movie to go to and pass my time. I just sat there and watched the world pass by. I noticed one person who just passed nearby had a very strange nose. I couldn't keep my eyes away from it. He looked at me, I looked back and smiled at him. He smiled back and went away. After a while one person came and sat beside me on the bench. I was very surprised. IT WAS THE NOSE! I got scared. We conversed in Hindi as follows:

He said, "Hello."

I replied reluctantly, "Hello."

"Are you a student?"

"Yes."

"What are you studying?"

"Pre-matriculation."

"Which school?"

I didn't want to tell him where I was studying, so I said, "I haven't joined it yet."

"Which one will you join?"

"I don't know."

"Where do you live?"

Now I got really scared. I was fifteen then. His features including his nose were really ugly. His face was full of lines and wrinkles. It seemed he had seen and passed a lot of hard life.

"I have to go now. My brother is waiting for me at Flora Fountain," I told him.

Before I could leave he gave me a small packet and said, "You and your brother will like it."

"What is it?" I asked.

"You smell it, you will feel happy."

I didn't take the packet and just thanked him and left very hurriedly. After a few steps, I ran as fast as I could. I looked back to see if he was following me. He wasn't. To be on the safe side, I came home in a very roundabout way. There was a park on the way home. I went in and sat under a tree and rested. After a while I looked at my watch, it was 3pm. I knew it would take me an hour to arrive home. I had another two hours to kill before I should go home. Before I had left home I was not well at all. With this experience I felt sick. I decided to go home.

I arrived home around 4pm. My sister said, "You are early, what happened?" I narrated my experience with the Nose.

"Perhaps he was giving you cannabis powder. It is good you didn't take it."

"Can I have a cup of tea please?" I sat in my favourite chair near the window. I loved to sit in that chair and look at the sea. The tea came. I was looking forward to it, so I started drinking it even though it was hot. There was a knock on the door, my sister opened the door. They had already told me not to open the door. Also it was agreed among family members that if for any reason I was present in the house when the Air Force official happened to visit us, we would say that I was their cousin.

When my sister opened the door, a person rushed in and asked, "Is this Jaik's house?" As soon as I heard it I went deathly white. Actually we all went deathly white. It dawned on us that he was the Air Force Officer and he had seen me in the house.

My sister blurted out, "Yes." In the meantime he looked at me and I looked at him stunned.

He asked my sister, "Who is he?"

"Oh. He is our cousin. He was in town, he has just visited us." She didn't know what else to say, we were all confused. She added, "I have given him a cup of tea to drink." After a short pause and a presence of mind she asked him, "Would you like to have a cup of tea? It is ready."

"No, thank you."

Very quickly I finished my tea, wished everyone in the family a "Goodbye, see you soon" and left.

He asked me, "Where do you live?"

"Kalyan." Kalyan is about thirty miles away from Mumbai. Everyone knew that many families from our community were housed there. It was easy for me to give him that reply I wished him "Goodbye" as well and left.

Instead of looking at the sea from window of our house, I walked towards the sea. I sat down on a stone near the sea.

Fishermen were drying their fish on racks. The smell was very overpowering. I couldn't care less. I just sat down. The waves had a hypnotic effect on me. They just kept coming and going away. I just gazed at the sea. All the time I was thinking about Jaik. 'I have blown it now. The officer has seen me. He will write a report that there was a male member in the family. Jaik had lied to the Air Force Authorities'. I was so engrossed in my thoughts that I didn't realise that it had gone dark. When I came to my senses, it was quite dark. With a heavy heart I went back home. All the family members were very concerned about me. I had taken a long time to come back.

"Now Jaik will not get discharged, the officer has seen Vasu." My mother sadly announced. We all thought on those lines. My sister wrote a letter to Jaik telling him that the officer had visited us. In case the Air Force Authorities open and read letters, she didn't mention anything that had transpired. From then on we all held our breath and hoped for the best. Jaik replied to my sister's letter saying, 'I haven't yet heard from the authorities. If I don't hear from them next month, I shall go to their office and remind them and tell them that my mother is very sick'.

Time didn't pass quick enough. There was no news from Jaik either. We had lost hope and after some time even forgotten about it. One Saturday morning, we were all having a late breakfast, when the postman came and delivered a telegram. In those days, telegrams would bring either good news or a bad. One never knew which one it was till one opens it and reads it. At that particular time, it had brought very good news. It was from Jaik. It said, 'Discharged, coming home Friday'. During those days telegram charges used to be on the number of words used. Jaik wanted to be economical. He did not specify which Friday, we assumed that it would be the next Friday. Luckily we received on the Friday a letter from Hiranand who was in Kolkata. 'Jaik has got his discharge, thank God. He will be arriving this Friday by Mumbai Express'. We were all delighted. On Friday morning my mother sent me for shopping. She cooked all kinds of dishes that Jaik liked. No one had to tell me what I must do. I found out the train timing and went to the railway station to receive Jaik. It was a very long journey from Kolkata to Mumbai. The distance is about 1,800 miles. I remember in 1945, when Jaik and I had travelled from Hyderabad, Sind, to Kolkata, it took us 48 hours, it took 36 hours for Jaik to come to Mumbai from Kolkata. At the end of the journey, one used to get very weary and tired.

The station was very crowded. The train was also full of passengers. In the crowd I couldn't locate Jaik. At that time there was no special reserved compartment. One would grab a seat and had to hang on to it. Here I was parading from one end of the platform to the other without much luck of finding Jaik. With a heavy heart I came back home to tell the family that Jaik was not there. I entered the house and opened my mouth to say, 'Jaik was not there'. But my mouth remained open. Suddenly I spotted in the room, Jaik was sitting and smiling at me.

"Jaik, I didn't see you?"

"I didn't expect anyone to come to the station. I just hired a porter and came home." Possibly he did it so quick that I couldn't spot him. Of course the train was very long as well.

I just said to myself, 'All is well that ends well'. When I did not see Jaik at the station, I had a negative thought that perhaps they didn't allow Jaik to be released.

The first couple of weeks we were all very happy to see Jaik released from his nine year contract with the Indian Air Force. He described to us how stubborn he was with the Air Force authorities and how he was punished. A few times he was punished with hard labour. Finally twice he was put into solitary confinement. That broke his spirit to work in the Air Force. He realised that there was no fun and enjoyment working with them. On top of that he saw so much discrimination that he was disgusted. He wanted to come out of the so called 'Hell'. He was very relieved when he came out. I also was very thankful to God that my slip-up when the Air Force Official had visited our house did not spoil his chance of discharge.

He wanted to work and earn some money to help the family. At that time getting a job was very difficult. Whenever he went for an interview he found that there were many candidates for just one clerical job. He had passed matriculation. Most of the other candidates were graduates. He never got selected. More over many candidates had personal recommendations from someone in that company. He realised that he would be wasting his time to look for a job in Mumbai. My mother thought of her two sons who were in Kolkata. She wrote a letter to them, 'Jaik is not able to get any job here. I am sending him to you. Please arrange to fix a job for him'. Very obediently Ramchand and Hiranand (two sons in Kolkata) wrote Jaik a personal letter, 'Come immediately to Kolkata. We shall fix a job for you. Enclosed please find a train fare'. Jaik was delighted and booked a ticket to Kolkata. I sent a wire to them, saying what date and what train Jaik would take when leaving for Kolkata. I did not make the same mistake that Jaik had done by giving the day not the date of arrival.

In 1951 I finished my matriculation examination. I felt that I should follow Jaik to Kolkata and get a job there. It looked impossible to get any employment in Mumbai. At the same time my eldest brother Motiram was not getting good treatment from his employers in Mumbai. Also his salary was not sufficient for our family to live comfortably. He had an offer of a job in Nairobi, Kenya. It was a three year contract he had to sign. He decided to go to Kenya. My mother was very depressed when she heard that I also was thinking of going away. She said to me, "We need at least one male member in the family. You shouldn't go away. Get a job here. It may take some time, but there is no hurry, don't worry." I tried very hard to get a clerical job. I had the same problems that Jaik had. One of my sisters suggested, "There is a college not far from here, just walking distance. Why don't you study for Batchelor of Commerce? With a degree you will get a job quicker and will get more salary." Then she added, "I have heard that you need not pay any fee. The government is going to pay the fee for 'Displaced Persons'. As you know we are classified as 'Displaced Persons'." I liked the idea and joined the college. At the same time I was applying for jobs. But there was no luck with any job.

I joined the college. They told me that I need not pay any fee for the course. The college is owned by a businessman from our Sindhi community. He has exempted fees for Sindhi students. I also found out that the government was going to pay our fees. I immediately submitted an application form to the government department for repayment of my fees.

My college course started. It was just a mile and a half away from where I used to live. I found a dirt road which shortened my journey to a mile. It was a new experience for me to go to college. No one in our family had studied at a college. I made some good friends in the college. There was one student who used to walk on the same route. His name was Gope Kundnani. Many times we would walk back together. On the way we would discuss various ills in our country and what should be done. I had a very enjoyable time at the college. I shall describe in chapter 17 my surprise meeting in London with Gope after nearly twenty years.

One day during a lunch break I was having lunch in the college canteen. I couldn't believe my eyes when I spotted two boys sitting at the next table eating their lunch.

"Are you Satu? Are you Kishin?" I asked them. I was very excited. They replied, "Vasu!" We were very excited and happy to meet each other. Both of them used to be my classmates in Hyderabad, Sind. In August 1947 India was partitioned into India and Pakistan. When Hindu families heard and witnessed the massacre, Hindu families just fled as quick as they could. Due to that we lost contact with our friends and families. That meeting with Satu and Kishin was so unexpected that we couldn't contain ourselves. We just talked and talked. When lunch break finished, we didn't want to attend lectures, we came out of the college, and went to a nearby café and continued our talk. We wanted to know so much about each other. I wanted to know, "How did they get out of Hyderabad? Where did they go? When did they come to Mumbai? Where do they live now? etc, etc." They also wanted to know answers to similar questions. How the time passed, we didn't know. I looked at the clock, it showed nearly 5pm. That was the time class finishes and we used to go home. We parted and promised to meet again on the next day.

While I was walking back home, I recalled that their family was quite wealthy. Their fathers were business partners. They had a business in Curacao. Curacao is a Caribbean island. I remembered that when I used to walk to my school, Satu and Kishin would come by in a huge Victoria carriage pulled by two very hefty horses. They were very famous in Hyderabad. There was only one Victoria carriage pulled by two horses. I had never been to their house. I had heard it was like a palace. They had half a dozen servants working in the joint household.

The next day we continued with 'give and take' of our news and views. It came out that they also had to leave their palace and their personal belongings. In Mumbai they rented a flat in 'Nanik Niwas'. It had a good location with a beautiful sea view. I didn't know then that it was a very expensive flat as well as location. A few years ago in London, I read the *Guinness Book Of Records*. It said that accumulation of wealth per inch of that building was the maximum in the whole world. It seemed that residents in that building were very rich. Each of them had huge businesses out of India, mainly in Africa.

After that we would have lunch together. My mother would give me a packed lunch, so would their mother. We would share it and supplement it with food we would order from the restaurant. The restaurant owner would allow us to eat our food. The restaurant had a few cubicles where we would eat our lunch in private. Satu and Kishin were very fond of cheese. They would get a supply of the imported Kraft cheese from their business in Curacao. I had never eaten cheese before, I had heard of it. At that time, it was food for rich people. They gave me cheese to eat. I didn't like it. It tasted like soap to me.

A few months after he joined college, Kishin was called away. His father had died. Kishin had to go and look after the business. It seemed he couldn't manage on his own. He called his cousin Satu to join him. A few months after that, before Satu could finish his first year college studies, he was also called to Curacao. I shall describe and mention in chapter 17, how I located them after nearly forty years. I could not meet Kishin as he had died by then.

Before Satu left Mumbai, he said, "Do you pay fees to the college?"

"No. Why?"

"There is an international company owned by Kishinchand Chellaram. They are ready to pay fees for any Sindhi student who goes for further studies."

"I don't pay fees. Can I still apply for it?"

"You can try." He gave me their office address and whom I could approach for it.

I went to their office. They gave me a form to complete. I completed it and handed it over to them.

After Satu and Kishin left college, I got busy with my studies. While Satu was in college, we would be together most of the time. Once we didn't like the lecture or the lecturer. It was Friday. Every Friday there would be new film releases. It so happened that there was a cinema hall adjacent to our college. They had a 9.00am show. Satu and I decided that we should go to the show. We went to the show. I don't remember the name of the movie, but we enjoyed it. It was like forbidden fruit. We were supposed to be attending college and here we were going to the movies. When we came out, we didn't feel like going to college. I said, "Satu, if we go to college they will ask us why we were so late."

"What shall we do?"

"There is a new release being shown, not far from here. If you want we could go there."

"Why not."

"Why not indeed." I replied. So we went to their 12 o'clock show. We ate our packed lunch in the cinema hall.

It is said that with anything the first time is difficult, the second time is easier. As soon as we came out of the cinema hall it was about 2.30pm. It was too early to go home. We then decided to go to another movie starting at 3pm. We glanced through the newspaper and located a cinema hall not far from where we were. We arrived just in time for the movie. When we came out of that third movie, our eyes had gone funny. Everything was blurred. For a moment we couldn't see properly. Also we were very thirsty as well. We went to a nearby café. We had a cup of tea and water to drink. In the meantime our eyes adjusted to the outside world.

After Satu left for Curacao I devoted more time in college and towards studies. I did extremely well. Also I had heard that I wouldn't get my fees paid if I didn't do well in studies. I am very glad to write that I did extremely well in my studies. After my examination results my teacher asked me, "What would you like to do now?"

"I haven't decided yet. Possibly I shall try to find a job for myself."

"You have very good marks, specially in mathematics. You could even go for engineering, if you want to."

"I shall think about it."

I was a bit concerned about the money. If I didn't earn, not only would money be needed to pay the engineering fees, but also I will not be contributing towards my family. I was very keen to contribute towards upkeep of the joint family. Out of the blue, I had very good news which came by post. Not only the government department sanctioned money to be paid to me for my, fees but also the 'Kishinchand Chellaram Trust' had sanctioned the fee money to be paid to me. It was a stroke of luck that not only did I not pay fees as they were exempted by the college, but also got cash for two lots of fees. Immediately my family decided that I need not work to contribute towards the family fund, the family would get sufficient funds from my four brothers.

There was another stroke of luck. One of my classmates told me that he had a job as a teacher. I told him that if there was any vacancy he should let me know. After a month or so he came running to me, "Vasu, there is a vacancy for a teacher. I have mentioned to the head teacher that I know a person who would be interested. The head teacher wants to meet you."

The next day I went along with him to meet the head teacher. She was quite a nice lady. After asking a few questions, she hired me and told me to start the following Monday. I was very glad that now I could study as well as earn money. But my whole lifestyle changed. To manage to study in college, and teach in school became nearly an impossible proposition. College timing was from 10am till 5pm. School timing was from 8am till 11am. The journey time between school and college was an hour and three quarters. My classmate had found a solution. I just followed his routine, which was as follows:

Leave home   6am
Walk for a mile as bus didn't start that early
Catch a train. Train journey time was about 20 minutes
Come out of station and catch a bus. Bus journey time was half an hour
After bus journey walk through a fishing village for about 15 minutes
Catch a ferry to cross sea to go to an island
After ferry ride walk for 15 minutes to reach the school

It was a very tight schedule. The bus, train and ferry all had to be on time. Then I was on time. The head teacher knew my schedule. So if I was a bit late sometimes, she was very considerate. I would arrive at college about 12.30pm when it was lunch break. I would then continue attending classes after lunch. But I would miss the morning lectures. I used to borrow notes from my mates for classes I had missed. It was a struggle but I managed anyhow. I used to be so tired at the end of the day that a few times I dozed off in the train and missed my station where I should have got off. But I was very happy that I was studying as well as earning money.

There was one incident in the school which I feel is worth mentioning. One of my students would not do what he was told. He was very obstinate. He would just stare at me. I had warned him that homework must be done. If he had a problem, he should let me know so that I could help him. He would neither do homework nor tell me his problem. Once I lost patience with him and slapped him. Next day while I was teaching in my class, I was called to meet the head teacher. I went to her office. In the office there was my obstinate student and his parents.

The head teacher said, "Your student complained that you slapped him."

"Yes I did. He never does his homework. I told him if he had a problem, he should let me know so that I can help him. He did not do that either."

"Did you know that we teachers can't slap a student. It is against the law."

"No, I did not know. What should we do if the student doesn't do what he is supposed to do?"

"We must not slap students."

"I am sorry if I did. But I don't want him in my class. He is spoiling the teaching atmosphere. Students will not learn in that atmosphere. Parents send children to school to learn and not to while away the time."

I was very surprised when the father said, "He is very disobedient at home as well. I give permission to you to slap my son, if you feel it necessary." He said that in front of his son. Even the head teacher was astonished. After the parents had gone she told me, "See if you can teach him without slapping."

Since the father had given me authority to slap his son, his son behaved in a very different way. He was a different person. He started coming to class on time. He would pay attention to studies. Also he would try to do his homework. He would even come to me and let me know what he couldn't understand. I was amazed. Initially he was a dead-end kid. But now there had been so much change in him. After that I never hit him. I had no reason to slap him. In this particular case a famous saying was true. The saying is, 'Spare the rod and spoil the child'.

At the end of the year examination, he not only passed but passed with fairly good marks. No one expected him to pass let alone get good marks. Even he was very surprised. It seemed he had been brain washed in his family that he was no good at studies. Due to that he had misbehaved at home as well. His father was sick and tired of him. the father wanted his son to learn. Perhaps that was the reason he had given me permission to slap him, if needed.

The day before the closing of school for annual holidays, the student and his parents visited the school. I was again called to the head teacher's office. I was confused and surprised to see the parents. I thought 'I have not slapped the student, what reason could there be for a complaint?' I sat down in a chair. The father had a packet in his hand which he handed over to his son. The son came to me and handed over the packet. He then touched my feet. In India we are taught that we should touch the feet of parents, teachers and any other elderly people. Elderly people then bless the person who had touched their feet. I blessed the student. The student had tears in his eyes. His crying was full of gratitude. The packet he gave me was a box of Indian sweets. It was Diwali time as well. Diwali is a Hindu festival. It is also called 'Festival Of Lights'. His father said, "We are very thankful and grateful to you. Even my son wouldn't stop talking about you saying how much you helped him in his studies. My son has been a very good son, he has become very obedient and hard working. It is all because of you. You had mentioned very sincerely that parents send their children to learn in school and not to while away the time. You opened my eyes. I am glad that I gave you permission to slap him. I have heard that you never had any reason to slap him after that." When he said that I was really touched. Noticing tears in the student's eyes my eyes got misty as well.

I had a very good time in that school. I was not much older than my students. It was just a few years difference between our ages. During lunch I would play with them. With heavy heart I had to leave the teaching job. I had applied for an engineering education course in Mumbai. It was difficult to get admission to Mumbai. My mother would not allow me to go away to any other far away university. Many of my classmates had to go to far away universities to study engineering. Luckily I got the admission to Mumbai due to my very good grade in my examination result. I had mentioned previously that my friend Mr Gope Kundnani used to walk with me to college. Once he mentioned that he had applied to an engineering college in a city called Anand. He had got the admission and he would go to Anand for studies. That was the last time I saw him. I did not hear from him or about him for many years. I shall mention him again in chapter 17 and describe how I came across him in London after nearly twenty years.

It was 1953 when I joined the engineering college in Mumbai. During the first period our lecturer gave us a list of books needed for the first year. Now our family finances were not bad at all. Six years ago we had lost everything. Our family just survived. It took us six years to be comfortable. Now we five brothers were earning and contributing towards the family fund. I bought all the books recommended. As the year progressed I noticed that my classmates were borrowing books from me. I had gladly lent the books to them. I didn't do very well in the first year examination. I realised why I didn't do very well. The reason was I had not studied hard enough. All the time I knew that I had all the books needed, which I could study any time. Due to that I never studied them. From the second year onwards I decided not to buy any books recommended by the teacher. Either I borrowed from the college library or from my classmates. It worked wonders. Because I knew that I had to give back the borrowed book within a certain time, I would read them. In that way I studied quite hard without realising that I was. I did extremely well in my examination after that. I was glad that I passed engineering in first class. I felt that it should be quite easy to get a job but I got a shock when I found out that no engineering company wanted me. Each one of them wanted an experienced engineer and not the one just fresh from the college. It took me about six months to land my first job. My first job was very far away from home. It was in the middle of a barren location erecting a steel plant. I shall come to that a little bit later.

During my six months of inactivity I came across two very good writers. During that time in my spare time I would read books by Edgar Wallace and Max Brand. Both of them have written many books. I feel that I must have read most of the books they have written. The local library was not very far from my house. During the Second World War, a few publishers had published lots of books in cheap paperback editions. These were now available very cheaply, sold on the footpath by second-hand dealers. I would look for my favourite books and buy. That way I collected quite a few books.

My three sisters were ready for marriage. At that time in India, most marriages were arranged marriages. There were many matchmakers who would look out for eligible boys. Matchmakers would have a portfolio of these boys with full details on them. Families with girls would contact these matchmakers to find good husbands for their girls. These matchmakers would also discuss about the dowry. My mother was very worried for my three sisters. According to our capacity we would agree to the amount of the dowry. Since I was the only male member at home and also I had no job yet, I did a lot of leg work by visiting matchmakers. Matchmakers would show us few photographs of eligible boys. Once photographs are viewed and exchanged, parents would also meet and view the would-be bride and groom. Once both parties had agreed to proceed further, birth charts of the boy and girl would be shown to the family Brahmin (priest) to confirm that both of them are compatible. This would be done individually by both parties. Brahmin is the highest caste in Hindu society. Brahmins are qualified not only in giving their view on compatibility for marriages, but performing marriage ceremonies as well. They know all the rituals to be performed according to Hindu Vedic rites. Hindus have four major Vedas. These are very old books giving details on everything worth knowing. One of them has described how all kinds of rituals should be performed. We Hindus have been following and performing the same rituals for thousands of years.

Once parents had agreed to proceed, the Brahmin had okayed it and of course the boy and girl had also agreed to the wedding, the priest was asked for an auspicious day for the marriage. The priest would refer to the holy book to see what were the various auspicious days. Both parties would then agree to one of the days given by the priest. Then and then only all the other programmes and ceremonies are finalised and fixed.

Around that time, my youngest sister would burst into tears for no reason or a very minor reason. First my mother did not think much of it. One day we had a visit from my mother's female cousin. During that time without reason my sister burst into tears.

"What is the matter with her?" The cousin asked my mother.

"Lately she cries without much reason," my mother replied.

"Last year my daughter did the same thing."

"What did you do?"

"I consulted a doctor. He visits 'Ramkrishna Mission' daily. He doesn't charge any fee, you just pay a donation to the centre. It is not very far from your house."

After cousin left, my mother suggested that I should take my sister to the doctor. My sister wouldn't agree to it and again burst into tears.

"Vasu, why don't you go to the doctor and explain the symptoms to him and get some medicine for your sister. Let us hope it works. I am sick and tired of her crying without any reason."

Next day I went to the centre. There were about 20 people waiting for the doctor. The doctor was very efficient. He would listen to what the patient had to say, ask a few questions and then prescribe the medicine. My number came and I went to him.

"We need some medicine for my sister. She is shy, she didn't want to come."

"What is her trouble?"

"She bursts into tears very frequently."

"Does she have a lot of saliva in her mouth?"

"When she talks, saliva drops fall from her mouth."

He looked at me, thought about something, referred to a book and wrote the medicine on a piece of paper. He told me to give it to the compounder who was nearby. The compounder gave me seven little packets of medicines. On one of them he put an 'X' mark. He said, "Let her take the medicine with 'X' today. The other six medicines she should take for next six days. Come back after seven days to consult the doctor."

I had looked through the hatch and noticed that the compounder had put some powder in each of seven packets. In one of them he put a few drops of colourless liquid. He then closed those packets and marked an 'X' on the one to which he had added the liquid.

"The doctor has prescribed Nat.Mur200. What medicine is it?" I asked the compounder.

"It is a biochemistry medicine."

I had never heard of it before. I didn't ask any more questions and went home.

I gave the packet marked 'X' to my sister to take immediately. The medicine was just sugary powder, it was not bitter at all. Generally medicines are bitter. We didn't think much of it. My sister finished the course of seven days medicine as a routine.

It was a miracle. My sister did not cry during those seven days or even after that. We realised that the medicine had worked. I was still looking for a job. I had plenty of time on my hands. I thought that I should find out a bit more about the medicine as well as about the so-called biochemistry. I went to the doctor to tell him that the medicine had worked. He said, "There is no need to give any more medicine." When the compounder had a minute I asked him, "I want to know more about biochemistry. Where can I get a book on it?"

He gave me an address of a chemist who sells homeopathic medicines. He said, "biochemistry is a branch of homeopathy. That shop should have a book on biochemistry." I bought a book recommended by the chemist in the shop. First thing I did was to read about Nat.Mur medicine. I was very surprised to read that Nat.Mur is nothing but sodium chloride. During my studies I knew that common salt is also nothing but sodium chloride. It was a mystery to me that a few drops of Nat.Mur could work wonders for my sister.

In the meantime, in 1951 my eldest brother (Motiram) had

gone to Nairobi, Kenya, to better his prospects. In 1953 my other brother (Hiranand) had gone to Lagos, Nigeria on a three year contract. His contract finished and he was returning from Nigeria back to India. He decided to come via London. After a stay of a month in London, he came back by an Italian luxury liner called *Lloyds Tristino*. I went to receive him at the Mumbai docks. He didn't look too well at all. He had a terrible bout of cold. Every now and then blue phlegm would come out of either his nose or mouth. He said that he had suffered from the cold for the last two weeks. That had made him quite weak. As soon as he saw me and then met the family, he felt much better. He is a good storyteller. He described his exploits in Nigeria as well as in London. While he was giving us this information, he would blow his nose. The blue phlegm would come out of his nose. It was a ghastly sight.

"Why don't you go to a doctor and consult him about your cold?" my mother suggested.

"It will be alright. Just give me Aspro." At that time, we had never heard of paracetamol. We used to get Aspro rather than aspirin.

My mother said, "Vasu, why don't you take him to consult the doctor in 'Ramkrishna Mission'?"

My brother wouldn't agree to visit a doctor. I had to go to the doctor on my brother's behalf.

"Doctor, my brother has just come from London. He has a terrible cold."

"Does he have any discharge from his nose?"

"Yes."

"What is the colour?"

"Blue."

"Any blood with it?"

"No."

He thought about it, referred to his book and prescribed a medicine. As usual I took the prescription to the compounder. He again gave me seven small medicine packets with one marked 'X'. The medicine with 'X' was to be taken immediately.

I came home and handed over the medicine with 'X' marked to my brother.

"Please take this medicine now. The other six packets are to be taken for the next six days."

He took the sugary powder and exclaimed, "Is that all? It is not bitter. It will not work. Will it?"

"We shall see," I replied. Even I was not sure about the effect of this medicine.

Next morning my brother said, "I got a very good sleep last night. Cold in the nose did not give me any trouble throughout the night."

"You have to take six more to have the full benefit." I gave him his second dose.

We all felt that it was a miracle. His cold gradually and naturally vanished. He had a headache, that also went. His appetite came back and so did his jolly mood. The cold and headache had made him very miserable.

The doctor had prescribed Bryonia 200. Last time I had bought a book from the homeopathy shop. I couldn't find that medicine in the book. I went to the shop and asked, "Where can I find Bryonia medicine in my book?" I showed my book to him.

"You can't find Bryonia in this book. This is a biochemistry book. You will find Bryonia in homeopathy book." He showed me a book which had listed the medicine. I bought that book as well. I wanted to know more about these miracle medicines. As the time went on, my family and I consulted the same doctor quite a few times. He was quite clever and efficient. His medicines never disappointed us. We had faith in him. I still had not found an engineering job, I had plenty of time to read these two books, and understand what the medicines were and how they worked. I also worked out why only one of the packets has an 'X' mark and why seven packets of medicines were being given. The reason was as follows:

The real medicine was in the packet with 'X' marked. All

other six packets had sugary powder without medicine. According to the book, the medicine works naturally for at least seven days. The doctor wanted me to come back after seven days and not before. In the meantime the medicine would have worked. Moreoever patients felt that they got 7 days medicine and not only one day's medicine. Slowly and gradually I developed a full faith in homeopathic medicines.

After a couple of months, Hiranand got tired of doing nothing. He didn't want to go to Africa again on a three year contract. He decided to go to Kolkata where Ramchand was. He didn't want to work as an employee. He decided to open a shop in New Market. New Market always did a good business. Most of the British residents would do their shopping in that market. Hiranand is now nearly eighty years old. He still has the shop which he runs with help of two employees.

I was again the only male member staying in the family. I had finished my engineering education. Still I had no luck with a job. I was getting very upset about it. We were all very pleased that one of the three sisters got engaged. I did a lot of legwork doing various jobs needed to be performed whilst arranging a marriage in the family. The wedding day was fixed. Sadly I couldn't attend the wedding. With a bit of luck my job application was successful. I was appointed as an Erection Engineer in Bhilai Steel Project. At that time India had a lot of industrial help from the UK, Germany, USA and Russia. With the help of the Russian government, Bhilai Steel Project was to start producing steel for industries. I had to leave my family and go far away to start work.

Bhilai was a barren area and very hot. Due to living conditions and the hot climate people would get sick. Also the water we used to drink was polluted. We would all get sick and suffer from loose motions. Due to that there was a huge turnover in the workforce. It was a living hell for me. I was so used to a comfortable life at home with good food and clean water. Within a month I suffered from loose motions. There was not many medical facilities either. For the next three months I lived with my sickness. But I was getting weaker and weaker. I still remember that once we were coming back from work by a coach to our living quarters, one of the engineers was telling a joke. We all laughed, but for me it was an effort even to laugh. I just smiled. Then I realised that my sickness had reached a dangerous point. I had to go home and consult a good doctor. The next day I went to the Chief Engineer and asked for one month's leave so that I could consult a doctor and get better. That same night I caught a train and came home.

I came home without informing my family. They were very glad to see me.

"What have you done to yourself? You don't look well at all. What is the matter?"

"The weather was very hot, the food was filthy and the water was contaminated. I have got loose motions.

"Go to the doctor in 'Ramkrishna Mission'. He should be able to cure you." My mother suggested.

Sure enough the doctor gave me appropriate medicine and within no time my health was back to normal. I didn't want to go to Bhilai again. I started applying for jobs in Mumbai. I was very pleased that I had good responses to my applications. It seemed my experience in erection engineering had a very positive effect. The economy was expanding. New engineering companies were coming out like mushrooms. I landed a good job not far from where I used to live. It was just a short bus ride from my house. I was appointed as a design engineer. My job was to calculate, specify and draw the steel frame work of a factory. There were six engineers in our section. The atmosphere was congenial. The working conditions were good. Our Chief Engineer was also like a friend. I had a very good time in that company.

One day one of the engineers said, "Do you know today the Queen in her car is passing through the main road? She should pass around midday." We had heard that the Queen was in town but didn't know her programme. Hurriedly I had my lunch and went out to the main road to see whether what my friend had said was true. He was right. The main road was very crowded with people standing on both sides of the road. I realised that it was impossible to see the Queen in that crowd. I was in luck. Our company's boundary wall near the main road was quite high. I asked the company's watchman, "Please help me climb the wall so that I can sit on top and see the Queen clearly." He smiled and helped me. At that time in India, executives never did that sort of thing. Executives generally behaved with stiff upper lips and not the way I behaved. When the Queen passed I had a very clear view of her. I never realised then that in a couple of years time I would be living in the Queen's country. Even though two years ago one of my classmates by the name of Shyam Gogia had gone to the UK. I had no intension of visiting the UK. Frequently I used to meet Shyam's uncle. He used to catch the same bus as mine. The uncle told me that Shyam had won an award for his amazing research work from the Duke of Edinburgh.

One of the six engineers called Mr Mohan Chawla became my very good friend. He used to live with his brother's family. He was never in a hurry to go back home. Both his parents had died a few years ago. We would go to the sea which was about a mile away from our office. We then would walk by the sea for an hour or so and then go home. My house was also near the sea but five miles away from my office. His house was about ten miles away and in the same direction.

One day Mohan said, "Why don't we walk right up to your house. I shall then catch a bus from there."

"It is a good idea, Let us do it today," I replied.

We walked about four miles and came across huge boulders. We could have climbed them, but they looked treacherous. We dropped the idea of climbing them. Instead we did the rest of the walk on the road and arrived my house. I told my mother that we had walked from our office. She couldn't believe it. She thought we were joking. Looking back I could see that no one in their right mind would walk that far when there was good public transport available. My mother realised that we were telling the truth. She immediately gave us a hot meal. We were famished after that walk.

One day Mohan announced, "I have got a very good job with an American company. The pay is also very good – nearly double what I am getting here." That started my mind working. I thought, 'Perhaps I should apply for a better job'. Very shortly I got an interview with the Otis Elevator Company. It seemed it was now easier to get a job having good experience in the engineering industry. I went for the interview. After the usual questions from the Chief Engineer, he asked me, "How much do you expect?" I quoted about 60% more than I was getting.

The Chief Engineer commented, "It is quite a lot, isn't it?"

"Because I am worth it," I replied.

I GOT THE JOB. I nearly fainted when I came out of the interview room.

I found out that Otis Elevator was an American company. It has branches throughout the world. Otis was doing very good business at that time. There were many high rising blocks of flats being built. All of them needed a lift or two. After three months probation period I got a raise. I was very happy. The company knew how to look after their employees. Everyone was very happy working there. That was the time India declared war on China. China had attacked Tibet and annexed it to China. India felt that it was her moral responsibility that it should defend Tibet. India didn't do very well in the war. Otis was a big company. It had employees from all over India. Throughout India there was a nationalist atmosphere. Everyone wanted to join forces and defeat China. Suddenly regionalism had vanished from India. I had an idea. Why not we form a group of friends. The group should have at least one person from each of our Indian regions. It was not difficult. We had already formed a group of friends who used to meet at the end of the day and go to a café and spend a couple of hours. I found out which region was not represented. I would then approach the person and explain what we intended to do. At that time we had sixteen regions in India. Finally our group was formed of 20 persons. It so happened that we had four from Goa. We would discuss what we should do for our country. Perhaps it was just an idea and hot air, but intentions were real. I even wrote a letter to the Editor of the *Indian Express* explaining what we had done. I had suggested that everyone in the country should think of India and forget the differences between regions and religion. I was very proud that they published my letter and I got good feedback from the public as well. In the meantime war was over: India did not do very well at all. China never let go of Tibet. They still have a hold over it. Perhaps the situation may have been different if at that time the Western world had morally supported India against China.

Most of our group worked in the Otis factory. One of our group used to work in the Otis office in the city. He was a shipping Ezecutive called Mr Harry Jagasia. He would visit the factory frequently and sort out shipping documents. One day he came to the factory. He was all smiles and very excited and said, "I have got it, I have got it." He had a piece of paper in his hand. We all surrounded him and were curious to know.

"I have an employment voucher from the British government. Now I can go to the UK and can work over there." When I enquired more about it he said, "Vasu, you are an engineer. The UK needs engineers, doctors, nurses and handymen. You could get the voucher very easily."

"Where can I get it?"

"Go to the British Embassy. They will give you a form to complete."

He was right. As soon as I gave them the completed form, I got the employment voucher by post. I had no intention of leaving my mother. I just ignored it. After about six months I got a letter from the British Embassy saying, 'Voucher has a validity of six months. It will expire shortly. If you want to use it we could extend it by a further three months and no more'.

I felt that the opportunity was too good to miss. I should go to the UK for about two years. During that time, I should earn as well as visit European countries. Perhaps it is ideal that I should learn more about the British and their way of life and their thinking. After two years I should come back, get married and settle down. It was difficult to convince my mother. She would be alone on her own. Finally she agreed when my four brothers suggested that they would visit her in rotation. My mother stipulated one condition, "Your dad had taken me for a pilgrimage and we had visited religious places. You must take me there before you go." I agreed.

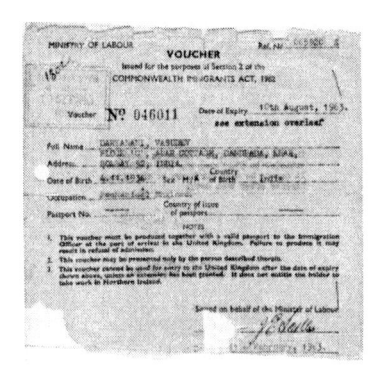

[voucher image]

I had to give three months notice to Otis. There was not sufficient time for me. The voucher was to be utilised before a certain day. I requested Otis to adjust my annual holiday with my notice period. Very reluctantly they had agreed. Now I had a problem. I had to take my mother on a pilgrimage of about a month. I again went to my Chief Engineer and requested.

I said, "My mother's wish is to go on a pilgrimage before I go to the UK. I need a months holiday."

"You can't do it. We already have adjusted your annual leave into the notice period." He was adamant about it. I then replied, "You can consider my request or not, I am taking my mother for a pilgrimage. If you want you may deduct my salary." Obviously I said this in such a way that he agreed and said, "Okay." I thanked him profusely.

In the meantime Mr Harry Jagasia had left for the UK. He

never left any forwarding address. I didn't know anyone else in the UK. Luckily I came across one of my classmates from my engineering college. He mentioned that another of our classmates had gone to the UK. He could help me. He gave me his address. I immediately wrote to him and described my intentions. He promptly replied that he could arrange to receive me and also arrange accommodation for me. I was very glad to get that kind of reply. After that I arranged my passage to the UK. Regarding Harry there was no news of him. No one knew his whereabouts. I shall describe later how accidentally I met Harry in London after nearly twenty years.

From the beginning my intention was to go away for about two years. I treated it as a long holiday. I thought that going to the UK by plane was too quick. There is no fun in travelling by plane. Why not go to the UK by a luxury liner? My brother Hiranand had travelled by a luxury liner when he was returning from Africa via London. He encouraged me to go by boat. It was more expensive by boat. My brother had travelled economy class. I thought that I was going on a long holiday, why not travel first class? I went to P&O shipping company. I got all the details from them. I found out that there was one of their ships called *Chusan* leaving for the UK a few days before my employment voucher was to expire. I was delighted that everything was fitting like a jigsaw puzzle. I had in the meantime booked train tickets to go on the pilgrimage with my mother. I got my tax clearance certificate so that I could apply for a passport. Everything went fine for me.

For a month my mother and I visited a few religious places. My mother was very happy that I had obliged and managed to fit this trip into my busy schedule. She blessed me from the bottom of her heart. I feel that all these years her blessing has given me a very good and happy life.

I was now ready for my 'Journey into the unknown'. Everyone in the family mentioned that it would be very cold in the UK. I got various gifts from each of them. It became my survival kit. It was as follows:

A pair of jeans	by eldest brother, Motiram
A whiskey hip flask	by brother Ramchand
A leather jacket	by brother Hiranand
A nail cutter	by brother Hiranand (I still use it)
A Longine watch	by brother Jaik
A woollen scarf	by eldest sister
A pair of woollen gloves	by middle sister
A hand-knitted slipover	by youngest sister
A black woollen cap	I used to wear it, I still do
Lots of kisses and hugs	from my mother
A small hand machine to make Indian savouries	from all the family (still use it)

In addition I had two homeopathic books I had purchased and constantly used. For your information I still use them. Due to constant use of them during the last 45 years, they have disintegrated. I am very careful not to lose any sheet.

My mother could read and write only in the Gurmukhi language. Sind and Punjab was highly influenced by Sikh teaching. Most Hindu families would have their holy book called 'Granth Sahib' in the house. They would regularly read it. Gurmukhi is the language used by Sikh. I didn't know Gurmukhi though. My mother suggested that I should write letters to her in Gurmukhi so that she could read them. I had brought a book on *How To Learn Gurmukhi*. I thought that I would learn the language and write letters to my mother. She then wouldn't have to go to someone else to read my letters to her.

I also had a book, *Teach Yourself Sindhi*. I thought that if anyone in the UK wanted to learn, Sindhi my regional language, I could give them it to learn.

Finally I had brought with me a book called *Bhagvad Gita* in Sindhi.

That completed my survival kit.

NOW I WAS READY FOR THE UNKNOWN WORLD

Chapter Five

Journey into the Unknown

I left Mumbai for London in August 1963. I felt that it would be a great adventure. Even though I had decided to be away from my family for two years, I was very excited about visiting a new country. I had decided that while I was in London I would not waste any time. I would visit as many places as I could. Also I was determined to meet many people in the UK. In that way I would be able to know how Europeans live, think, behave. In short I wanted to know all about them.

It was my first overseas trip. I did not know what to expect in the wide world. Also I was very concerned about my mother. She would be living on her own. I was very grateful to her that she allowed me to go away leaving her alone. My brothers encouraged me to go saying that they would visit her in rotation. I also felt that with my employment voucher I was able to go to the UK, and that kind of opportunity may not come again. With lots of blessings from my mother I left her on her own. That was the reason I did not want to be away more than two years.

I had been practising homeopathy and biochemistry medicines for my minor illnesses. Very rarely I went to the doctors. I had found quite a few new effective homeopathic medicines for my use. Due to that I never had any need to go to the doctors. I made a list of books I should buy and take with me to London. Finally I decided what should be in my 'Survival Kit'. I have listed it in my previous chapter.

I travelled by P&O luxury liner *Chusan*. It was a 17 day cruise from Mumbai to Tilbury. It was a very expensive trip. I thought that it could be the holiday of a lifetime. Why should I travel in a second class berth when I could travel in a first class berth. I felt that I should enjoy myself and make it a good two year holiday. I went to

P&O's office to enquire about the availability of first class and the fare. It was well within my means. I felt that I could spend all my savings on the trip. While I am in the UK, I should be earning sufficient to look after myself in the best possible way. The ship was coming from Australia. It was full of Australians. At that time, I never could distinguish between Australians, British, Americans or Europeans. They looked the same to me. Slowly I could see the difference in their behaviour, language, accent, etc. The food we got on the ship was not to my liking. I was used to my Indian spicy food. In 1963, Indian food was not popular at all. On the contrary, it was being ridiculed about its taste and smell. Initially I was very unhappy with the food I was getting on the ship. As the time passed, I got used to it and ate what I liked. They had given us a very wide variety of food. There was plenty of choice.

Every day on the ship they would issue a newsletter giving us a lot of information about where we were and which longitude we had crossed. In addition to it, they had organised trips for all the passengers, whenever we docked. First we docked at Eden, then at Post Said/Suez, Naples and then finally at Tilbury. In the newsletters they would inform us where the trip would be and when the coach would take us away and then bring us back. In Eden it was a very small trip. There wasn't much to see. But at Naples they took us around to Mount Vesuvius, the ruins of Pompeii, and Sorrento. The trip was really fantastic. It was a memorable trip, visiting those ancient sites. I had read about them but never dreamed of visiting them. I took lots of photographs with a Canon camera I had bought in Eden. Eden is a free port. I got the camera for just £12.

After I purchased the camera I noticed that I had another two hours before I needed to join the ship. I wandered around. I came across a huge entrance to what looked like a park. I was curious. I wanted to know what it was. There was no one at the gate. I went in to find out more about it. Shortly I came across a swimming pool and a bar. It was a hot day. I thought that I should have a glass of beer. I went to the bar.

"Can I have a glass of beer, please?"

"What is the name of your host?"

"What do you mean? I am not a guest of anyone."

"Sorry, sir. I can't serve you. I can only serve officers and their guests."

"What place is this?"

"This is a British Air Force base."

Then it dawned on me that unknowingly I had walked into a British Air Force base.

"Didn't someone stop you at the gate?" he asked with surprise.

"There was no one at the gate."

He immediately called security office who immediately escorted me to the gate. I am sure after that the base would constantly have had a security officer at the gate.

My camera was a new Canon model. In the UK it was sold for £32.00. In 1963, £32.00 was a good amount. It was two weeks pay for an average worker. I was very pleased and proud to use it wherever I went. At the back of my mind I always had a thought that I am here for a limited time. I found lots of things amusing and interesting. I would then take photographs of them. I remember one woman was carrying a dog in her lap. I found it very amusing. With her permission I took her photograph with the dog in her lap. In India where I come from, women carry their children in their laps and not a dog. I couldn't imagine that a dog would be carried in a lap. A few days later I saw a policeman in shirt sleeves. Again I couldn't perceive that a British policeman would be in shirt sleeves. We had a good and robust concept of a British bobby in his uniform and policeman's hat. Within a short time I had accumulated lots of photos. I sent a selected few good photographs back home to my family.

I had another important thought in the back of my mind. I realised that I was here for a short time and that the normal local person doesn't know much about India and Indians except what they had heard and read in history books. I should impart a very good image and impression of an Indian. I thought that I was like a self-appointed ambassador. My whole behaviour and attitude changed as soon as I realised that I was representing India. I became very proud of Indian history, Indian culture and Indian moral behaviour. I started mixing with lots of people wherever I went. I started wearing a black cap which I had brought from India. The black cap promoted lots of responses from people wherever I went. It was one of the items in my 'Survival Kit'. I was easily recognised. Everyone knew that there was a person who was not one of them, who was very different from the others. At the drop of a hat I would talk about India, its history, its old books, its old fashioned 'joint family' concept. I used to tell them that in India we look after our elders. Because of the joint family concept there would be three generations living in the same house. Old people not only are looked after by their children, but there would be grandchildren who would give grandparents a very happy and entertaining life. I also used to tell them about our caste system. I would tell them that the main idea behind the caste system was 'division of labour'. Thousands of years ago it worked well. It doesn't work now. On the contrary, it has become a curse on society.

I also explained to local people why Sikhs wear 5 Ks, 5 Ks are Kes (hair), Karpan (sword), Kangan (steel bangle), Kanga (comb), and Katcha (the wearing of specially tailored underwear). In addition to it whenever anyone asked me anything about India and Indians, I would try my best to explain in great detail so that local people understood Indians and their behaviour.

At that time on TV they used to show a cow passing through a high street in an Indian town. The business and traffic in the high street would stop till the cow was gone. Many would ask me in a ridiculing tone, questions like, "Why do Indians allow cows pass through the high street and disturb the business and traffic? Why don't Hindus eat beef?" They would be asking these questions jokingly and make fun of me and Hindus in general. I would very seriously explain to them why we Hindus do not eat beef. My explanation would be as follows:

India consists of about 80% villages. A village family generally consisted of a wife and two children. The family had a small amount of land on which they would grow grains/vegetables/fruit, etc. He would work from early morning till sunset. He would use the ox for tilling the land. During lunchtime the wife would come with a lunchbox and both would eat lunch together. In the meantime, the two children after eating their breakfast would go to school. They would walk to the school with their packed lunch in their schoolbag. The wife would come back home and do all kinds of housework and cooking. Finally she would get ready for the children and her husband. The family needs milk, butter and all kinds of dairy products. Due to that each farmer would have a cow. The cow provided lots of milk for the family and also provided an ox for farm tilling. The cow would have a name. The cow would be treated like a family member. The whole economy of the family was dependant upon her.

In olden days, many women would die during childbirth. That little child would be without a mother. It was found out that cow's milk is nearly as good as mother's milk. From then on the cow is like a mother to the child. In Britain many families have a rabbit as a pet. They are even named and treated like a member of the family. That family would be very reluctant to eat that rabbit as food. Similarly an Indian farmer wouldn't dream of eating a cow. This sentiment has been going on for centuries. So when Hindus don't eat beef, it has nothing to do with Hindu religion, it is the sentiment of the Hindu society.

Let us clarify what is Hinduism. It is not a religion started by any one person. Christianity follows Christ's teaching. Islam follows Mohammed's teaching, Buddhism similarly follows Lord Buddha's teachings. Hinduism was never started by any one person. It just evolved as the world evolved. Hindus called it 'Sanatam Dharma' (perpetual religion). It has no starting date and so it will not have a termination date. Hindus believe that each one of us has a soul. The soul is a tiny part of the super soul (God). That means we all have the same father and we are all brothers and sisters. If all of us thought that way, there would be very little friction, arguments and fighting in the world.

I thought that as I was a qualified mechanical engineer, I should have no problem getting a job. How wrong I was. Every employer I applied to wanted an engineer with experience. After a few months I realised that it would be impossible to get a job as an engineer. I started applying for a job as a draughtsman. Finally after about four months I landed a job of an engineering draughtsman. I thought that it would be economical that I should stay near my job and walk to work. I saw an advertisement in the newspaper shop for a room. The following Saturday morning I rang the bell of the address given in the advertisement. An Irish lady opened the door.

"I have come for the room to let. Can I see it?"

She looked at me and said very hesitantly, "The room is gone." The husband also came to the door.

"I have just got a job nearby in an engineering company. It is within walking distance from here. It would be very handy to have this room. I can then walk to work. At the moment I have to travel a good distance."

Both were very hesitant to give me the room. While they were thinking I added, "Just give me the room for a week as a trial period. If you don't like it, I shall go away after the end of the week."

"You will go away after the end of the week, if we don't like it?"

"Yes I will." Then I added, "Your advertisement mentioned £3 per week. Can I give you £3 in advance?" I produced £3 from my pocket and handed it over to the husband. As soon as he took the money, I knew I had made a deal.

"Tomorrow I shall bring my stuff. What time in the morning is convenient for you?"

"About 11 in the morning would be fine."

They were very nice to me, I also was very nice to them. One week became a year. After a year when I changed my job I had to leave that place. I could see that they were feeling very sorry to see me go. During the year we had been quite good friends.

At that time my income was quite low. I wanted to visit many places in the UK. I thought that perhaps I should have my own transport so that every weekend I could visit different cities and the seaside. From my low income I saved £1 per week. Finally I had sufficient money to buy an old scooter. The scooter gave me a lot of freedom to visit many far away places as well. I didn't want to spend any money on newspapers, so I would go to a nearby library and read various newspapers. I would go through 'situations vacant' columns so that I could get a better job.

We used to have two evening newspapers – *Evening News* and *Evening Standard*. After that both of them merged and now we have only one newspaper called *Evening Standard*. The *Evening Standard* once invited readers to write in not more than 50 words their own 'Finest Hour'. In 1964, a film based on Sir Winston Churchill's wartime was being released. The name of the film was *My finest hour*. The paper mentioned that the first ten best entries would be awarded a double ticket for the premiere show of the film. The premiere show was to be shown in the newly built Royal Festival Hall where the Duke of Edinburgh would be the guest of honour. Also winners would be allowed to attend the cocktail party after the show. I liked the idea. I thought it would be great if I was one of the winners. I had mentally noted down the last date for the submission of the entry. Every day while I was walking to my work and back I would think very hard about my 'finest hour'. The last day was getting nearer and I couldn't think of any special finest hour. Suddenly the day before the last day I found out about my finest hour. I wrote it down on a postcard and carefully counted the words so that they were not more than 50 words. I felt that I couldn't rely on the post. On the last day of submission I personally went to the office of the newspaper in Fleet Street and handed over my entry. Every day after that I would look for the names of the winners. The day came when five of the winners' entries were published in the paper. I was very sad that mine was not one of them. I anxiously waited for the day when they would announce the remaining five names. I had a very pleasant surprise when I saw my entry in print with a cartoon. The copy of it is shown on the opposite page.

My Finest Hour

The following day I went to my office and said, "I have been to the Royal Festival Hall."

"What concert did you attend?"

"No, it was not a concert. It was a film premiere show attended by the Duke of Edinburgh." Then I described to them what and how it happened. I could see that they were very jealous of me thinking, 'We live in this country. We haven't been to the Royal Festival Hall, nor attended a cocktail party in the presence of Duke of Edinburgh. This person who has just arrived in this country has been all over the place'.

Within a short time I joined the local Tory party and regularly visited their centre. I would meet many people there. They would ask me a lot of questions and I would answer in the best possible way. Sometimes they would ask a silly question to be funny and make fun of me and of Indians. I would very seriously reply back to them. By that time I made them understand that what they said was not funny. After a couple of months I got a job in GEC, it was a huge company. They had a very good social club. The social club had various sections and activities. I joined five sections so that I could visit the club every day of the week. These five sections were snooker, table tennis, bridge, photographic section and stamp collection section. Every weekend would pass in visiting various parts of the country. I went to the Isle of Wight where I learned boating, sailing and canoeing. I visited many cities in England. I also visited Scotland, Wales and Ireland. Possibly I was the most busy person on earth. I was thoroughly enjoying myself. I remember in the Isle of Wight one person asked me, "Do Indians live in trees?" This question may have been a joke, may have been to ridicule Indians or it was just ignorance. I did not laugh. Very seriously I replied, "Yes, we live in trees but use elevators to go up and down." I said it with a very straight face. Initially the person did not understand the joke. After a while the person laughed and said, "Really?"

"Oh yes," I replied. Wherever I went I thoroughly enjoyed myself. All the time I was doing my best since I had limited time in this country. Also I was not shackled in any way. I was free and my mind was free, my thoughts were free so was my behaviour. My behaviour I felt was first class. All the time I was imparting a very good impression of Indians on local people. I made many good friends. I learned to drink beer and Guinness. We would go to a pub every Friday night. I found out a method of keeping up with locals in drinking sessions. They would drink a pint of beer, I would drink a half pint. In that way I could keep up with them.

When two years finished , I felt my job was not done. I had to learn so much about the British. So I stayed on, till I got pressure from my mother in India that I should now return. In the meantime I had changed my job and was working with Imperial Chemical Industries in North East England. In 1967, after four years stay in the UK, I decided to go back to India, but not for good, just to see my family and decide what I was going to do next. At that time, from North East England, it was difficult to get tickets for India. I couldn't find any travel agent who could give me a ticket for India. I had to come to London and meet the travel agent. Now I had a car. Early morning I started from Middlesborough for London. There was not much traffic on the road, so I was driving quite fast. Suddenly I had a puncture in the front tyre. I tried my best to control my car, but my car somersaulted three to four times and landed on the other side of the dual carriageway on the A1. During those days they never had central barriers. I didn't know what was happening. I was just going round and round and finally my car stopped. I was very dazed and couldn't think clearly. Suddenly my car door opened and a person peered inside. "Are you alright?"

"Yes, I am alright."

"OK, come out now."

"Yes, I am coming out." But I was dazed, I just sat there looking down and couldn't think of anything. After sometime he again asked me to come out. I nearly fainted when I saw the state of my car. It was a complete wreck. I couldn't believe that I came out of it and survived. I just had a few scratches on my knees. A long line of cars were waiting for my car to be removed – the carriageway was blocked.

I came out of the car and everyone asked me the same question, "Are you alright?" Perhaps no one could believe either that I had come out of that wreck and survived. Shortly the police came and immediately after that an RAC van came as well. I was a member of the RAC. The RAC asked me what I wanted to do with the car. Suddenly I started shivering. It wasn't winter and it wasn't cold either. But possibly due to shock I started shivering. Policemen wrapped me in a blanket and asked. "Where can we drop you?"

"I am going to London, can you take me to London?"

"Yes, where in London?"

In London I used to live in East London with a family. I gave the police that address.

He asked, "What about your car?"

"It is no good to any one now. It looks like scrap," I added. "Has it got any scrap value?"

"Not a lot," he replied.

"Please scrap it," I responded.

He took me to the police station where he came from. Before we started for London we had tea and a sandwich in the police station. Then we set off to London. He was quite a nice person, he came from Doncaster. He had been in the force for the last five years. He said, "This is the first miracle I have seen. People don't survive this kind of crash. You are very lucky. If you had been wearing a safety belt you would have been strangled by it. Please drive carefully and don't push your luck."

The policemen brought me to the house of Mr Sajjad ali Khan and his wife Naushi, with whom I used to stay before I went to Middlesborough. They were very surprised to see me and very glad as well. I had been away for three years, and there was so much to talk about. We were very good friends. Even though I was their tenant, I was like one of the family members, even though I am a Hindu and they were Muslims from India. At that time in 1965 the relationship between India and Pakistan was not very good. On the contrary, the war between the two countries was going on. We used to sit together and watch it on TV.

I explained to Mr and Mrs Khan everything about my accident, and also let them know that I was going to India on holiday. We talked and talked. They told me the next day that while talking I had dozed off.

The following morning I went to the travel agent and purchased a return ticket to India. He could get a seat for me the following day, provided I gave him cash. I was delighted and gave him the required amount and got my ticket.

In those days, an hour before flight time was sufficient to check-in. My flight was at 18.30 hours. I started around 16.00 hours for the airport. During those times, the Piccadilly line used to terminate at Hounslow West Station and then one would catch a bus to the airport. It so happened that the bus I caught suddenly developed trouble with its engine. By the time the next bus came, we had lost a bit of time. Quickly I got off the bus and went to check-in counter at the airport. It was 18.15. They said I was too late to board the plane. I was very upset, I said, "Just give me a boarding pass, I will carry my luggage."

"It is not allowed. With that same ticket we shall allow you to travel by the next available flight. It will be the day after tomorrow." I thanked him and went back to Khan's house.

The Khan family were again very surprised to see me. This is the second time I had surprised them with me visiting without any warning. Last time I did this, I came with the police after my accident. Now I was feeling very rotten. I wanted to go to India and see my family, but now there was a delay of two more days. Two days compared to the four years I had been away was nothing but, it was like a child gets a toy, but at the last minute it is snatched from him, he is going to get upset and cry very loudly to show his annoyance. That was my situation. I didn't do anything except take the Khan family for shopping. They had a small child. We visited a park and played with the child. It was a beautiful day. Many families with their children had come. Luckily I did not tell my family in India which day I was arriving. I had just said that I was planning to visit India in the month of September. So they were not as anxious as I was. Finally the day came; I boarded the plane, arrived in Mumbai, caught a taxi, arrived at our house and knocked on the door. I wanted to see their faces full of surprise. For a few minutes, we were all silent with shock and surprise. Then all of us talked together.

I had stayed for four years in the UK. My initial idea was to spend only two years. So I thought I should go back to India, see my family, then decide what I should do. Either I would come back to the UK for good or come back for a short while to finish my personal assignment of finding out about how to 'Know Europeans Better'.

I got a shock of a lifetime. I could not identify myself with my family and friends. It seemed that after I had left India for London and then went North-East of England, to Middlesborough, I was all the time with British society. I had little contact with Indians, the reason was that I didn't want to waste my limited time in the UK. I wanted to know as much as possible about British people. Due to that, slowly, but gradually, my thinking and nature had changed and I possibly nearly had a British way of thinking. In addition, I was so used to being among white people that in India I felt I was an odd man out. My food habits had changed. I didn't want to have tea with a lot of sugar, didn't want tea boiled. I was used to eating less spicy food. I didn't talk much either. When I went to India, I had at the back of my mind to look for a suitable Indian girl as my wife.

During my stay of about three months in India I went to Kolkata, Pune and Bangalore and met all my brothers and sisters. Finally I decided that perhaps I would be a misfit in India. I should go back to the UK and establish myself for good there. Since I decided that I should live in the UK, I felt that perhaps an Indian wife would not survive there, as there is so much difference in the way of life. In the UK one has to do everything – cleaning, cooking, driving, shopping, ironing, practically everything. In India we have cleaners, cooks, chauffeurs, washermen, milkmen, papermen, vegetablemen, and full-time servants. It would have been difficult for Indian girl to cope with all those duties. There were a few girls interested in getting married to me and coming with me to the UK. I didn't go ahead with any one of them. I had finally decided that a British girl is more practical. She is so used to all these chores.

In the UK I had a few girls who were interested in me, but I was not interested in any of them. All the time I was thinking that I should go to India and then decide. Now I have come to India and have decided what I want to do. So I came back to Middlesborough and continued with my life with an additional assignment. Now not only was I studying 'How Europeans Live and Think', but with my roving eyes I was searching for my future wife. I started going with my friends to clubs, dances, outings, theatre, concerts etc, it was like finding a needle in a haystack. As the time passed I looked through quite a few haystacks but no luck.

One of our office mates was getting married. He gave me an invitation to attend the reception and said, "Come with your girlfriend."

"I haven't got a girlfriend." He said, "Come any way, you may get your girlfriend there." He laughed. I smiled thinking that one doesn't get a girlfriend like that. Anyway, I went to the reception even though I did not know anyone except the groom. The groom was very busy surrounded by his family and friends.

At the party I spotted a familiar face and went to him with a brandy glass in my hand and said, "I think I know you, I have seen you somewhere." Then added, "Do you work in ICI?"

He said, "Yes. Do you?" I said, "Yes, in the design section." That was our start and I found out that his name was George and he was working in the piping section. While we were talking, a beautiful girl approached him and asked, "Where is John?"

"He is over there." Before she left, George introduced me to her and said, "This is Anita, she is my younger sister. She works in ICI." Then George turned towards me and said to his sister, "This is Vasu. Vasu also works in ICI." After a short talk with us she went over to John. After she left, I kept thinking about her, I was stunned by her beauty; white suit, shoulder length hair, beautiful smiling eyes, slim, not too fat, not too thin. I felt she was just right. But the main thing which caught my eye was the way she screwed up her nose when George asked her, 'Do you want a drink?' That really bowled me over. While I was talking to George, I kept thinking about her and planning that I must meet her again. I knew in which section of ICI George worked. The following week, I walked over to the piping section to meet him. He was busy with his work. I casually talked with him, saying that I was just passing by and noticed him. He was very glad to see me. It seemed Anita had asked George about me. George said, "I was thinking about you, Vasu."

"Anything special?"

"No. Just Anita was asking me lots of questions about you."

"She is pretty, isn't she?" I commented.

I asked George for Anita's phone number so that I could phone his sister. He very gladly gave it to me and told me what was the best time to phone her. At the first opportunity I phoned Anita. It seemed her mother picked up the phone.

"Can I talk to Anita, please?"

"Who shall I say wants to talk to her?"

"Vasu," I said and then added, "I met her last week at the wedding reception."

"Oh, yes, George was talking about you, he said that you would phone for Anita."

Then I heard the mother calling Anita saying that George's friend, that foreign gentleman, is on the line.

"Hello, Anita speaking."

"Hello Anita, I am Vasu. Do you remember me? I met you and George last week at the wedding reception."

"Oh yes, I remember."

I didn't know what to say next, so I blurted out, "It is a nice day today, isn't it?"

"Yes, very nice, there is no rain today. Yesterday it was raining very heavily." Then she added, "I got soaked yesterday, caught in a heavy shower."

"Didn't catch cold, I hope."

"Oh, just a sniff." This small talk gave me a chance to think what to say next.

"I would like to meet you," I said, before she could respond, I asked her, ""What are you doing tomorrow evening, after work?"

"Nothing much." After a pause she asked, "What do you have in mind?"

"*Bonny and Clyde* is running at the Elite Cinema, I have heard it is quite good." After a pause, I asked, "Would you like to see it?"

"I don't mind," she replied.

"I finish my work at 5.30pm. What time do you finish?"

"I finish at 5pm," Anita replied.

"The show starts at 7.30pm. That gives us sufficient time to go home, freshen up, have something to eat and we can meet around 7pm at the cinema hall. You know where it is, don't you?"

"Yes, I know it."

"OK, I shall see you then."

"See you."

I was over the moon, I couldn't think straight, all the time I could see her and visualise her. Every now and then I could see her face screwing her nose in her typical way. After that whenever I wanted to visualise her, I just would close my eyes and see her.

I don't remember much about the film, I don't think Anita did either. We were in our own dream world. Looking back I don't remember what I was thinking, but I remember that I was very happy and felt like climbing the nearest hill and shouting at the top of my voice, I don't know what, but definitely would have said 'I am the happiest man on earth'.

I had come in my car, which was parked not far away. After the film, I thought that her mother may be waiting, it was quite late. But with hesitation, I asked, "Can we go for a drink?"

"I don't mind."

I was very surprised but glad at the reply. We went to a bar in a nearby hotel. The atmosphere in the hotel pub was much better than just in a normal pub. At that time, pubs were generally quite rough with rough characters visiting them. We talked and talked and exchanged our views, our aims in life, about our families, etc etc. I very much liked what I heard. Obviously Anita liked what she heard as well. We went to my car so that I could take her to her house. It seemed Anita was not in a hurry to go to her house. On the way to her house, we passed a public park. There were a few swings in the park and the park had no gates, anyone could enter at any time. When Anita saw the swings, she said, "I want to sit on the swing." Who am I to refuse? I stopped the car and there we were swinging on two swings and talking about this and that. Strangely time passed so quickly and nicely that suddenly it was dawn. In North England during summer time, the sun rises very early. Finally I dropped her near her house. "When can I meet you again? Can we meet tomorrow?" I was very glad when she said, "Yes. Tomorrow you can pick me up at the same place where you are dropping me today."

Around 5.30 in the morning we wished goodnight/good morning and I departed to my house.

After that every evening at the same time, same place I would pick her up and we went wherever we fancied. During these meetings we would talk about our future together. I thought that my parents/family are 5,000 miles away. Anita also should be far away from her parents. At that time the Canadian government were advertising a fare of only £10 to go to Canada and immigrate to that country. We thought it was a very good idea that we should get married and immigrate to Canada. We went to their Embassy and got all the relevant details regarding housing/job etc.

It came out suddenly in our conversation that Anita's mother didn't like the idea that Anita should marry a non-English person. Anita told me that a while ago she wanted to marry an Irish boy called Kenny. Her mother didn't like him. Since then Anita would call her mother 'a silly cow'.

When I heard that Anita's mother wouldn't like me, I got very upset. Up to now I had never been to Anita's house, so I said, "If your mother doesn't like me what shall we do?"

"My mother doesn't matter, if you can convince my eldest sister, Roberta, then Roberta will sort everything out." But she said, "Roberta is a tough nut to crack, if you can handle her, then we will have no problem."

"Are you with me?" I asked Anita.

"Always," she replied.

"Where and when can I meet your sister?" After serious thinking, Anita replied, "You could come this Saturday around 6pm to our house. I have shown it to you from the outside. I shall tell Roberta to come as well, she is married and lives about 10 miles away from here." Then she added, "But, be strong with her, otherwise she will chew you up."

I was a bit worried about it as I had never met Roberta, and it seemed their brother George had no say in these matters.

Saturday came. With pounding heartbeat I knocked on their door. Roberta opened the door. "Yes?" she asked.

"I am Vasu, and have come to meet Anita." She just stared at me. I saw Anita was lurking behind her sister. She came forward and guided me to the reception room. Her mother never came, it seemed my first interview was with Roberta.

I don't remember what she said or what I replied, it was nearly forty years ago, but I remember that she indicated that they are English and do not marry with any other non-English. To cut the story short, I said to Roberta," Anita and I are going to marry each other, you like it or not. We shall invite you, it is up to you to grace the occasion or not." I said it with such conviction and authority that she backed away and all her hostile attitude melted away. I noticed Anita was standing in a doorway. When I saw her, she gave me a thumbs-up sign and was very pleased and smiling broadly. Roberta went away and brought their mother into the room. Anita also came and the four of us sat and talked in general. Anita went to the kitchen and brought tea and biscuits. Then I realised that I had scored.

Chapter Six

Lyke Wake Walk

It was early 1968. I had been in ICI for the last two years. During those two years I had been very active. I had joined ICI's social club. There were quite a few sections pursuing different activities. I had joined five sections in such a way that I was from Monday to Friday in the clubhouse pursuing varied activities. They were as follows:

Monday	Play Duplicate Bridge
Tuesday	Photography
Wednesday	Small Bore Rifle Practice
Thursday	Writer's Section
Friday	Wine and Cheese Tasting

The atmosphere in ICI was very friendly. All the employees behaved like a very big joint family. There were mainly two big employers in the area, ICI and British Steel. Due to that most of residents were either employed by ICI or British Steel. Many people knew me either by face or by name. During weekends I would take my car and visit nearby villages and towns. All the time I used to tell myself, 'Vasu, you are here for a short time. Make the best use of it. Visit as many places as you can, meet as many people, make them aware about your country, culture and everything about India and Hindus'. I remember one Saturday I visited a seaside town called Whitby, about 30 miles away from Middlesbrough. Who do you think I met walking on the beach? A bridge player and his wife. Similarly I went to Scarborough on another occasion. I was having fish and chips for lunch, when I heard someone call my name. I looked around and was surprised to see a couple sitting on the next table in the restaurant. They regularly attended 'Wine and Cheese Tasting'. I immediately went and joined them at their table. I had joined ICI as if I had joined a huge joint family. This family was like a huge octopus with tentacles reaching all over the place. Our engineering section had ten mechanical engineers. We had an invisible bond among us. As the time passed, bond became stronger. It so happened that during lunchtime we would play football, go for a swim, play green bowling, or anything similar we fancied. After that we would go to the canteen and eat double lunches. Six of us had become very close. No one could separate us. It was like 'one for six and six for one'.

In our group, Ken Hornby was always looking for something new to do. One morning he said, "Why don't we go to a pub for a drink this Friday evening?"

We all liked the idea. Douglas Macdonald, another one in our group said, "Joan likes shopping on Friday evenings. Let me check with her and let you know tomorrow."

The next day he came and said, "Joan doesn't like the idea, but I have convinced her that shopping on Saturday is better."

Friday came and all six of us met around 7.30pm in a pub specified by Ken. I was not happy at all. I had to miss my 'Wine and Cheese Tasting' party. But as I said our attitude was 'one for six and six for one'. I don't remember how many pints of beer we had. I had already learned my lesson of keeping up with these heavy drinkers. I would order half a pint against their one pint. I could survive the night without getting drunk. That idea had served me well.

A few times I could see that my mates were too drunk to drive a car. I would take them in my car and safely deliver them to their wives. Their wives would be very grateful and offer me a supper before I drove off to my house. A few times I had accepted their offer.

Another day Ken came out with another idea. He said, "Why don't we walk 'Lyke Wake Walk'?" It seemed everyone knew what he was talking about. I had never heard of it so I enquired, "What is it?"

"It is a walk, Vasu. Would you like to come?"

"Of course I will come. When are we going to walk?"

"It is getting hot now. We should walk in the night."

"Then we should select an evening when there is a full moon," Lenny Pope suggested.

"We should start the walk Friday evening and finish Saturday afternoon."

"I shall find out the full moon Friday and let you know tomorrow," Lenny suggested.

The following day Lenny said, "Friday the 24th May will be a full moon. We should start our walk on that day. We have about four weeks during which time we should organise what to carry and whose car we will go in to the starting point." I was completely ignorant of the distance or the terrain we were supposed to walk. Finally everything was decided. The four who agreed to walk were:

Ken Hornby
Lenny Pope
John Pearson
Vasu Daryanani

I had agreed to pick them up and take them to the starting point at a village called Osmotherly. We arrived around 7.30pm. It seemed that before the start must sign a register located in a pub called the Queen Catherine. We went in the pub, had a drink, signed our names and were ready to start the walk. When I had picked up my friends I noticed that they were wearing heavy walking boots, wind cheaters, scarves and gloves. I heard one of my friends commenting to another, "Look at Vasu. He has come as if he has come for an evening stroll." I was in my normal shoes and wearing my normal jacket. But to be on the safe side I had an extra pullover, scarf and my black cap which I had brought with me. It was one of the items in my survival kit. Suddenly I felt sorry for myself when the realisation came to me that I was not dressed correctly for the occasion. Obviously they knew the walk and the terrain.

We started at 8.00pm. Ken Hornby was our leader. Lenny and John had a general idea of the walk. They also had a map. The evening was very pleasant. Spring was in the air. We also had a spring in our step and very briskly went ahead. We were in a good mood. After a couple of miles we came across a hill to climb. It wasn't difficult. Then the next hill came for us to climb. That wasn't too bad either. We had nearly completed ten miles. The full walk was forty-two miles. We stopped to have something to eat and drink. It seemed Ken was struggling to climb the second hill.

Ken said, "I had a touch of flu last week. It has drained away my energy. I don't think I will be able to walk further. I feel very tired. I am sorry to say that I shall go down the hill to the main road and thumb a lift to go home." It was nearly midnight.

"Ken, can you manage on your own?"

"Yes, I can. I am just tired. I will be alright. You go ahead and finish the walk."

I had never walked and climbed so many hills. They were making me tired. I was very green and ignorant about the terrain and the place where we were walking. I was curious. I asked Lenny, "Lenny, what is this area called? There are so many hills all around us."

"We are on the Yorkshire Moors."

The three of us got up to finish the walk. It was lucky that due to the full moon and clear sky we could see the terrain very well. More hills came to climb. They were getting more difficult to climb as the time went on. It seemed it was equally difficult to come down the hills. It was getting chilly as well. Due to that we walked faster to keep ourselves warm. We had now finished nearly half the walk and were coming down a hill. John Pearson complained that his new boots were hurting him, and said, "I can't carry on. It is very painful." He also had no choice but to go down to the main road nearby and make his way to his house. It was good that I had brought them in my car. Ken as well as John just had to find their way to their house. John was very sorry to leave us half way. He was determined to finish the walk. His new boots had betrayed him. Now it was only Lenny and I. We were both determined to finish the walk. We ate and drank what we had left in our backpacks. Most of our food and tea was gone except one sandwich each, one apple each, and a mouthful of water for the remainder of our walk.

All this time I would jump across any water or mud which came along so that I did not spoil my shoes. I would jump and land on my left leg. Due to that my left leg was very painful. I then tried to jump on my right leg. By this time both legs were hurting. My leg muscles had become very tight due to climbing hills, coming down and then jumping across the mud and so on. I decided that I should conserve my energy and be gentle with my leg muscles. After that I would just walk through the mud, water, or whatever came in my way. I remember that once I went up to my knees in a bog, but I had passed caring. I could see that Lenny and I were not in any shape to finish the walk. Finally we arrived at a point and noticed that there was a main road below. According to our map we had about another ten miles to go. We had finished all our food and drink. There was nothing left except one apple each. It was nine in the morning and the sun was shining, but we both were shivering. We felt very cold. We were definitely not in shape to continue and finish the remaining ten miles. My leg muscles had been very tight. I was sure Lenny also would be in a similar state. Lenny was determined to finish the walk.

"Lenny, if you want to finish the walk, I shall come with you. I can't let you go on your own. I am not fit to go further. I am cold, my legs are painful, I feel like fainting." I looked at Lenny, he was very determined. I then added, "Why don't we go home now. Next time we shall definitely complete this walk. But we have to bring more food and drinks. My shoes are falling apart. I shall have stronger shoes." With a lot of persuasion I finally convinced Lenny. We came down to the main road. It took us nearly half an hour to get a lift to a nearby bus station. Finally we arrived at his house in the afternoon. After his wife, Joan, gave us something to eat and drink, he dropped me at the Queen Catherine where my car was. I realised that my leg muscles were so tight that even pushing the accelerator and brake pedal was an effort for me. I arrived safely home, had a shower and rested till the following lunchtime.

I was in agony. My legs were very painful. I thought it would be foolish to attempt that kind of walk again. The next day I did not go to work. Instead I went to my GP to consult him. When I told him that I had attempted the Lyke Wake walk, he said, "It is good that you didn't push yourself to do the last ten miles. You could have done permanent damage to your leg muscles. It seems that there is no harm done now. Every evening before you go to bed, sit in a bath full of hot water, as hot as you can manage. Come and see me in a weeks time."

I thanked him and did what he told me.

The next day I went to my office. Ken asked me, "We have decided that we will walk on Friday 12th July. It will be a full moon. Are you coming for the walk?"

"Of course I am coming, Ken."

There was a wild cry from Lenny's throat. "I won the bet, I won the bet," Lenny shouted. It seemed Ken and Lenny had a bet. Ken had said that this time Vasu wouldn't dare to attempt the walk again. He was in a bad shape. Obviously Lenny knew me better than Ken did.

I thought that I was not physically fit and ready for the walk I had agreed to do on the 12th July. I had an idea that I should walk regularly to tone up my leg muscles. I lived six miles away from my office. I would use my car to come to my office. Why not change my house and live nearer to my office, say two miles. I would then walk every day to and from my office. Still I had six weeks before the walk started. By that time my leg muscles should be sufficiently toned up. I found out that it was not easy to get a room. Last time I got a room in a house which was owned by an Indian. This time I tried but it was very difficult. As soon as the owner of a house who had advertised a 'room to let' heard my accent, he would say, "Sorry, the room has just gone." At that time I was courting Anita. I told her to phone for the room.

The landlord gave her the address. At the appointed time we both arrived at the house. The landlord saw me and hesitated. Anita, who later became my wife said, "My boyfriend works in ICI. He is a mechanical engineer. Can we see the room please?"

"Oh, you work in ICI?" he asked me.

"Yes."

"What section?"

"Pressure vessel design."

"I work in ICI as well. I work in the administration office," he replied.

As I had mentioned earlier that working in ICI was like working in a joint family. He showed us a room. It was quite small. There was a small Baby Belling cooker in the room. The bathroom and TV room were for common use. I immediately paid him two weeks rent and thanked him.

It was a very wise move I had made. Not only did it help me in toning my leg muscles, I saved money on not using my car. The walk would take me about half an hour. By car it would have taken at least twenty minutes due to heavy traffic on the road. Also Anita and I had more privacy in that house.

Friday the 12th July came. I felt quite fit. This time seven of us agreed to walk. In addition we had a supporting party who would meet us at checkpoints and also at the end of the walk. They would feed us with food and drinks. The supporting party would look after any of us who were not able to continue with the walk. The following were the seven who started the walk.

> John Pearson
> Leslie Pearson
> Bob Hawkins
> Ron Kell
> Ian Macdonald
> Stewart Mcdonald
> Vasu Daryanani

The supporting party were:

Douglas Macdonald
Len Pope
Ken Hornby
Roger Mason
Bill Rogers

Douglas Macdonald was working in ICI in our section. He felt that he was not fit enough to walk forty-two miles. But he mentioned that his two young brothers Ian and Stewart would like to walk. Both were young and used to play in a local football team.

Lenny Pope was still not fit to walk. As you know I had been to my GP for consultation, so did he to his GP. His GP advised him. "Do not attempt the walk. Your leg muscles have gone very weak."

Ken Hornby was also was not fit yet. He had developed some kind of chest infection after he had the flu.

Roger Mason and Bill Rogers wanted to help us as much as they could.

This time I had two pullovers instead of one. Apart from that my attire was the same as for my first walk. The supporting party was very helpful. We didn't have to carry our backpacks. At every checkpoint we were greeted with a smile and were given food and drinks. It was real luxury compared to the last walk we had. We were well prepared for our second attempt at the walk. Also we were all in a happy mood knowing that we had a capable leader in Ron Kell. Also we were relaxed and not tensed and miserable as we were on our first attempt. I remember once on the way during a comfort stop, one of us broke wind. In the dead of night, there was silence all around us. The sound of 'break of wind' sounded very loud and odd. We all laughed and one of us said, "Now, John is relieved." After that for a long time we couldn't stop laughing.

John and his wife Leslie gave up after the first checkpoint. It was so easy for anyone to give up knowing that the supporting party would look after them. Leslie's boots were hurting her feet. John had no option but to accompany his wife. At the second checkpoint Bob gave up. Bob said, "I can't breathe. I am short of breath. I would like to stay with the supporting party." Now we were four, and were very determined to finish the walk. I was in good shape. My leg muscles were much stronger than they were before. Also Ron Kell had already done the walk during the night few years ago. This time he was our leader. The supporting party was very helpful at every checkpoint. The checkpoint was after every ten miles. When we were approaching the third checkpoint, we had done about thirty miles. I felt very weak and wanted to sit down. Luckily we spotted Douglas' car in the distance at the checkpoint. I made a huge effort to carry on till we arrived where Douglas was standing. I just slumped in the car's back seat. I faintly heard, "Vasu. What do want to eat?" I just raised my hand to indicate that I was not yet fit to reply. I could faintly hear they were saying, "Vasu is asleep. Let us finish his soup." Someone else said, "Let us finish his eggs."

After a while I recovered and sat down. I then had my soup, had my eggs and whatever else was available. After a cup of tea I was ready to finish the final twelve miles. I just went on mechanically determined to finish the walk. After a few miles I felt much better and stronger. Finally on Saturday morning around 12.15 we finished the walk. We were all very tired. We just slid down on the ground. Douglas had said that he would pick us up around 2.00pm. Ron our leader said, "We have to sign out." The register is kept in a pub in a village called Ravenscar. It is about half a mile from here." No one moved. I looked at the three of them. None of them had any intention to go to the pub and sign out. "I will go," I said. I was dying to have a cup of tea. I thought I could do both, have a tea as well as sign out for all of us. I dragged myself slowly and walked to the pub. Douglas was not due till 2.00pm. I had plenty of time. Douglas came at 2.00pm on the dot. He picked us up and took us to our houses. It was a luxury to be driven home. In the car I closed my eyes and went out like a light till Douglas woke me up and said, "Vasu, can you manage to climb stairs to your room?"

"Yes I can. Thank you Douglas."

I was in much better shape than I was during the first attempt. By Sunday evening I had recovered. I was ready to go to the office on Monday morning. Would you believe it if I tell you that I walked to the office as I had been doing for the last six weeks. I had continued walking to and from office till my last day in ICI. It had become my habit.

Do you know that now we were planning the walk again! Lenny had instigated it.

Lenny commented, "I missed the walk. I would like to do the walk. The next full moon is on Friday 7th September."

"Lenny, I shall be in the supporting party. But if for any reason you do not get sufficient members to walk, I shall accompany you," I replied to Lenny.

"I shall consult my GP to see if he has any objection to my walking."

A few days later he went to meet his GP. GP discouraged him and said, "Do not walk unless you want to damage your leg muscles permanently."

Lenny had no option but to listen to his GP. There wasn't much enthusiasm among others. The third attempt never materialised. I had done the walk. I wasn't very keen to attempt it again.

They told me that I should write to Lyke Wake walk club and let them know that I had finished the walk. I could apply for the membership. The club sent to me a tie and lapel pin. Both showed a coffin. It is said that during Viking times, if any of their priests died in an inland area, Vikings would carry him in his coffin across the Yorkshire Moors and bury him in the sea. That was the reason the tie and lapel pin showed the shape of a coffin.

Around that time I read in a national newspaper that the Canadian government were encouraging British engineers to immigrate to Canada. The fare to Canada would only be £10. I had left India to visit various countries. I thought that I should take advantage of it. At that time I was courting Anita and we were seriously thinking of getting married. When I mentioned to her that we could immigrate to Canada as soon as we got married, she was delighted. The Canadian Immigration Office was in London. We thought that we should visit London and find out more about it. My birthday was in November. We finally planned as follows:

> Resign from ICI and serve an appropriate notice period
> My last day in the office should be a Friday
> The following day, ie on Saturday, we should get married
> That afternoon a reception should be held
> Next day, ie on Sunday, pack our car with whatever belongings we had
> Leave for London
> Before that a hotel room should be booked in London for two weeks
> During that two weeks we should find a place to live
> Also find work on a contract basis
> While in London investigate more about immigration to Canada

Everything went according to our plan. I had made my friends aware of what our plans were. It seemed everyone in ICI knew me and my plans.

ICI used to publish every month a newsletter called *Billingham News*. The editor came to know about our successful attempt at Lyke Wake walk. They sent their reporter along with a photographer. Someone told the reporter that I was leaving the company, getting married and immigrating to Canada. The reporter gathered all the engineers in our section all around me while I was sitting at my desk studying the Lyke Wake walk map. When the paper came out it had the group photograph with me sitting and all the others standing around me while we all studied the map. The photograph had a heading:

End of trail for Vasu

The nearby ICI plant at Wilton also used to produce their own monthly newspaper called *Wilton News*. Initially I had joined ICI in their Wilton site. They came to know about my exploits as well. They sent their reporter and a photographer. They also displayed a group photograph with a caption: VASU LEAVES LYKE WAKE TEAM.

I was very pleased with myself that I had not wasted my time. I felt I had utilised and spent my time very well indeed.

After I left ICI in North East England I came to London. One evening I was standing on a platform at Oxford Circus tube station. One person approached me and asked, "Have you done it?"

"Done what?"

"Lyke Wake walk?"

I used to wear the Lyke Wake walk tie very proudly. I was wearing it on that evening. He had recognised it.

"Yes, I have. Have you?"

"Oh, yes. I did it while I was at Newcastle University, long time ago," he replied.

Chapter Seven

How I located my Friend in a Foreign Land

I have been racing ahead with my autobiography and ignoring quite a few interesting experiences. I feel that the following two experiences must not be ignored. How I located Luciana Boati and how I managed to meet the Pope and shook hands with him.

When I arrived in London way back in 1963, I used to stay with an Indian family in Golders Green, London NW11. I was quite keen to have a job. I was a mechanical engineer. It seemed it was not as easy as I thought. I thought I would get lots of job offers. After going through an advertisement in the *Daily Telegraph*, I was told that the *Daily Telegraph* had good jobs for mechanical engineers. I would send, say, four applications in one day. The advertiser would get it on the next day. The post was very efficient at that time. The employer would reply on that same day and I would get a reply on the following day. The reply would always be full of regrets. After a few months I got sick and tired of this kind of routine. Getting regret letters was soul destroying. I didn't know what to do except continue applying for jobs. I had heard that a few graduates, to earn some money, would take up a job to feed the chocolate machines during the night in the underground stations. I also was getting short of money. I was lucky that my eldest brother, Motiram, was in Nairobi, Kenya. I wrote to him to send some money to me so that I could survive till I got a job. To reduce my expenses I stopped buying newspapers. After my breakfast I would go to the nearby library and go through 'situation vacant' column. It became my routine. My first priority was to get a job before I could do anything. My main mission was to see the world as well as to know and understand the British and the Europeans. I could see that my time was being wasted and was not able to pursue my mission.

I noticed a young beautiful girl who also was very regular in visiting the library. She would also read the newspapers. I used to sit at a very large table, about ten people could sit around it and read newspapers. One day I was reading a newspaper and she sat in the chair beside me. That was the only chair vacant. I looked up, she smiled, I smiled back. We then continued reading. After some time she left. During those days I was very shy. I wanted to talk to her but couldn't. After she left I thought I would talk to her next time. Every day I would look for her but she never came. A week passed, I was very anxious. After a week she turned up. She sat across from me. The table was quite large, so we couldn't talk to each other. Shortly after that I mustered some courage and went round to her. "You didn't come for a week, were you away?" I enquired.

"I had a touch of flu."

"You are OK now?"

"Oh yes, thank you."

In the library one couldn't talk much nor talk loudly. I went back to my seat. When she was about to leave, I glanced up. She caught my gaze and wished me goodbye.

"Goodbye. See you tomorrow," I replied.

"Yes. See you tomorrow," she replied.

Again a week passed by and I didn't see her. I thought that I had lost her. I kicked myself saying that I should have asked for her name, phone number, etc. The next day she turned up. I was so glad to see her. For me she was like a sight for sore eyes. I immediately requested her to come with me to a far corner in the library, so that we could whisper. I gathered that she was from Italy and she was working as an au-pair with an English family. She came to London to learn English, then would go back to Italy. She was here only for a short time. I asked her, "When do you go back to Italy?"

"In two weeks time," she replied.

The Next day was Saturday. I asked her, "Do you work during weekends?"

"No, I don't work during weekends."

I suggested, "Why not meet tomorrow for a coffee?"

"Yes. Why not. Where shall we meet?"

I didn't know much about the area. "Why not meet around 11am here in the library. We can then go out." She agreed.

During the next two weeks we met every day, drank lots of coffee, and did lots of sightseeing. We both were new in the country. It was very interesting to go sightseeing together. I was proud of my camera, which I had bought in Eden. I took a few photos. We went to Trafalgar Square, Green Park and St James Park. We also visited the river Thames and other usual sightseeing spots.

We had a very good time. I came to know that she came from Milan. The next week was Christmas. We had Christmas dinner in a cheap restaurant. I didn't have much money. I was not earning then. Moreover I was not sure about myself. I came here with a mission. My mission was to earn, spend and understand Europeans in general. I didn't want to get involved with a girl. I restrained myself. Before she left for Milan, I asked and she gave me her address in Milan. I gave her a scarf as a Christmas present. She gave me in return an LP of an Italian singer.

Luckily in early January I got a job in a nearby small engineering company. I got busy, but my mind was very disturbed. For the last two weeks we had been constantly together. Suddenly she was not there. I felt lost. I remember when I used to work on my drawing board, I would see her face. I didn't know what to do. I was very confused. As the time passed, that kind of feeling wore off and I got back to normal. I remembered her but in a nicer way. My confusion was gone.

I used to live with an Indian family in Golders Green. My job was about three miles away. I thought that I should move my digs nearer to where my job was. Luckily I got a room with an Irish family. That house was very handy. Not only was my office just a mile away, but the local library and Middlesex University were not far either. It occurred to me that perhaps I should study further in engineering. In India, in addition to acquiring a degree in engineering, I had passed Part I and Part II examinations of the Institute of Mechanical Engineers (London). I knew that if I passed their Part III, I could get a degree called A.M.I. Mech. E. Luck would have it that nearby Middlesex University had an evening course which would help me pass the Part III. Now I got very busy with my work as well as my studies. My mind was a bit more settled and I could think of following my mission. I thought that it would be nice if I had my own transport rather than relying on public transport. My salary was only £8 per week. I started saving at least £1 per week so that in a few months time I could buy a motorcycle. I had gathered that one couldn't drive a motorbike before passing a driving test. But one could drive a scooter on one's own, by sticking an 'L' plate on it. I bought a scooter. Now I went everywhere. Every weekend I was away to various places. I even joined a scooter club. I remember when I went for their monthly meeting I was surprised to see boys as young as sixteen with their girlfriends. Some of them were skinheads. All of them were under twenty years. I was the daddy of them all. I was then thirty years old. They didn't give me a hard time. They would just ask silly questions like, "Do Indians live in trees?" Then they would giggle. I very seriously would reply, "Of course. But we use elevators to go up and down." There would be a deathly silence for a moment. Then they would giggle more. Once, I remember, in the middle of that winter, they had a visit to Brands Hatch. I went along with them. It was extremely cold day on that day. I had a hot cup of tea early in the morning. It didn't feel hot at all. You could very well imagine how cold that morning was.

After a year I got a much better job as a draughtsman-designer. The pay was nearly double what I had been getting. But it was in Stratford, London E15. I would travel by my scooter. Again I felt that I could move nearer to my work place. I saw an advertisement in a local newspaper shop for a room to let. At that time Stratford had quite a good percentage of Asians living in the area. The room I got was with a Muslim family. The house was very near to Plaistow underground station. Also it was quite near to my work place. The family, Mr and Mrs S A Khan had a little daughter. There were two more lodgers. The atmosphere in the house was very congenial. It so happened that we three lodgers and Mr Khan would finish work around 6pm. The kitchen was shared. Everyone was trying to cook/heat food at the same time. Then all of us would sit at a big dining table and eat together. It was a good mixture of people we had in the house. Mr Khan was a Muslim but came from India, one lodger was from Pakistan, another lodger was a Sikh. He and I had come from India. It so happened that suddenly there was a border dispute between India and Pakistan. The dispute turned into a war. The sitting room was common to all of us. We would sit together and watch the news, specially the news about the war between India and Pakistan. It was very disturbing to me. People in Pakistan and India are the same in appearance, they have the same culture, the same blood running through their veins and the same forefather. The only difference is between their faiths. The war between Pakistan and India was like a war between brothers. That was 1965. Now we are in the twenty-first century. Still the brothers are very hostile to each other.

The chief engineer asked me which days I would like my annual holiday of three weeks. I wanted to go to Europe and visit as many countries as I could. I came across a holiday brochure. The brochure had a few coach tours around Europe. I selected the three week tour. I liked the itinerary. From London we would go to Holland, Germany, Italy, France and then back to London. In Italy we would be visiting Florence, Venice, Rome and passing through Milan. I had a very pleasant thought. The girl whom I had met in the library two years ago was Italian. Her name was Luciana Boati. She had given me her address in Milan before she had left London. I thought, perhaps during this holiday I could meet her while our coach was passing through Milan. It was just a thought. Before I went on the holiday I made sure that I had with me her address in Milan.

During our holiday, while we were approaching Milan, I asked the courier, "Do we stop for a night in Milan?"

"No we don't. We just stop for half an hour for a coffee, then move on."

I showed him the girl's address, and asked him, "How far is this address from the coach stop in Milan?"

"I don't know."

My brain was working overtime. I thought that it was unthinkable not to meet Luciana while I was in the same city. She didn't know that I would be arriving in Milan. It was a very long shot. My plan was very simple.

"Which town are we heading for, and which hotel will the group staying at?" He gave me the details. "How far is that town from Milan and is there any rail link between Milan and that town?"

"It is not far. There is a frequent train service to that town from Milan."

One final question. "After breakfast what time will you and the group leave the hotel for the next destination?"

He told me the time.

"I am now going to this address to meet my friend. I shall join the group tomorrow morning before you leave. If I can't make it, please deposit my luggage in London with the tour operator's office." He agreed. I was very excited with my planning. It was just a long shot. I enquired at the coach station how to get to that address. They guided me and said, "It is not far. By walking it shouldn't take more than half an hour." It was around four in the afternoon.

The address was a shop dealing in stationary. It was on the main road. In the shop there was an elderly person behind the counter.

"Are you Mr Boati?"

"Yes."

"I would like to meet Luciana. Is she around?"

"Who is asking?"

"I met her in London two years ago. She gave me this address."

In the meantime an elderly lady had come down from the upstairs flat. I presumed she was his wife.

Mr Boati told his wife in Italian that I was enquiring about Luciana.

"What name shall we tell Luciana?"

"My name is Vasu."

"Where are you from?"

"I am from India."

Conversing with Mr Boati was very difficult. He knew very little English and I couldn't understand most of what he was saying. But anyhow, we managed to understand each other.

When I said that I was from India, he smiled and pounded the counter twice with his fist and said, "India Pakistan Bum Bum."

I didn't understand what he meant. Slowly I understood what he meant. At that time the war was still raging between India and Pakistan. He was saying with his 'Bum Bum' action that war between two countries was going on. Mr Boati was quite a jolly person. We conversed as much as we could till Luciana came from the flat above.

Before she had appeared my mind was wandering and asking lots of questions like, "Has she married yet? Has she changed in appearance? Will she remember me and recognise me? What would she think and feel to see me suddenly appearing on her doorstep?" All my doubts vanished as soon as she appeared and said, "Hello, Vasu. Why didn't you tell me that you were visiting us?" I tried to explain why and how, but I was very confused as well as excited. I was confused about what I should do now, and excited because I never expected to meet her so soon and sudden. It was a long shot that I had tried to meet her, but it seemed that my God had been very kind to me. He had favoured me with an opportunity, which, I felt comes once in a lifetime. On the other hand, I was very much restricted by my so called 'mission'.

"Hello Luciana. Can we go for a coffee. Is there any coffee shop nearby?"

"Yes. There is a nice one nearby. We shall go there." She turned to her parents and spoke to them in Italian. I gathered that she told them that we were going for a coffee.

We went to the coffee shop. All the time my brain was working overtime. I was thinking, Now I have met her. What is next? I would imagine that Luciana was also thinking and asking the same question to herself. I was sure that her parents must have been confused and did not know what was going on.

Slowly I recovered and composed myself.

"Have you finished your studies yet?"

"No. I have one more year to go."

"What will you do after that?"

"I would like to be an air hostess."

"Have you applied?"

"No, but my uncle works in Alitalia. I am very hopeful to get a job with Alitalia," she replied. "What do you do now? Last time when I saw you, you were trying to start an import-export company. How is it doing?" Luciana asked me.

"No. I never started it. In the meantime I got a job as an engineer. I am a mechanical engineer." Then I described and explained how I happened to be in Milan.

"You will stay for dinner. Won't you?"

"Before I say yes, I would like to know the train times so that I can join my group in the next town."

"We have a train timetable in our house. We can find the times from it."

We went to her house. It was time to close the shop as well. Her brother Angelo had come from work. Her grandmother was also staying in the flat. I noticed that there was one early morning train. It would be ideal to catch that train and reach my hotel on time. Since I was having dinner with them, I could see that I would not be able to catch last train on that day. I decided to catch the morning train.

"Do you have a spare room for me?" I asked.

"Yes, we have," Luciana replied, then added, "don't worry about it. In the morning we shall take you to the station to catch the morning train."

You can very well imagine that it was a very strange situation. A man had come out of the blue to meet a girl in her own town. There was no relationship before it. It was just a chance meeting two years ago. Each of us were thinking very hard. As follows:

Parents may be thinking, 'Is the man a suitable boy for our

daughter? He is not a Roman Catholic. Is it appropriate for our daughter to select him?'

Luciana may be thinking: 'Vasu has come all the way from London just to meet me. Surely he has more in mind than just to meet me. I shall wait for his next move.

I was thinking very hard. But I was very confused. All the time I was thinking, 'I am not ready yet for a relationship, or marriage. I know it was a Godsent opportunity. But marriage/relationship will spoil all my planning'. My main purpose would be defeated. In addition, I was at that time reluctant to marry a non-Hindu girl.

I took out my camera from my shoulder bag. As soon as Luciana saw it she cried, "Oh! You have brought your photographic machine." It was a big joke between us during our meeting two years ago in London. The first time I had heard from her, I was hysterical. I had told her that it was a camera. But it was a standing joke between us. She had remembered it and used the same name for the camera. Again on that evening we laughed and laughed. Her family didn't know what the joke was. Luciana explained to them. They just smiled. I wanted to be in the photos so I requested Angelo to take our group photos. I still have copies of those two group photos.

The dinner time was very enjoyable. It was a typical Italian meal with Italian wine. The conversation with the family was very tiring. Her father would ask me a question. Luciana would translate and ask me in English. I would then reply in English and then she would convey my reply to her father. After dinner we all retired to our own rooms. Next morning they woke me up, gave me a coffee and a salami sandwich and took me to the station to catch my train. Before we parted I gave Luciana my address in the UK. I told her to keep in touch. I was standing at the train door and waved them goodbye. Maybe it was my imagination, but looking back, all three of them had a strange look on them, perhaps thinking, 'What a strange person he is. He came all the way from London to meet us, but did not tell us what is in his mind'.

Chapter Eight

How I met the Pope and Shook Hands with Him

I was very lucky that my train came in time. We arrived on time in the other town. I have forgotten the name of the town, it was 43 years ago. The hotel was not far from the station. I had only my shoulder bag as luggage. I walked to the hotel where the group was staying. The group had just finished their breakfast. The coach was being loaded with our luggage. I hurriedly got my breakfast and located my suitcase. I wanted to make sure that my luggage was on the coach.

The courier asked me, "Did you meet your girl?"
"Yes. I did."
"Is she alright?"
"Yes. She is alright. But I am not alright."
"What do you mean?"
"I was very indecisive. I am still not very sure about myself."

It was time to leave. We all boarded the coach and went ahead to other places to visit. We came to Venice. I had read that Marco Polo had come from Venice. I was very interested to find out a bit more about Marco Polo. When I was about fourteen years old I had seen the Hollywood film called *Adventures of Marco Polo* staring Gary Cooper. My brother Jaik and I were crazy about Gary Cooper movies. At that age we hardly knew English language. We couldn't understand Gary Cooper's accent either. But we used to enjoy Hollywood movies. In Venice, when our group visited St Mark's Square, I came across a building with Marco Polo mentioned on it. It so happened that renovation work on the building was going on. It was shut for a while. By the time they opened it again, I and the group would have gone.

After the usual sightseeing in Venice, we proceeded to Florence. I was very impressed with Florence. The whole town looked to me like a huge painting. We didn't see much on the first day. The next day during a city tour, our courier had hired a guide to take us around and explain and give us more details about various art galleries and museums. Luckily we had a very good guide. She was very knowledgeable. She explained and gave us lots of information about the arts and paintings displayed in Florence. She made a huge effort to explain in a very interesting way. We thoroughly enjoyed the trip to Florence. I felt that so far the visit to Florence had been the most enjoyable one.

I had heard so much about Rome that I and others in the group had been anxiously awaiting the visit there. But luck would have it that our guide in Rome was not as clever as the guide we had in Florence. It looked like the guide was giving us information because it was her job. She was not enthusiastic at all. At the end of the day we had a gala dinner. The gala dinner made it up to us. We all thoroughly enjoyed the occasion. At the end of the evening our courier announced, "Tomorrow is a free day. You can explore Rome in your own time and visit the Vatican City as well."

In the group most of the members were in pairs. Looking back I think I was the only single person in the group. I hadn't joined up with anyone. There was no one to tell me what to do and when. Next morning I had a leisurely breakfast. I thought that I could explore Rome till lunchtime, have lunch, and then make my way towards the Vatican City. It was around 3pm that I arrived at the Vatican City. Generally 3pm is my afternoon tea/coffee time. I went in a nearby café and had my coffee. I was getting bored being on my own. I could see everyone else was in pairs. I was feeling miserable at my own plight. I then decided that at the first opportunity I would go back to India and meet my family. I could then work on 'getting married'. But how, I had no clue. At least I wouldn't feel so low when I was with my family.

I finished my coffee and went in the cathedral. It was beautiful. I am a Hindu. We Hindus do not have that much fascination for Christian arts and churches. I am sure that if I had been Roman Catholic I would have gone mad and perhaps kissed the ground, etc,

etc. It was about 5.30pm when they announced that it was closing time and all must leave. Slowly we left from a side door. When we were coming out of the door, I noticed that there was a queue of people standing next to a closed door, which was next to the door we were emerging from. I went to investigate. I was just wondering why they were waiting to get in when we were all coming out. I asked this question to a man in the queue. He was one of five in a group. It looked like he was their leader. All five of them had a badge on their chest.

"How is it that we have just come out of the hall and you are going in?"

"We are going to meet the Pope."

"Can anyone meet the Pope?"

"No."

"How can you meet the Pope?"

"We have an invitation to meet him at 6.30pm."

"Where can I get an invitation?"

"You can't get it now. All invitations have been distributed. We are members of the Radiological Society, who have provided us with the invitations."

"It is a pity I can't meet the Pope. I have travelled 5,000 miles just to meet him," I said jokingly.

The leader looked at me intensely. He was touched by my remark of travelling 5,000 miles. After a moment he put his hand in his inside pocket and produced a slip of paper. He handed over the slip of paper to me and said, "You can have it. One of our members is not feeling well. He is resting in the hotel room. This is his invitation. You can use it." I thanked him and looked at it. It was written in Italian. I couldn't understand. I could just understand the writing which was '25 Set. 1965 - Ore 18,30'. I guessed that the appointment was on 25th September 1965 @ 18.30pm. We waited patiently. It wasn't time to meet the Pope yet. A copy of the invitation is displayed on the next page.

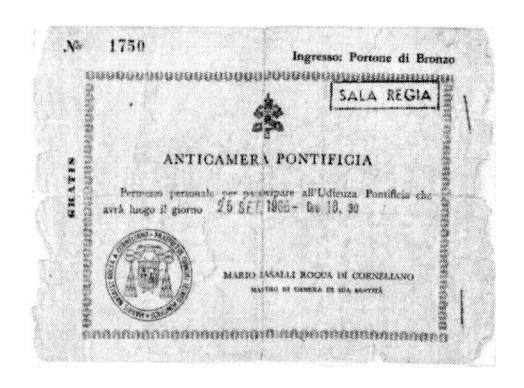

One of the group asked me, "Do you know Cardinal Joseph in Bombay?"

"No, sorry I don't. Where does he live?"

"He is Cardinal in St Xavier's Cathedral."

"Do you know Father Dominic?" asked the leader. "We met him last year in one of our religious gatherings.". Suddenly it occurred to me that they thought I was a Roman Catholic from Bombay. I thought that I must clear their doubt. I replied, "I am a Hindu. I don't go to church. I do not move in the circle you move in."

"Oh." There was a deathly silence. Possibly they were thinking, 'He is Hindu but he has made an effort to travel 5,000 miles to meet the Pope. There is something funny about him'.

"I have quite a few Roman Catholic friends in Bombay. Mainly they are from Goa. One is Pinto, the other is D'Souza, the third is D'Silva." After a pause I explained, "Now I have come from London." I gave them a true picture of myself and who I was. We talked about this and that for some time till the small door opened. As soon as the door opened, many people from the queue rushed in. I also rushed in with them. There was a staircase ahead of us. Most of them had come either in pairs or in a group. I was on my own. I climbed the staircase two steps at a time and was well ahead of all of them. At the top of the stairs there was a small hall. I went as far as I could. There was a barrier. I and some other first comers waited at the barrier. I didn't know what to expect. We waited expectantly for something dramatic to happen. By that time everyone had arrived in the hall. There was a lot of pressure from the crowd pushing me forward. I was squeezed between the crowd behind me and the barrier in front of me. The metal barrier was hurting my body due to the pressure from behind me. I had no choice but to push back. I put my two hands on the metal frame and made sure that there was a gap between my body and the metal barrier and waited anxiously. About five yards in front of me a door opened. There was a commotion at the door. Suddenly the Pope, sitting in his chair, appeared at the door. He, in his chair, was being carried by four people on their shoulders. He started blessing the crowd. Suddenly he came down from his chair and started shaking hands with people standing across the barrier. Every one of us extended our hands so that he could shake ours. There were lots of us across the barrier. It was ages before he grabbed my hand and shook it. I was very lucky to see that he shook hands with only few more people after he shook my hand. He sat in his chair. They carried the chair with the Pope in it and went back in the door where they had appeared a few moments ago. The whole crowd went crazy. They were so happy and excited that they hugged each other, shaking hands with anyone around. People who had shaken hands with the Pope were the chosen ones. Lots of people from the crowd saw me shaking hands with the Pope. They came and congratulated me, hugged me, and shook hands with me. I was very embarrassed. I didn't know what was happening. One beautiful woman hugged me and said something in Italian, I don't know what she said. But looking at her and her behaviour I gathered that it was far more than excitement due to the Pope. I got scared and blushed. She had a female companion who called her in Italian. Perhaps her companion was telling her, 'Leave him, he is a cry baby'.

I came out of the cathedral. I looked back to make sure that the two women were not following me, then went back to my hotel by Metro. I was quite late for my dinner. I was famished. All the time while I was in the cathedral I never realised how hungry I was. My group had just finished their main meal and were eating the dessert. My courier was very happy to see me.

"Did you lose your way, Mr Vasu?"

"No, I did not lose my way. I met the Pope."

"What?"

"I met the Pope."

"How did you do that?"

I started telling them what and how it happened. After a few minutes I asked him, "Have you saved my dinner?" He called the waiter who said, "No. Food is all gone."

"What about dessert?"

"Yes. We shall give you your dessert."

"Can I have two portions, please. I am very hungry."

Very kindly they gave me two portions. I was lucky that they had cheesecake as a dessert. One member didn't want cheesecake. I was so grateful to the member who didn't eat their cake. I went to him and said, "thank you for not eating your cheesecake. I love cheesecake." After I had my cheesecake and coffee I was ready to tell them my story. It was a very hot evening. I had been rushing around. I had literally devoured the cheesecakes. I was sweating profusely. I wiped my face and composed myself. Now I was ready. We had an Irish couple in the group. They were Catholic. So was our courier. They were more anxious than others in the group to hear how I had managed to meet the Pope. After I finished narrating how it had happened, I went to the lounge and sat down in a corner. I was tired.

The Irish couple who were in our group approached me and said, "Now you will not wash your hands. Will you?"

"What do you mean?" I didn't understand why they were saying it. "Of course I shall wash my hands," I replied.

They explained, "Now your hand is blessed and holy."

I was in a joking mood, I said, "I can transfer sacredness to your hand, you just shake my hand." Then added, "I will not charge you for it." I gave them a very broad grin. Do you know what they did? They both shook my hand and imagined that they were shaking hands with the Pope. I was very pleased with myself that I had been of some service to the Irish couple. After that other group members also approached me and shook hands with me. I felt very important, not as much as the Pope but a mini Pope.

After that we went ahead with the rest of our tour. We passed through Italy and France and finally arrived back in England. The trip was an experience for me. During the three week trip, we visited many cities and European countries. But I would say, from my point of view, the highlights were locating Luciana in Milan and shaking hands with the Pope.

Chapter Nine

Life in ICI

And what a life it was. I was fortunate to work in a very good organisation, make many good friends and find a wife for myself. Let me give you the full details. You then decide if it was as good as I thought it was.

It was the end of 1965. I had been working with a small engineering company in Stratford, London, E15. I was very happy working there. The directors were very helpful. The staff were very friendly. I was working as a mechanical engineer in their engineering section. One couldn't ask for better working conditions than we had. My office was within walking distance from where I lived. Every lunchtime my section leader and I would go to a nearby pub for our lunch. The work was not stressful either. I could, every weekend, take my scooter and go far away to visit places. I wanted to visit as many different places as I could while I was in the UK. Most evenings I would be out to socialise. I had joined the Conservative Party. Very frequently I would visit their social club. I would meet lots of people in the club and play snooker, cards, darts, domino, table tennis and so on. Many times I would visit the club wearing the black cap which I had brought from India with me. The cap would promote comments from others. That was how I came to be mixing with others in no time. I thought that after a year or two, I would go back home and settle down. Whatever spare time I had, I would spend in the nearby library. I loved reading books, magazines and newspapers.

One Thursday evening I visited the library. On Thursdays the library was open till 8pm. I casually looked through the *London Evening News*. As you know, the *Evening News* is not now in circulation. It was merged with the *Evening Standard* a few years ago. I don't know what prompted me to look at situation vacant columns. A large advertisement caught my eye. It said:

Imperial Chemical Industries
Immediately wanted, Engineers for the Petro-Chemical division in North-East England
Open evening in Charing Cross Hotel, London
Thursday and Friday between 6.00 to 8.00pm
No appointment necessary. Just pop in and meet the Chief Engineer

I had not wished to change my job. I was very secure and happy with my job. But I had heard the name ICI in India as well. Everyone in India knew that ICI was a good, well established and reputable company. Their Dulux paint was very famous in India. I thought that there was no harm in me meeting the chief engineer during the open day. I noted down the details. I had seen this advertisement on Thursday. The open evening was on Friday as well. The next day I briskly finished my work and went straight to Charing Cross Hotel. I had taken my certificates with me in case they wanted to see them.

ICI had hired a huge hall for their open evening. I was amazed when I saw so many people had come for the interview. All of them were in their suits and carrying briefcases. I was not very keen for the job so I did not come in a suit, nor carry a briefcase. I felt that I should go back. I wouldn't get a job here. There were so many engineers with their suits and briefcases who had come for appointments. While I was thinking on those lines, one lady wearing an ICI badge approached me and asked, "Can I help you?"

"I have come for the open evening."

"Are you an engineer?"

"Yes, mechanical engineer."

She guided me to a desk and handed me a form to complete. I completed it and handed it over to her.

She guided me to a room where a few people were sitting.

"Please take your seat here. We shall call you."

After about twenty minutes or so my name was called. The

same lady guided me to a room. I entered the room. At the far end there was a huge desk with three people seated. I went towards it. The person sitting in the middle indicated to a chair across the desk.

"Please take your seat."

I still remember how casual I was on that evening. Because I was not keen for a job I was not nervous at all.

The interview was very strange. They had seen my application form which had given them sufficient information about me.

"So, you are from India?"

"Yes."

"You came to the UK on an employment voucher?"

"Yes."

"It seems you are now working as a design engineer."

"Yes."

"Why do you want to leave them?"

"I work with a small company, compared to your company. I presume prospects in a well established and well organised company such as yours would be good." Then I added, "In India, ICI has a very good name. Dulux paint is very famous in India. I would like to work with your company if I can."

"The division you would be working in doesn't make Dulux. It is made by our other division. We are looking for engineers to work in the petro-chemical industry. We notice that the company you are working with is serving petro-chemical industry."

"Yes. We are sub-contractors in the petro-chemical industry."

All three of them consulted each other for a few minutes. The leader then spoke. "How much do you expect?"

"You gave the salary scale in the advertisement. I am quite happy with it."

They looked at each other, then the leader spoke, "When can you start?"

The question was so sudden and unexpected that I was stunned.

I composed myself and said, "I have to give one month's notice to my employers."

"Today is the 25th. Can you start one month from the 1st?"
"Yes I can."

"In a few days time we shall send you an appointment letter in duplicate. If you agree to join us, please sign the duplicate copy and send it to us as soon as possible."

I thanked them and left the room. I was in a daze. I didn't expect to get the job. I did not come here to get the job. I just attended their open evening to see what was happening.

While I was going back home, I thought that perhaps it was a blessing in disguise. I had come to the UK to see and visit various parts of the country and to meet as many people as I could. The new job in a new location would suit my plan. Now I was anxiously awaiting the appointment letter. As soon as I got the letter, I signed the duplicate and sent it back to them. I lodged my one month's notice with my employer. They were very sad to see me go. I was equally sad to leave them as well. They were so nice to me. They wished me all the luck with the new company. They were very pleased for me when I told them that I was joining ICI.

Along with the appointment letter, they also had sent to me a rail ticket and instructions on where to go. They also allowed me to stay in their guesthouse for a week. During that one week I should find my place to live. Their guesthouse was in Saltburn, Teeside, North East England. I travelled on Sunday to Saltburn and arrived around 4.00pm. A van had come to pick me up from the station. By the time we got to the guesthouse it was 5pm. I went into my room, had a wash and came down. I was very surprised and upset that I couldn't see anyone else in the guesthouse. I was the only one. I wanted to have a cup of tea. Since I couldn't see anyone, I thought I should go to the kitchen and help myself. The kitchen was closed. I thought that I should go out of the guesthouse and get a cup of tea. Nowadays the situation is different. In 1965, on Sundays, the streets were deserted. No shops/restaurants were open. Pubs open at certain times, they would serve alcohol, crisps and peanuts only. When I came out of the guesthouse I couldn't get a cup of tea. I was feeling hungry as well. I couldn't get anything to eat either. I was so miserable. There was no one in the guesthouse. There was no one in the street either. Saltburn is a very small seaside village. That Sunday happened to be very cloudy, cold and miserable. Apart from the odd car on the road there was nothing. The streets were so empty that I remembered a scene from a film called *On The Beach*. The scene is where a ship with its crew has just come back from a long voyage. When they docked and the crew disembarked, they saw a similar sight. No one was moving, the streets were empty, tumbleweed was blowing in the wind. I don't remember how I survived that night without tea and a meal. The following evening I pointed this out to the manager of the guesthouse. He said, "On Sundays you don't get anything to eat here. Didn't you eat a meal on the train?"

"I was not hungry then. Also I thought that I would eat an evening meal after I arrived."

Every day a pick-up would pick me up and take me to the site and bring me back in the evening. I had to find a place to live by the end of the week. I had to vacate the room in the guesthouse. On Monday evening, after the evening meal I went out to look for a room to rent. It seemed that residents in Saltburn never rented a room for longer than a week. They suggested that I should try my luck in the nearby town called Middlesborough. After that, every evening I would visit Middlesborough, and look at the advertisements displayed in the newspaper shops. It was quite tough to get a room. It seemed there was much more 'discrimination' in North East England than in London. No one was ready to give me a room. On Friday evening I told the manager of the guesthouse, "I haven't yet found a room to rent."

"You have to vacate the room by this Sunday," he replied.

The following day was Saturday. I started early so that I could visit as many houses as possible. It was a long day for me. By 4.00pm I must have visited five addresses, but there was no luck. Each landlord said, "Sorry it has just gone." In London I had known that 'Sorry, it has just gone' mostly meant that 'We don't want to give you a room, you are different'. I had in my mind one more address to visit and try my luck. With a heavy heart I went to the address and knocked on the door. A white boy of towering height opened the door. My heart sank, I thought that his family would say the same thing, 'Sorry, the room is gone'.

"I have come for the room advertised." Hesitantly I added, "Is it still available?"

"Dave," he called from the doorstep. "Someone has come for the room."

After a few seconds an Indian came down.

"Dave, he has come for the room," the white boy's name was Billy.

"Come, I shall show you the room," Dave told me to follow upstairs.

The room was a small one. Beggars can't be choosers, I thought.

"It is £3 per week. Kitchen, bathroom and sitting room are common for all of us."

"How many of you are staying here?"

"Just three of us. Each of us will have our own room."

"Can I take it from tomorrow? Tomorrow is Sunday. It would be easier for me from tomorrow."

"Yes you can."

"Tomorrow morning around 11 I shall come with my belongings."

"That is fine."

"By the way I work for ICI in their Wilton site. Do you know if any bus goes from here to Wilton?"

"Yes." I thanked him and gave him £3.00 as the first week's rent.

I found out that I had to go about ten minutes walk from home to the bus stop and another ten minutes walk from the bus stop to the Wilton site. I also found out that Dave was not his name; Billy had given him that name. Billy said that Dave was easier to pronounce than his original name. It didn't take me long to settle down with Dave and Billy. Dave used to work on the railways. Billy was an artist. One day I asked him, "Billy, with due respect to you, why are you staying with us Indians?"

"I am an artist. I do lots of paintings. My luggage is very strange compared to others. I carry various paint tins and canvases in frames. Landlords don't like it. Dave very kindly has accommodated me."

As the time passed we came to know each other very well. We were amicable and accommodating. I am pleased to write that we never had any friction between the three of us. After a year, Billy moved out and moved in with his girlfriend, Carol. We got another lodger called Leo in place of Billy. Leo was an elderly person. The whole atmosphere in the house changed. Billy was quite a jolly fellow. His girlfriend, Carol, used to visit him when he was with us. The atmosphere was very different when a woman was around. Carol became, in a way, a part of our family. Leo was different. He was elderly and a very serious type. Leo liked his beer. Most of the evenings after dinner he would go to the nearby pub and stay till they closed. But he never gave us any hard times.

ICI was expanding fast. At that time in 1965 they were spending £1 million per week on constructing and expanding, and that was only on the Wilton site. Now, in 2009, £1 million doesn't amount to much. ICI had another similar site in Billingham. Billingham was just six miles away from Wilton. They were spending quite a lot at the Billingham site as well. Six months after I had joined, the company decided to centralise their engineering design section. It was decided that our design section in Wilton should be transferred to Billingham. Billingham is about same distance from Middlesborough as Wilton, but in different direction. The only problem was that there was no direct bus route to the site. I had to change three buses to reach my destination. I would spend a lot of time in travelling to and fro. A few times I got a lift coming back from my office. I thought that I should have my own transport.

My salary was good; I could afford a car. After consulting a few of my friends I bought a second-hand Renault Gordini. It was a small car and very economical to run. My problem now was that I didn't know how to drive a car. After enquiring around ICI, I located a person who did not have a car but used to come from Middlesborough by public transport/lifts from his friends. He agreed to sit with me in the car so that I could drive after I had displayed an 'L' plate on my car. At the same time I joined a driving school. Every day I would drive my car to the office and back. When my driving test came, I was confident that I would pass. But I didn't pass the test. I was very disappointed. I was hoping that once I passed the test, I would be able to go far away every weekend.

The house I was living in was just 200 yards away from a football ground. Every weekend residents had to move their cars parked in front of their houses to a different area. During football days police designated our road a 'No Parking' area. It was a nuisance, not only to have to move our car far away, but to listen to the noise and singing and shouting from the supporters and the football ground. I felt that if I had passed my driving test, I would have gone during weekends to visit nearby towns and villages.

It was 1966. That was the year World Cup football games were being played in England. Middlesborough football ground was designated as one of the grounds where world teams would play. I vividly remember the day when South Korea and Russia were playing in Middleborough. The atmosphere in the town was electric. The town was literally taken over by football fever. We would watch football games on television. One comes out of the house and one would listen to crowds singing and dancing. The crowd would wear scarves and make noises with rattles and blowers. The crowd would make noises with anything and everything. Once I remember, on the day Russia was playing against South Korea I went shopping in the morning. I noticed there was one hydrant in the high street which was tilting. A group of football supporters were passing by. All of them had a stick in their hand. One of them hit the hydrant with the stick. It made a funny noise. He liked that noise so he hit it again. His friends also had sticks. All of them one by one hit the hydrant till it broke. Oh, what a mess it was. Water started pouring out. Within no time the high street was flooded. The group giggled and quietly walked away. Everyone knows what happened that year.

ENGLAND WON THE WORLD CUP.

I realised that when I joined ICI, I had joined a brotherhood. Every other person in the area was either working in ICI or knew someone who worked for ICI. I was never far away from ICI influence. I went to Whitby and came across ICI staff. I went to Scarborough; a couple recognised me. I had joined ICI's social club. Every evening I would visit it; I had joined all the different sections. Many people in ICI knew me. I remember one evening during wine and cheese tasting, I commented to the group of people I was talking with and I said, "Do you know, on this day I have finished one year in ICI."

"No. We have known you for quite a few years."

"Yes. Really. On this day, last year, I joined the company."

The people in the social club had seen me so many times that in a short time they thought that I had been around much longer than one year.

That was the year the Indian Cricket Team visited England to play test matches. One day an Indian employee working in the piping section said, "Vasu, Indian cricket team is playing this weekend at Leeds Cricket Ground. Would you like to come? I know one of the players. Come along and I shall introduce him to you after the game."

"I can't come, I haven't yet passed my driving test."

"Come on Vasu. Make a day of it."

I thought that I would not get this kind of opportunity again.

"Okay, I shall come."

"See you this Saturday at the cricket ground."

I had failed the driving test. It was a hassle to ask someone to sit with me while I was driving my car. I had already removed the 'L' plates from my car and had been driving my car. I went to the cricket ground and watched the Indian team not doing very well in the first inning. In the second inning, Rusi Surti was out for a low score. Farouk Engineer and Ajit Wadekar did very well and scored 190 for one. Nawab Of Pataudi was the captain of the Indian team. At the end of the day's play, my Indian friend met me.

"Indian team is staying in so and so Hotel. I am going there. I shall see you there and introduce the team to you." I was a bit concerned about me driving around in a new city without a full driving licence. Hesitantly I made my way towards the hotel. At one place I came across a wide road with a central grass verge. I thought that it was a one-way system. I was horrified when I noticed that it was not a one-way system. Both parts of the road had two-way systems. I nearly got involved in an accident. I noticed that there was one policeman standing at the corner of the road. He had witnessed what had happened. With very quick thinking, I drove straight to where he was standing and asked him, "Officer, how do I go to so and so hotel? Indian cricket team is staying there. I am going there to meet them."

He gave me the correct directions and said, "Drive carefully. Give yourself a chance, mate."

I arrived safely at the hotel. I met my Indian friend who introduced me to the team. I remember that I met Nawab Of Pataudi, Kundaram, Vishwanath and Chandu Borde. Borde was the vice captain. One person asked Borde, "Your team is following on. Didn't do very well in the first innings. Now what do you think? Will the Indian team lose the test match?"

"No. We will not lose. We are doing well in the second innings. We will make sure that we do not lose the test." He uttered the words so confidently that we were all delighted to hear those words.

It was nearly midnight when I left for my home. On the way I lost my way. I was driving through a village, I don't remember the name. I saw an old man waving at me to stop.

"Can you give me a lift please?"

"I am going to Middlesborough. Where do you want to go?"

"My house is on your way. I can tell you where to drop me."

He entered the car. He had too much to drink. I could smell the strong smell of alcohol.

"Have you been to the pub?"

"Yes. We had a party. I had too much to drink. I am not able to walk. Generally I walk home. My house is not very far. Just drop me at the top of this road." He thanked me profusely when he left. When I arrived home, it was quite late. I was very tired. I went straight to bed without disturbing anyone else. The following Monday I narrated this incident of giving a lift to this old man, to my friends in my engineering section. They said, "You are lucky that nothing happened to you. Many times people get mugged. One old man stops you for a lift. As soon as you stop, a few more people who are hiding nearby will come and take over the car as well as mug the driver. Please don't do this again."

While I am writing about the cricket test, I remember during the following year, the Pakistan cricket team had visited England. I thought that perhaps I could go and watch them. I had done it before when I went to Leeds to watch the Indian team. The Pakistan team was playing in Nottingham. The Pakistan team did not do very well at all. At the end of that day's play, I went to the town and looked around and had my dinner. It was quite late when I finished. I didn't want to drive in the night. By this time I had passed my driving test. Last time I had lost my way driving in the night from Leeds. My friends had warned me to be careful driving in the night. It was the month of June. The day was quite long. I realised that if I stayed a bit longer, it would be daylight. I could then drive in the daylight. There were still a few hours of night left. Why not sleep in my car for a few hours? A thought occurred to me. I drove to find a convenient place to park my car. I saw a park which had no gates. I drove in, parked my car and went to sleep. I don't remember after how long, but it was daylight when a policeman knocked on my car window.

"You can't park here. This is a park and not a parking place."

"Sorry Officer, I was very tired, I have been to cricket test match. I had to drive to Middlesborough."

"No, you can't park the car here. You have to move."

Since it was daylight, I drove towards Middlesborough and safely arrived home.

During the first week of joining ICI, I had a phone call from the admin office. In my section Mr Alec Wright picked up the phone. "Who is Mr Dar...?" Alec enquired around the office.

"Daryanani?" I said.

"Yes. It is a phone call for you." I picked up the phone and talked to the admin person. He called me to the office and handed over some documents to me. When I came back I asked Alec, "Alec, don't you know my name?"

"No. It is a difficult name to remember."

"Alex, what is easier. To remember one name and a surname or to remember nine names and surnames?" At that time we had ten people working in the section. This sentence had a magic effect on all the people working in that section. After that everyone knew not only my name and surname but could pronounce them correctly.

Every Monday evening I would go to the ICI social evening and a play card game called Bridge. I did not do that well at the game. A few years after that when I came to London, I joined ICI plastic division in Welwyn Garden City. I did fairly well, possibly because my partner and I understood each other. I found out that they would play every Monday around 7.30 in the evening. On the first day I went a bit early to the Bridge room to investigate and play. I was amazed that there were so many people waiting to play.

"Hello," one person approached me. He was the captain of the Bridge club. His name is Ron Howarth.

"Hello," I replied.

"Can I help you?" He had never seen me.

"I would like to play Bridge."

"Have you played before?"

"Yes."

"Have you got a partner? Here we play in pairs."

"No. I haven't."

I noticed that most of the people were sitting in pairs. One person was sitting on his own.

"Ian, you wanted a partner. Here is a partner for you." Ron turned towards me and asked, "What is your name?"

"Vasu."

"What is yours?"

"Ian Rankin."

"Ian. Vasu is your partner for this evening."

Ian approached me and asked, "Which system do you play?"

"What do you mean?"

"We play the Acol system. It is the British system."

"I haven't heard of it. What system is that?"

His heart sank. He realised that I had never heard of Acol; how can I play Bridge?

"Ian, it is 7.15pm now. We have still got 15 minutes before the game starts. Why not tell me what it is. Perhaps I can grasp it, since I know how to play Bridge."

He had no option but to oblige me and started telling me all about the Acol system. He explained that the Acol system is for bidding the Bridge contract. I understood what he meant. It was now time to play. There was another thing I never knew, which was that they were playing duplicate Bridge. The cards are dealt once and preserved so that the same cards could be played by other pairs. The same cards are played around tables and scores are noted. At the end of the evening, it was decided which pair came second and which came first. I came to know it is called Duplicate Bridge. All international Bridge competitions are played in Duplicate Bridge.

Since everything was new to me, I was very careful in bidding as well as in playing. It was a very intensive atmosphere. Every player was very serious and played with full concentration. I remember that at the end of the evening I developed a terrible headache. We had a tea break when Ian and I discussed a few points on how we played and what we should do from then on. The game started again. Finally we had played all hands to be played. Ron, our captain, went through the score sheets to see which pairs were going to be first and second. All of us were anxiously waiting for the results. In the meantime Ian and I were discussing our play.

"I don't think we made many mistakes this evening," Ian commented.

"No, possibly not."

"I could have played better during the last hand. I could have made the contract." Ian's voice was sorrowful.

"Let us see what happens."

Ron finished counting the points and announced, "C Schutz and F Simpson are second this evening. But the pair who came first this evening are newcomers. They have never played together before this evening. They are Ian and Vasu."

I was very surprised and delighted to hear my name as the winner. Not only Ian was very surprised, but all the players were astonished. Ian had never come first before. This was the first time he had won. Everyone looked at me. One by one they came and shook my hand. In one night I had become a famous Bridge player.

Before Ian left that evening he asked me, "Vasu, are you coming next Monday?"

"Of course."

"Have you got a partner?"

"Oh yes. I have a partner." Ian looked very disappointed. After a pause I added, "His name is Ian."

Ian gave me a very broad smile when it sunk in. He shook my hand. You could see that he was as pleased as punch.

"Good night, Vasu. See you next Monday."

"Yes. See you next Monday."

We did fairly well regularly. Ian and I had a good understanding between us. I was quite careful to play well. Ron, our captain, one day told us, "You could play in the regional competition. You could do very well." He put our names in for the regional tournament. Ron had very high hopes in us. He was talking about regional, national and finally international tournaments. He talked quite a lot about Omar Shareef. Omar had become a very good international player. We went to play in the regional tournament. Unfortunately we didn't do well at all. Ron was very sad that we had let him down. But we continued to do very well in our ICI club.

One evening Ian looked very sad. "What is the matter, Ian?"

He didn't want to talk about it. During our tea break I asked him again. "Ian, are you feeling alright?"

"I am sick and tired of life."

"Why?"

"My girlfriend has left me."

We both were silent for a while.

"Your girlfriend may come back. She may be equally sick and tired of life without you."

He didn't say anything. After that for a few weeks he came but his mind was not on it. His mind was never on the game. We never won anything after that. One day he phoned me and said, "Vasu, I can't concentrate on the game. I can not concentrate on anything. I am very sorry that I have let you down. I shall stop playing. You have to find another partner." Ian sounded very disturbed.

I tried to get another partner. I did play a few times when someone was without a partner. Sometimes I would sit out without a partner. I was looking for a regular partner who I could rely on and understand. Ian and I had a very good understanding. After that I lost interest and stopped playing altogether.

I had also joined the 'small bore rifle' section. It was held every Tuesday. I had done some rifle shooting while I was in India. When I was in college I had joined the National Cadet Corps (NCC). Every Tuesday, Thursday evening and all day Sunday we would have military training. At the end of the year we attended camp for a month. In the camp we had full military training including rifle shooting practice.

On Thursdays I went to their photography section. I was very proud of my Canon camera which I had bought in Eden while I was coming from Bombay to London. It was a new model. When I attended my first night in photography section, many members had not heard of Canon cameras. They had heard of Canon gas cookers. One member innocently asked me, "Does your camera work on gas?" I didn't understand his joke. He explained that he had never known that Canon made cameras as well. He knew that they made Canon gas cookers.

The evening which I enjoyed most was the 'cheese and wine

Tasting' party. It used to be held every Friday. They would have a different theme every Friday. They would call them French wine night, Spanish wine night, German wine night, English wine night, etc, etc. Also some nights were based on variations in cheese. These nights were very popular with members. Friday being the end of the working week, members were relaxed. I was surprised that some of the members were very knowledgeable about wines; they would tell you about the bouquet of wine, colour, taste, etc. I would just ask a question and listen to their ramble. Every one would be very relaxed after a few drinks. As the evening progressed, they would be very jolly as well. They would laugh at the silliest jokes. I was very careful. I knew that I couldn't hold my drink like they did. I would therefore take half the quantity they would take. By this way I could survive the night. Sometimes a member would have had so much to drink that they lost control of their speech. They wouldn't know what they were saying. I remember one evening one member called Alec was ready to go. He wished good night to one and all. He came to me and said, "Vasu, good night."

"Good night, Alec."

I noticed that he was not steady. I went to him and said, "Alec, can I drive you home?"

"No. I am alright."

He stood unsteadily for a while and said, "Vasu, you are a good man."

"Thank you, Alec."

"No. No. Really you are a good man."

"Thank you for your compliment Alec."

He couldn't stand so he said, "I want to sit down."

I brought a chair and let him sit down.

"Alec, I shall take you home," I replied.

"No. No. James will take me home."

"James is not here."

"Where is he?"

"James did not come this evening. He was not feeling well."

"Oh."

With gentle persuasion he accepted my offer. I drove him home. On the way while I was taking him home, he repeated I don't remember how many times, 'Vasu, you are a good man'. When we arrived at his house, he was fast asleep in my car. I had a tough time to wake him up and take him upstairs to his room. His wife was very grateful to me. She offered me supper. If Alec had been sober, I would have accepted her offer. I didn't want to have supper on my own with her. I had to refuse and said, "Next time I will have supper."

I used to arrive early at my office. I would avoid a lot of traffic on the way coming from Middlesborough to Billingham. On the way there was a bridge to be crossed. There would be a lot of traffic during office times. I found out that by crossing the bridge just ten minutes early, I could make a big difference to my journey time. While coming back I would be involved in the traffic jam. I found a good solution to my problem. We used to finish at 5.30pm on the dot. Every one of them would rush to their car and leave at the same time. This would create a traffic jam not only at the bridge but in the ICI site as well. I used to park my car not far from my office. I could see the car park and my car from the window in our office.

We had a back door to the office, not far from where I sat. About three minutes before 5.30pm I would very quietly slip away from the back door. I would run to my car and before any one arrived at the car park, I was on the way. The chief engineer's office was further away. There was less chance of him noticing me slipping away three minutes early. A few engineers in our section would moan about me leaving early. I just ignored them and carried on with it. One day after lunch break I came to the office. There was a note on my desk, 'Vasu Daryanani alias E.A.R.L.Y. Leaver sits here'.

I didn't understand it. All the other engineers were looking at me to see what my reaction was. I didn't understand what it meant. When I looked closely I noticed that my alias was nothing but the words Early Leaver. We all laughed, but I continued with my routine, justifying that I came to the office nearly fifteen minutes early.

One of the engineers in our section was Lenny Pope. He was always smiling and laughing. He would always give us details of what strange things happened to him the day before. He would tell us in such a way that they would sound very amazing. He had a knack of giving details about them. One day he came and said, "I have just bought a Triumph car. It is very zippy. Do you know I can do 120 miles per hour?"

"No, you can't do 120mph in a Triumph car."

"Yes I can. The handbook says so."

"The handbook is lying."

"Have you opened it up yet?"

"Yes I have. I have done 120 mph."

None of us believed it. So we said, "This lunchtime show us that you can do 120mph."

Lunchtime three of us accompanied him in the car. The car had a small body. But it was not a Triumph Herald. It was a Triumph Vittese.

The Billingham site is not far from the highway. Within no time he was driving on the highway. He stepped on the accelerator. The car picked up speed and within no time reached 110mph. Then it started struggling. He explained, "There are four of us in the car. When I was alone I could do 120mph." We believed him because he reached 110mph in no time.

Another day he came to the office and told us, "We have a very strange neighbour. He is never around. Most of the time he is out of the town or out of the country."

"Have you found out why he is out?"

"I think he is some kind of reporter with the BBC."

"Where does he go?"

"According to what we hear, he is all over the place. Sometimes he is in the Middle East, sometimes he is in Europe somewhere. We haven't yet seen him. He comes home very late. Then by early morning he is away to his assignment.

"What is his name, do you know?"

"Martin Bell. Wait a minute, my mistake. His name is George Lambelle."

We all know that Martin Bell became a famous man. A few years ago he stood as an Independent candidate against Neil Hamilton, a Conservative candidate. Martin Bell won the election. I believe Martin Bell is still a Member of Parliament.

ICI has a magazine which comes out every month. Once, Sir Paul Chambers, Chairman of ICI wrote an article, 'My three years in ICI'. It was published in the ICI magazine. That gave me an idea. Why don't I write an article and send it to the editor of the ICI magazine. My article would be 'My two years in ICI'. When I mentioned it to one of my colleagues, he said, "Why not write an article, 'How I moulded ICI HOC Division'." Our petro-chemical section was a part of the Heavy Organic Division (HOC). He then added, "Using a brown colour." I commented, "But not made by ICI." We both laughed. I liked his sense of humour.

It was 1967 that I went back to India. Four years ago I had arrived in the UK. I wanted to stay for two years only. After two years I realised that my job was not done. But this time I had known lots of people in ICI. I had even mixed socially with their families. When I came back from India after a five week holiday, I had brought many sarees for ladies and cigarettes and cigarette holders for men. We had good fun in our office. There was not strict supervision in the office. Within limits we could do anything. I handed over sarees to girls in the office and gave sarees to my friends for their wives. In the office girls to whom I had given sarees would come back in a short time wearing sarees. It was like a fashion parade. Of course we made sure that we kept our noise level low so that the chief engineer wouldn't know what was happening in the office. He was a very considerate person. As and when he noticed that we were doing something different, he would smile and ignore it and go away. At that time there was no 'no smoking' ban in offices. Many smokers with their cigarettes in the holders which I had given them would be smoking very proudly showing off their holders. It was good fun. Girls would come to my section and ask me how to wear a saree. I had a general idea. I would wrap around the saree over their skirt. During those days most girls would wear a skirt. It wasn't like now – in 2008 most girls wear trousers and jeans.

Looking back I would say that I had a very good time in ICI and in North East England. Initially it was difficult for me to break the barrier and mix with the locals. Once they knew me they accepted me as I was. I had a chance to play with them, went pub crawling with them, walked 42 miles with them, socialised and mixed with their families. To a certain extent I was one of them.

Chapter Ten

Start of Married Life

We couldn't decide on the wedding day as the Canadian visit was taking a long time to organise. So we thought that initially we should go to London. Anita would be far away from her parents. Now I had to plan and act fast. I had to give three months notice to ICI, get accommodation and a job in London. Finally our plan was finalised. My last day in ICI would be a Friday, we would arrange to have a registry office wedding on the following morning, have a reception in the evening, load all our belongings in our car and drive away to London on Sunday in the early morning. A hotel room would be booked where we would stay for two weeks. During those two weeks we would try to get a room as well as getting an engineering job on contract. At the same time we would work on the Canada trip/immigration.

I am very glad to say that everything went according to our plan. Our hotel room was in Muswell Hill, London. Shortly we found a room near Turnpike Lane Station and I got contract work in Ealing. As the time passed, we got busy with our life; nothing much happened about the Canada trip. Perhaps we lost interest, and we continued with our life. Our son Krishna was born in the nearby Middlesex Hospital.

While I was working in ICI we had formed a group. Every Friday evening we would go pub crawling, have supper in a pub and come back home. Four of our group had beards, I and another member were clean shaven. I wanted to grow a beard as well. Anita would not agree to it, saying that I would look older. Amongst the wedding gifts, I was given an electric shaver. During Christmas holidays in 1969, Krishna was born. It was a difficult birth for Anita, the time for me was also difficult. Pregnant women's demands are very strange. Once Anita wanted chicken soup on Sunday evening.

At that time, all the shops were closed. On Sundays, one could not get anything from anywhere. I didn't know what to do till I came across a petrol station which happened to have a vending machine. I got chicken soup from the machine. It looked horrible, but Anita loved it. Once she wanted a pickle. Again I couldn't get it anywhere. Luckily her craving for a pickle was short lived. With that kind of life and the arrival of a new baby, I was very tired and suffered from flu. I was in bed for a week. When I recovered I had one week's growth on my chin. Anita said, "Vasu, you wanted to grow a beard. Now is the time, just stop shaving. Since 1968 I had grown a beard, until 1995. Why I shaved my beard will be revealed in the later part of my story.

We had one room only. It was difficult with the arrival of a baby. We started looking around for a house. I saw an advertisement in the local paper that a cottage was to be sold in Buntingford.

Buntingford is about 40 miles north of London, on the way to Cambridge. The following Sunday, we put our son Krishna in a carrycot, put the cot on the back seat of our car and went to view the cottage. The cottage was very small; no bathroom, just a tub in one corner. In a corner there was a baby Belling cooker. It was a very small cooking area. It was so small that one could say 'You could not swing a cat in it'.

Opposite to the cottage there was a big board saying 'For Sale three bedroom new houses, from £4,500'. We were very surprised. The price of the cottage we saw was £4,600. Here for less you could get a three bedroom new house with central heating and a garage. We couldn't believe it. When we went to the site, we noticed a big housing estate with lots of houses already built and ready to move into. Lots of people were moving about. We located a person with a clipboard jotting down names. It seemed he was from W H Lee, Estate Agents, who were the sole agents of the whole estate.

"We want to buy a house," I said.

"Go around. Whichever house has a 'For Sale' sign, you can buy and I shall reserve it for you."

"We want to buy an end of terrace house."

"They are all gone." We looked around. Suddenly we came across number 265, which was an end of terrace house and had a 'For Sale' sign on it. I immediately ran to him and gave him the number. He referred to his notes and said, "It is sold, but the person hasn't confirmed it; you can have it if you want." We immediately reserved the house.

I organised the mortgage with Halifax and we moved into our first house. The house in Buntingford was very convenient. I had started working with ICI in their plastic division in Welwyn Garden City, on a contract basis. They welcomed me with open arms as I had worked with ICI in Middlesborough.

Life was good. God had been very kind to us. Marriage, child, good house, good job, good income, everything was fine for us. We didn't realise that life could have ups and downs. So far we had only seen and experienced ups, not downs.

It was 1970, my mother had been writing to me that I should go and meet her and the family.

I immediately went and booked my ticket to visit India. A week later I had a letter from my eldest brother, Motiram, who was in Kenya. The letter said, 'situation in Kenya is too hot for Indians. Kenyans are killing British as well as Indians. Kenyan government is pushing Indians to either denounce British citizenship and accept Kenyan or get out of the country, I prefer to be British. I am allowed to come to the UK. Can you accommodate me?'

I immediately replied, 'You are welcome. I have a three bedroom house. Please let me know your arrival details'.

Anita was pregnant with our daughter Nina. Anita mentioned that while I was away in India, she would like to go and stay with her mother. Suddenly I was getting very busy with my brother coming from Kenya and staying with us. Anita was pregnant and I had to take her and Krishna by car to Middlesborough, come back, get ready to go to India and buy gifts for my family in India. I mentioned to Motiram that he could come with me to India, but he was not ready yet.

I had a very good time with my family in India and told them all about Anita and Krishna. I told them that next time I would bring them. All the time, I was concerned about Anita and Krishna and wanted to go back to the UK as soon as possible. The day came when I made my way to the UK. I got to Buntingford and noticed that my brother Motiram was coping very well on his own. It was winter. Snow was everywhere. It was a sudden change from the hot climate in India to cold and snowy weather in London. The following day I drove to Middlesborough to bring back Anita and Krishna. Because of heavy snow everywhere there was not much traffic. It didn't take long for me to arrive in Middlesborough and reunite with my family.

Soon my holidays were over and I went to work on the following Monday. There was a letter waiting for me in my office. I got the shock of a lifetime when I read the letter. It was from the chief engineer. Up to that day I was riding high; everything was going right for me. Marriage, children, house, job etc. everything went smoothly. But now the letter from the chief engineer turned everything upside down for me. The letter said that due to the economic situation in the country, ICI had to reduce contract staff. I was on a contract. According to the contract only one week's notice was needed. ICI gave me just one week's notice. My situation then was as follows:

I had spent a lot of money on the trip to India and had bought gifts for my family in India.

My eldest brother whom we all called Dada, was with us.

I had just taken on mortgage.

I had a one year old child.

My wife was pregnant with another child.

I had only one week to find another job. I had spent my cash reserve on the trip to India.

Normally I could get another job on contract quite easily. But due to the economic situation of the country all companies were reducing staff; no company was taking more staff till the situation improved. I was in a fix, I didn't know what to do. I tried many engineering companies, all gave the same negative reply. So I tried to apply for any job. Most of the advertisements were for salesmen. Companies wanted salesmen for double glazing, shower units, freezers, etc, etc. I went for a few interviews, but due to lack of selling experience, it didn't work out. Finally I came across an advertisement saying 'Is the atmosphere in your office electric? Are you happy with your job? Are you getting sufficient income? If not, phone us for immediate employment with unlimited income'. This advertisement grabbed me because not only was it an immediate vacancy but had an unlimited income.

It was Abbey Life Assurance Company Ltd. They wanted agents to sell their life assurance products. Initially I didn't like the idea of selling life assurance. I was a qualified mechanical engineer. I delayed in replying to them, hoping to get an engineering job. But there were no engineering jobs. So I decided that I should go along with the Life Assurance company till I got an engineer's job.

I didn't realise then that I was wasting my useful time. All the time I was hoping to get an offer of an engineering job. I was not concentrating on selling life assurance policies. I was not getting anywhere, even though I was trying hard. It was Christmas and New Year holiday time. No one was in the mood to listen to my sales pitch for life assurances. Many people would talk about 'New Year resolution'. They would talk about 'reducing weight' or similar resolutions.

I asked myself, what should be my resolution?

Due to worrying about 'not supporting family properly', I was not getting a good nights sleep. All the time I was thinking that I should earn more. But how? I couldn't see how I could earn more money. I was doing my best. Suddenly I saw the light. There and then I resolved:

I am a life assurance salesman
Abbey Life is my company
I want to make a success of my life assurance career

As soon as I made the resolution, I went to sleep. I had such a beautiful and peaceful sleep, which I had not had for a long time.

Now I was ready to do my job. I waited anxiously for the holidays to finish. I was full of enthusiasm. It so happened that as soon as the holidays finished I developed a severe migraine headache. I pushed myself and went to my office and arranged a few appointments to meet people and tell them all about life assurance and its benefits. I still remember when I went to meet my first appointment around 5.00pm in a businessman's office. I had such a terrible headache that while I was telling him about life assurances, I had my left hand on the left side of my head and pressing it. He asked, "Do you have a headache?"

"Yes," I replied.

He opened his desk drawer and gave me a tablet to relieve my headache. I found out that he had three daughters. I suggested that he should take three investment plans for his three daughters. He agreed and took a substantial amount of plans. His partner was watching us. When I finished, his partner came to me. "Can I have investment plans for my two daughters?"

"Of course you can." I couldn't restrain my delight at getting substantial business on the first working day of the year.

It was magic! I continued with lots of sales in that first year and by the end of November I qualified for the Million Dollar Round Table (MDRT). It is, and still is, an elite organisation: only top salesmen would qualify for it. My manager said that I was one of the top salesmen in the company. I was baffled. I was not a forceful salesman like other top salesmen, but according to the manager and other salesmen I was one of the top salesmen. Now other salesmen in the office would approach me for advice on 'how they could increase their sales'. I didn't do anything differently except that I had a New Year resolution and stuck with it. I would tell them that it was as easy as that, just resolve to do good, and stick with it. It seemed that it was too easy a formula for success and they wouldn't understand it and accept it.

In the office once, they had arranged a special meeting; they called it 'Cavalcade Of Stars'. Top salesmen would sit in the big hall and other salesmen would go to them and ask the question 'How to increase sales and income'. Would you believe it that I was one of the stars!

My income increased substantially. I bought another house which I rented out. I was on a high, everything was happening to my liking. We went for a few good holidays with the family.

I was getting sick and tired of driving from Buntingford to Hertford North Station, leaving the car and catching a train to London. Many times the return journey was not very good either. British Rail would cancel trains. There was nowhere to go except wait for the next train which would be in an hour's time. Once I remember that it was very late. British Rail had cancelled their last train to Hertford North. I didn't know what to do. One railway employee approached me and asked me, "Where do you want to go?"

"I would like to go to Hertford North."

"I am also going to Hertford North. We have a special train for railway employees. You could come with me." There was a train on the platform. We and other employees boarded it.

"Thank you very much for helping me." I thanked the person.

I thought that we should move nearer London and have a bigger and better house. That is what we did.

We moved to a house in Enfield Chase. It was a four bedroom semi-detached house. In the meantime my eldest brother, Dada, had moved to his own house. He had asked for a house from Sainsbury, his employers. He had a job with them in their accounts section. Sainsbury has a huge warehouse in Buntingford.

The location of our house in Enfield Chase was very good; the children's school was nearby, shopping was quite handy and above all our house was only seven minutes walking distance from the railway station. It would take only half an hour's journey to reach the heart of London. My travelling time to my office and back was shorter and was very comfortable.

I kept getting more and more business, so much so that I sold a million pound policy to two of my clients. My company was very happy and displayed my framed photo in the reception along with other star performers. I was very pleased with myself. Now I expanded my life assurance business whereby I was selling to clients in other countries. Due to that I would visit Spain, Germany, Africa, the Middle East etc. I would be away but not for more than two weeks at a stretch. One day I came back from my two weeks trip. I was very disturbed when I saw two strangers in our sitting room. I had never seen them before. My wife was with them. They were engrossed in a very serious discussion.

My mind raced. It was full of questions which were to be answered. Who were they? They did not look like salesmen selling household goods. What did they want? Why had my wife allowed them inside? Surely they were not neighbours. I knew all our neighbours. What was the book all three of them were studying so intently? Surely they didn't look like my wife's relations. I knew all of them.

Chapter Eleven

Troubled Waters

I was very disturbed when I saw those two boys with my wife in our sitting room. I had just arrived back from my very tiring business trip overseas. I didn't want to ask too many questions to find out 'who and why'.

"Hello," I wished them. They wished back. "I shall go upstairs, have a shower and come down," I told my wife. My mind was very disturbed. I thought that when I went down I would find out what was going on. When I came down they were gone.

"They have left these two magazines to read." I looked at them, they were called *Watch Tower* and *Awake*.

"Were they from Jehovah's Witness?" I asked my wife.

"Yes," my wife replied. "They will come tomorrow at the same time."

"Why?"

"To study the Bible with me."

My wife was never that religious. She was born Church of England Christian but never went regularly to a church. We did not even get married in a church; we were married in a registry office in Middlesborough. I felt that if I told her not to do Bible study and not to invite them again, she would do it just to defy me. I kept quiet and did not say anything. Perhaps it was just a fad, she could grow out of it. I had brought a substantial life assurance business. I wanted to complete all the paperwork and submit them the following day.

I was horrified when I found out that they would visit her twice a week for two hours each time. This went on for a few weeks when one Sunday morning she announced, "I am going to a meeting after lunch."

"What meeting?"

"Those two boys will come after lunch and pick me up. We three will go to a meeting."

"Do you have to go to this meeting?"

"Yes. They have invited me. There will be at least 200 people attending. There will be a lecture by a well known person coming from the USA."

I had no option but to let her go to the meeting. At that time I thought that I should give her a 'long rope'. She would possibly get sick and tired of these strange ideas of Jehovah's Witnesses. I had glanced through the magazines they had left. I was not impressed by them at all. My wife was getting more and more involved with them. After a few months she got very much involved with the Jehovah's Witness Society, if you can call them Society. Tuesday and Thursday afternoons she would go and knock at other people's houses and persuade them to attend Sunday meetings. Saturday mornings, an old lady would visit her. Both would do Bible study together. On Sundays she would go to the meetings held in the local 'Kingdom Hall'. Twice a year they would have a very big meeting which was generally held in Twickenham. People from all over the country would come in coaches. All this time she used to go on her own. She was obviously persuaded to bring the children and her husband to these meetings as well. The children had no choice. They went along with her. I didn't want to interfere with the system. To tell you the truth I did not want any argument in the family. I had quietly asked my two children if they wanted to go to these meetings. They were quite happy to go. Many times they would bring with them a Chinese takeaway to eat when they came home from the meetings. The children loved Chinese takeaways.

And it seemed she was pressurised to bring her husband for meetings. She would come from these meetings and would say, like:

"It was a very good meeting."

"Six hundred attended. We had a very good lecture from a person from the USA."

"There are lots of Indians attending these meetings."

Since I had no intention of attending these meetings she would get very nasty. Looking back I could say that this was the start of the break up of our married life. Before she joined them, every Sunday lunch time we as a family would go for a walk after our lunch. Then it all changed. On Sunday after lunch my wife and children would go to the meeting and I would go for a walk on my own. I felt very miserable. After they came back from their meeting she would argue with me and ask me again, "Why are you not coming with us for the meeting?" That kind of question would turn into a row. Our life was getting less and less pleasant. I got very busy in my life assurance business. I don't know if I made myself very busy because of the unhappy atmosphere at home, or because I was busy that was why there was an unhappy atmosphere at home. It was the 'chicken and egg' situation. I was fairly well organised whereby we as a family would go on holidays during the children's holidays. By that way we had at least three holidays in a year.

I am Hindu. We have many festivals in a year. Most festivals are linked with attending a temple. It seemed the Jehovah's Witness society do not visit churches, temples etc. In addition they do not celebrate birthdays and festivals. Many Hindu marriages take place in a temple. She would refuse to go to these weddings. Many of my life assurance clients were Hindus. They would invite us for weddings and various festivals. Because my wife wouldn't accompany me, I would go on my own. My client would ask me, "Where is your wife?"

"She was not feeling well."

"What is wrong with her?"

"Oh, just a touch of flu."

Once I remember that my son's birthday was in a few days time. He came home from his school and said to us, "I would like to invite my friends for my birthday party."

"No. You can't invite them. Don't you know that we do not celebrate birthdays?" My wife told him.

"But, Mum, last year I invited them. Why not this year?"

"Last year was different, You know that during meetings they told us not to celebrate anything."

I tried to encourage my son to hold the party, but he was helpless against his mum.

The situation was getting worse. We couldn't hold any party in the house. We couldn't go to any party either. Also not attending wedding receptions as well curtailed our social life. The only thing my wife and children would do was 'Bible study'. Life really became a drag. I got more busy with my life assurance business. The charm in life was gone.

My son passed GCSE and was ready to go to college. He selected Nottingham University. I don't know if he was glad to be away from us and away from these meetings and Bible study classes. I had never asked him. But my wife got very hostile to me saying, "You have arranged it so that he is away from me and away from these meetings." I did not arrange it that way. He wanted to study business studies and chose Nottingham University. The situation was such that whatever I said or did was wrong by her.

When I was young I never learned to play any games. I thought that my children should not miss out the way I missed out. When my daughter was just three years old and my son five years old, I had admitted them into swimming classes. Even though I was very busy with the life assurance business, I would take a day off and take them to a swimming pool about ten miles away. We used to live in a village called Buntingford. The nearest pool was either in Stevenage or in Ware. Both of them were about ten miles away. Buntingford was a very small sleepy village. There wasn't much happening. We had to find our own entertainment for the children. Even the nearest railway station was about ten miles away. We then decided that we should move to a place with some life and also a railway station nearby. We moved near to Hertford North Station. Life was a bit easier. I would catch a train and travel to London. There was no need to use the car. Even the children's schooling was much better. The children could just walk to school and back. Shopping wasn't bad either. We saved a lot of time in Hertford compared to

Buntingford. My wife would shop on her own without my help. Now I was free to devote more time towards my life assurance business. My business increased substantially and I started going overseas to sell life assurance products to businessmen overseas. My businessmen clients in the UK would suggest to me to go overseas and meet their business contacts and sell to them similar products. My clients were very happy with the life assurances I had given them. They wanted their family and friends to benefit from these products. My clients in this country would even give me letters of recommendation addressed to their contacts overseas. I was doing extremely well in my business. I had qualified for the Million Dollar Round Table (MDRT). I continued to qualify and became a life member of MDRT. Everything was fine for us. It was a good living, good holidays and a happy family. One couldn't ask for more. But from the day the two boys visited us, our life became upside down.

I continued to progress in my business and had very good earnings. I thought of having a four bedroom house nearer to London. We saw a good four bedroom semi-detached house not far from Enfield Chase Station. We moved to Enfield Chase in November 1977. It seemed we moved to Enfield at the right time. No sooner had we exchanged contracts to buy the house, prices started increasing. Our estate agent pleaded with me to sell the house at a good profit. He said he had a confirmed buyer for the house. Prices increased so fast that within two years our house price had doubled.

I found out that Enfield council was quite good for children's activities. At every mid-term, term, or annual holidays the council had organised teaching classes for various sports free of charge for school students. I don't know if they still do. I found these classes very useful. As I mentioned I didn't want my children to miss out. I arranged to admit them in various sports activities. My children learned most sports in that way. I was very surprised and glad that the council had even organised free classes for water skiing.

Initially I went on my own to West Africa and then to East Africa on life assurance business. After that I was encouraged by my clients to meet their family and friends in Spain to sell them life assurances. I didn't want to be away from my family. I found a very good solution. Why not take the whole family with me to Spain? It worked very well. We visited the Canary Islands and Malaga/Toremolinos quite a few times. My clients overseas became my friends. We would get a very good welcome from them. It was definitely 'A business with pleasure'. After breakfast I would take my briefcase and go off on life assurance business and my family would enjoy a good holiday. We always had good weather. In Malaga I had a nephew who we used to visit as and when we would visit Malaga. In addition we visited Greece, Morocco, Thailand, Hong Kong and Singapore and of course a three week coach tour of Europe. My son one day had remarked, "Dad, did you know that I have visited many more countries than anyone else in my class."

There is one incident which is worth mentioning here.

We went to Rhodes Island, Greece. We stayed at the Holiday Inn. The children and I were swimming in the hotel swimming pool. The water in the pool was sea water. Suddenly a thought occurred to me. A few months ago I had been to a Life Boat Exhibition in a seaside town in England. It had given a diagram and description of 'how to survive in the sea by conserving your energy'. It had mentioned that while you are awaiting relief to come to you while you are in the sea, do not lose your energy by swimming to keep afloat. You could just relax and stand still, and you would float. By that way you could survive in the water for a very long time. I thought that I should try it while I was in sea water. I tried but was unsuccessful. I was not relaxed sufficiently enough. I tried again and this time I was very relaxed. I was amazed that I could float vertically just by standing still. I was so excited that I called my children, "Kris, Nina. Come here quick." They were terrified. They thought I was in trouble. When they came near to me I explained to them what I had experienced. They tried and they were successful as well. Everyone around us was swimming wildly and we three of us were just standing still and not doing anything at all, not even moving a muscle except muscles in our face. We three were grinning very widely indeed.

I used to go to attend annual MDRT meetings generally held in the USA. Families were not allowed during those meetings. Once in a while families were allowed. In 1981 the meeting was in New Orleans. MDRT had announced that families were allowed during that meeting. We as a family had never been to the USA. We thought that not only should we go to New Orleans, but visit many more cities in the USA. At that time Pan Am Airways had a special deal whereby not only the return air fare to New York was quite cheap but also would allow us to travel by their sister company, National Airways, for four weeks all around the USA for just an additional $100 per person. It was like the bargain of the century. I grabbed it. We travelled and visited many cities in the USA. We had an opportunity to visit Disney World, Disney Land, Kennedy Space Centre and Sea World, just to name a few places. The list would be too long to mention here. Even though as a family we enjoyed ourselves as much as we could, there was an undercurrent between my wife and I. Her belief in Jehovah's Witness would surface every now and then and we would be restricted in some of our visits to religious places.

I had joined Abbey Life as their insurance agent. We had a manager, Mr Clive Holmes, who had encouraged me to qualify for MDRT. It was all because of his encouragement and his presence in our branch that I progressed in my life assurance business. He was already a member of MDRT and every year would attend their meeting in the USA. One year there was a meeting held, I believe, in Chicago. During one lecture, the speaker was informed that Clive Holmes was needed as there was a phone call from his wife calling from London. The next day we heard that Clive had left for London as he had to leave in a hurry. After a month or so I happened to have lunch with Clive.

I asked him, "Clive. You left the MDRT meeting in a hurry. What was the hurry?"

"My wife had an attack of depression. I had to go and join her." Then he added, "Vasu, let me give you some useful advice."

He hesitated and continued, "Vasu, you are now very busy in the life assurance business, but make sure you devote sufficient time towards your family. I know you have two children. Once children are in their teens, they think they are grown up. Before they reach their teens, make sure you take them out, play with them and spend as much time with them as you can."

When I heard that I was very pleased that I was on the right track. I had been spending lots of time with my children and my wife. We had so many holidays together. On hearing what Clive had just said I paid more attention to the children. My wife didn't want more attention from me. She wanted me to attend Jehovah's Witness meetings. She was very angry that I had no intention of attending them.

My son, Kris, joined Nottingham University. My wife and I took him to Nottingham and made sure that everything was alright by him. After that I made it a point to visit him every alternate Saturday. We would go to a pub and have lunch and a drink and discuss his progress. When I told my wife that she should come with me to visit him, she refused saying that on Saturdays she had to do Bible study with one old lady. When his first year's result came I was horrified. He didn't do any good at all. He had barely passed.

I asked him, "Kris, didn't you study at all? What you have been doing with your time?"

"I have been playing drums," he replied.

"You could have done both."

He was silent.

"You have to work hard this year. Shall I talk with your teachers to help you?"

"No, Dad, I will work hard."

When he was in school, he had a great interest in playing drums. He became so much involved that he would play loud music till late at night. Once our next door neighbour complained. Kris did not pay any attention to the complaint. The neighbour had no option but to complain to the council. The council sent a policeman who threatened Kris to reduce the volume of his amplifier and not to play late at night. Otherwise he would be put behind bars. In Nottingham he had free rein and progressed quite a lot, so much so that he formed a group. In studies he didn't do well in the second year either. As usual I met him one Saturday morning after the end of the second year.

"Kris, I think you are wasting your time here. Instead of studying you are just fiddling around."

"I want to be a musician," he replied.

I was horrified to hear that. After due thought I told him, "Kris. Everyone can't be Beatles or Rolling Stones. 95% of musicians and artists are dying of hunger. Only 5% really make a success of their career. What I suggest you to do is this, you have only the final year to prove that you are good enough to get your degree. Once you have your degree, you have a choice. If you pursue music and make a success of it, well and good. But if you don't, you have your degree to lean on. If you don't have a degree and fail in your music career, you have no option but to carry on with music. Just imagine what situation you would be in at that time."

He did not say anything but obviously realised that it made sense. I was very pleased to see that in his final year he passed with honours. It seemed he had been studying as well as practising drums with his group. The group decided that they should tour the country and perform in pubs and nightclubs.

He sent to me his full programme of the tour. I thought that I should attend his performance when they were fairly near to London. I attended when they came to Stevenage, Hitchin, Milton Keynes, St Albans, Bishop's Stortford and similar nearby places. In London they performed in Camden Town and a few other places. Their last performance was a finale in Preston, Lancashire. It was quite far from London. But I really made an effort. I asked my wife to accompany me. I mentioned that Kris would be very happy to see both of us. But again that visit to Preston would have interfered with her Jehovah's Witness meetings. She refused. I went on my own. Their perofrmance was from 7.30 to 10.30 in the evening. I met Kris and his group before they started.

"Kris, after the performance I would like to take all of you for a nice dinner."

They agreed. The performance started. As usual it was very noisy. But the crowd as well as the group thoroughly enjoyed the performance. Kris mentioned that there were many youngsters who had been following them from performance to performance. It was a great success. After they finished I went to them so that I could take them out for dinner.

"Dad, the group has decided not to go for dinner. We are all very tired."

I was a bit disappointed, but glad that now I could leave for home. It was quite late. I grabbed fish and chips and drove home. It was nearly 3.30 in the morning that I arrived home.

He did not become a successful musician as he thought he would. Shortly after their finale in Preston the group members parted company. One of his classmates got a job in the IT industry in Nottingham. Kris was very good at computing. During schooling, his spare time was spent either playing drums or playing with the computer he had in his room. He went along with his classmate to see if he could get a job in computing. He was lucky. He worked with the company on an hourly basis on contract. They liked his work and he became their 'trouble shooter'. They would send him to various nearby cities to sort out and help their clients in computing. He liked the work and the money as well. This was the first time he had earned a decent wage. He came to know that the company he was working with was a branch of a big American company. He decided to visit the USA. For three months he worked and earned in the USA. Then he did the same in Australia. He liked Australia so much that he decided to settle in Australia rather than in the USA or the UK. He got a good job in Australia. He also liked the climate and the people. He applied for citizenship. Now he is a citizen of Australia.

Now we should leave Kris here and find out what was happening to my daughter Nina. Nina is an artist. She could sketch your caricature. You give her a few minutes and stand still and she will hand over your sketch. She wanted to join a 'graphic design' course. Initially she went to Maidstone University and then transferred to Middlesex University at Trent Park, Oakwood, Middlesex. In the meantime my wife got depressed as both children had gone away. The relationship between us was getting from bad to worse. Nina couldn't stand the horrible atmosphere at home. She had no choice but to find her own flat. She was not happy with that. She decided that she should also go to Australia. She went and was happy to meet her brother. She also liked the country, people and weather.

Nina worked as a graphic designer for a while. She was quite happy in Australia, but not settled yet. After a while she met a solicitor called Dan from the USA. They liked each other. Dan invited Nina to meet his parents in the USA. His parents fell in love with Nina. Shortly after that Nina and Dan got married in October 2004. The marriage was held in New York. I went and attended the wedding and blessed the couple. I also met Dan's parents. I was very impressed with Dan's family. The attitude and nature of Dan as well as his family was very pleasant and loveable. I am glad to write that Nina is now happily married and well settled in New York, USA.

Chapter Twelve

How I Helped my Children to do Well in Studies
Also
How we Lost and Found Them

My son is now a citizen of Australia. He is very happy with the country, its people, climate and outdoor life. In 2007 he came to London with his fiancée Sarah. Their plan was to be in the UK for three years only. During those three years they would work very hard and save money so that they can buy a property in Australia when they go back and settle down. Now Kris works with a good IT company. He is like 'man with the suitcase'. He is in charge of their European operation. He travels quite a lot to European countries and visits the USA/Canada for management meetings. Sarah is also doing well. She works with an international accountancy firm as a 'loss adjuster'. Both of them earn substantial salaries. Kris works in the famous building called the 'Gherkin'. It is very near to Liverpool Street Station. Whenever Kris has time he contacts me to meet up. We meet in Wetherspoons pub very near to Liverpool Street Station. He works from home and goes to his office only once a week.

We generally talk about the good old days. One day he was talking about his school days. He said, "Dad, I just remembered a funny incident. It was touch and go, I may have told this to you."

"Which incident you are talking about?"

"The incident about the 'Music Shop'."

"I may remember it. But tell me about it."

"One day I arrived late in my school. My teacher asked me to stand outside of the classroom. She had said the same thing to another five students. There we were, six of us standing outside. We got bored standing around. One of us said, 'Did you know there is a new music shop opened in the Trocadero, near Piccadilly Circus? Why don't we go there instead of standing here like a lemon'?

"We agreed to visit the shop. We had a look around at the music tape section. I was horrified when I saw my friends slyly pocketing tapes.

'I am going out. I shall wait for you at the entrance of the shop, I told them. As I was going out I noticed two policemen passed me very hurriedly. I thought that perhaps the store manager had phoned the police. I looked back and noticed that my friends were being arrested. I was mighty glad that I was not one of them, it was a near thing for me."

"Perhaps you may recall what I did when you were just three years old."

"What did you do, Dad?"

"When you were just three years old, we used to live in a small village called Buntingford. One day I saw you eating lots of chocolates. You had many more in your pocket. I asked you, 'Where did you get all the money to buy these sweets'? 'My school friend gave me the money'. 'Where did he get so much money'? 'His dad gives it to him'.

"I suspected that possibly his friend had pinched from his dad's jacket pockets. Shortly your friend came. I asked him, 'Where do you get money to give to Kris'? 'My dad gives me the pocket money'. 'No one gets so much pocket money, perhaps you have taken it from his coat pocket'?

"Your friend was silent. When I threatened your friend that I would let his dad know about it, he admitted it and said that both of you had been to the sweetshop and pinched sweets.

"I grabbed your hand and took you to the sweetshop. Buntingford was a very small village, had only one sweetshop. The shopkeeper recognised you and said, 'This boy and his friend have this morning taken sweets without paying for them'.

" 'Please remember my son's face. In future, anytime he pinches sweets, please do not phone me. Phone the police'. I said that in front of you. Perhaps that had a lasting impression on you that taking articles without paying for them is bad and is stealing. That may be the reason you detached yourself from your friends in the music shop."

"I don't remember it, Dad."

"You were only three years old."

After a while Kris remembered his life in Nottingham University. He said, "Did you know Dad that I did not do well in studies during my first two years. I just played drums. I wanted to be a musician. I had no interest in studies at all. I had formed my music group. We were very busy with making music. During the final year I picked up in my studies and passed with honours. It was like a miracle that I did very well in my final year."

"You may or may not remember what exactly happened so that you did very well in the finals."

"What happened Dad?"

"Do you remember I used to visit you in Nottingham every alternate Saturday. We would go to a pub, have a pub lunch. I knew you had struggled in the first two years. The third year was nearly finished. I said, 'I have seen your study reports. They are not good at all. Do you think you will pass?'

'No I shall fail'. You had replied.

'Do you want to pass?'

'Yes'.

'I suggest you study as hard as you can'.

'I want to be a musician'.

'Everyone can't be Rolling Stones and Beatles. Only 5% of musicians make it, but 95% are just passing the time. I suggest that from now on you work very hard and pass the examination and get the degree certificate. After that you can try your best to be a musician. If you succeed, well and good, if you don't succeed, you can rely on your graduate certificate to get a job and look after yourself. You have a choice. But if you don't acquire the degree, you have no choice whatsoever. A person must always have a choice. He should not be in a situation where he is forced to do what he doesn't want to do'. So I think our above conversation had an effect on you unconsciously. I had left you with thoughts of 'having options'. Possibly that was why you worked hard and passed with honours.

On that day while I was driving back home, I was hoping and praying that my thoughts may have some effect on you."

"So that was how it had happened. I don't recall that conversation. As you say it had an effect on me unconsciously. My actions were based on those thoughts."

"I was delighted when you passed with honours. After you finished your course you didn't come home, you continued with music and played drums. You had formed your group and had planned to tour the country. You had an agent who advised you to tour the USA after touring the UK. The group and the agent were very optimistic about the future. Your agent said, 'Once you tour the USA, your life is made'. You sent to me your tour programme. It was quite extensive. I decided that I would attend as many performances as possible. I attended performances in Bishop's Stortford, St Albans, Welwyn, Stevenage and Camden Town. Your finale was in Preston, Lancashire. I suggested to your mum to accompany me to Preston. I told her that you would be delighted to see both of us. She declined saying it would interfere with her Jehovah's Witness meetings. I came on my own. I had a good breakfast, packed my lunch and tea flask and met you just before you were to start the performance. I met your group as well. I told the group, 'I would like to take all of you for a nice dinner after the performance'. The group was delighted. The performance was good and very noisy. After the performance the group decided not to go for dinner saying, 'We are very tired'. Before I started back home I grabbed fish and chips and then drove back home. It was nearly three in the morning that I arrived home."

"I remember it. It was our best performance ever. Nearly 1,000 people turned up. Did you know, there were many youngsters who would follow us from performance to performance. We had very high hopes. We were riding high and were planning to go to the USA. Our agent said that we would be famous once we performed in the USA."

"I don't think you and the group performed in the USA, did you?"

"No. We did not. Our lead singer had a row with his girlfriend. She left him, he couldn't sstand the stress. Shortly after that he left us. Our agent tried his best to encourage him to carry on, but he couldn't. Our group tried to get another lead singer. After a while we gave up and the group was disbanded."

"What made you decide to get a job in the IT industry and not pursue the music?"

"I used to live in a house with three other boys. One of them was working in the IT industry. He worked on contract and was getting a very high hourly rate. It was contract work whereby he could work or not work, it was up to him and his mood. I liked the idea of 'working whenever I wanted'. I went with him to his office and met his boss. The boss gave me a test and immediately hired me. I was shocked to be hired so soon. It happened so quick that I didn't get a chance to think about it."

"You were very good at computing. At home you used to work on it for hours. Remember I had bought a BBC B computer for you? You even wrote music on it. Perhaps the test they gave you was very easy for you."

"Yes. I found them very easy." Kris had a mouthful of Guinness before he continued, "The IT company I worked with was an international company. It had its head office in the USA and offices all around the world. Through the internet I made lots of contacts with other employees in the USA. I finally decided to go to the USA. I travelled all over the USA. Whenever I ran short of money I worked in IT companies."

"After about three months you came back to London, didn't you?"

"Yes, I did. While I was in the USA, I decided that I should go to Australia. I had made a few contacts in Australia. After a short stay in London, I went to Australia and did the same thing that I did in the USA."

"Now you are a citizen of Australia. What made you apply for Australian citizenship?"

"I liked the weather, liked the people and above all liked the outdoor life. I decided that I should have a permanent job and not contract work. I found out what was needed to be a citizen and applied for it. Now I am a citizen of Australia. Sarah, my fiancée and I are here for about three years. We shall save as much as possible and then go back to Australia and settle down."

Our food arrived. We were very hungry. We started eating and talking.

Kris asked me, "It was a mystery to me. Mum used to complain so much about me playing drums very loud. You never complained. Why?"

"I did not want to restrict your progress in the 'art of music'. I just ignored it and was hoping for the best for you. You used to love Ravi Shankar's sitar playing and his drumming. Do you remember once our neighbour complained about your loud drumming? You just ignored him. He complained to the Enfield council. The council sent a policeman to meet you. The policeman threatened you that if you did not reduce the volume of the sound, he would arrest you and put you behind bars."

Kris first smiled and then laughed very loudly and said, "I don't remember it at all."

"After that you had kept the volume of the amplifier quite low and kept your room window closed."

"While we are talking about your schooling time, I think that I should mention to you an incident. It has a lot of bearing on your progress in your studies. Do you know you wouldn't have made it to the university if I hadn't done what I did then."

"Why do you say that I would not have made it to university? I came second in my class."

I smiled and reached for my Guinness. We had finished our meal. I had a mouthful of the drink and said, "I used to go to work quite early in the morning. One day I started a bit late. A phone call came. I picked up the phone as your mum was in the bathroom. It was from your school teacher. 'Can I talk to Kris' mum please?'

'She is in the bathroom. I am Kris' father'.

'Kris hasn't come to the school today'.

'He left as usual for the school'.

'His attendance is very poor. He hasn't been to school for some time. He is very poor in studies'.

"I was shocked. As far as I knew you and Nina used to go to school regularly. I felt very bad about it.

'I would like to meet you, perhaps there is a mistake somewhere. Where can I meet you and discuss the situation?'

'Can you come this Friday around 11 in the morning?'

'Yes I can. I am quite busy with my work. I would like to meet all Kris' teachers one by one on Friday. Can you arrange it, please?'

'Yes I can. We shall see you this Friday'.

'Thank you'. I replied.

"I never mentioned this either to you or to your mum. On Friday I went to the school and met all the teachers one by one. Each one of them had shown me the attendance register. I could see that your attendance was poor indeed. In addition they showed me your progress report. It looked pathetic. I was ashamed of the whole thing. I came home. You came home from school as usual. According to the register you were absent from the school. After our meal, I called you into my room to find out the truth.

'Kris, I have been to your school. I have met all your teachers. They have shown me your attendance register as well as your progress report. Both reports are horrible. Did you go to school today?'

'Yes I did.'

'According to the attendance register you were absent. Where did you go?'

'A few of us went to a music shop.'

'Your progress report also was not very good either. Don't you do you homework?'

"To cut the long story short you complained that the teachers were not nice to you, they didn't allow you to sit in the front row and they always victimised you.

'If I request your teachers to let you sit in the front row and don't victimise you, will you attend the school regularly?'

'Yes I would.'

"Next day I went to the school and met the head teacher and explained to her about your troubles.

'You are the only parent I have come across who has come and met us and sorted out your son's problems.' She was very glad to meet me. 'Leave it with me. I shall make sure that Kris is not victimised and is allowed to sit in the front row.'

"I thanked her and told you that from then on it was all up to you. You had only three months left for GSCE examinations. If you didn't do your homework or would attend classes regularly, I shall have no option but to phone Enfield Council and tell them that KRIS IS NOT MY SON. PLEASE ADMIT HIM IN AN ORPHANAGE. During those three months you worked very hard, and never missed any classes."

"I don't remember any of it. Yes, I did extremely well in my studies. But I remember that you allowed me to use your desk. I came second in my class. When the results had come out, everyone was asking, 'Who is Kris?' Overnight I became famous in my school. Before that I was an unknown student. Now everyone knew me."

"Yes, I remember you had come in from school. You were all smiles. You mentioned that even students you didn't know approached you and would talk to you. Then you thanked me profusely and had said, 'Thank you for scaring me to death and threatening to put me in an orphanage'."

While I am talking about my two children, let me tell you how we lost them and found them again during two incidents. We were really scared stiff.

I have two children, my son was born in 1969 in Middlesex Hospital, Edmonton. He took a long time to come out of the cosiness of his mother's womb. The due date had come and gone. One week passed, two weeks passed. He was keeping all of us in suspense. The doctors couldn't understand why there was no indication of labour pain at all. Finally they felt that it could be dangerous for mother and child if this continued. Finally the doctors gave my wife some sort of medicine/drug to promote labour pains. That did the trick. Unexpectedly my wife had pains in the middle of the night. I phoned the hospital and they asked me to bring her to the hospital immediately. She had been ready to go to hospital for the last three weeks, so she didn't take long to get ready. Immediately I put her in the car and drove to the hospital which was about four miles away. In the middle of the night, the roads were quite clear, so it didn't take long. The doctors were very surprised to see us so soon. They were not ready for us. Even though it was a short journey, I was very anxious and thoughts passed through my mind. What if we don't reach hospital on time?

Now the real trouble started. Again our son wouldn't come out, possibly he was too comfortable. For a long time, my wife pushed and pushed, but it was of no use. She was sweating profusely and very tired. Finally the doctors decided that it would have to be caesarean. All the time I was present and near to my wife holding her hand and encouraging her to push. Finally, after the doctors cut her open, my son's head appeared. Slowly and gradually he came out. Everyone was very relieved, specially my wife and I. It was such hard work on her part, but all went very well. I marvelled at nature and was very pleased to get this gift from God.

Naming our son was not difficult. There were lots of suggestions by friends and family. My name is Vasu which is short for Vasudev. According to our history, one of our Gods is Krishna, whose father's name is Vasudev. So why not name my son Krishna. Everyone liked the idea. Many people had a middle name as well, but since everyone was happy with the given name, we didn't find it necessary to give him an additional name as well.

I come from India, but have been in this country for the last 45 years. When I came, I had brought a few necessary books with me. One of the books I had brought was *Teach Yourself Sindhi.* When my children grew and went to kindergarten, I thought that I should teach them Sindhi as well, they could learn English in school. But it turned out to be a funny situation. I remember when we would sit at the table and have a meal, I taught the children that when they had had enough, they should say 'bus'. This means they had had enough. But the children said 'bus' in their school. The teacher couldn't understand and asked my son, "Where is the bus?" I realised that possibly I may be confusing my children, so I dropped the idea of teaching them Sindhi.

During the Easter holidays in 1977, we decided to go to Spain. We had bought a package holiday. Our flight was a night flight, so when we arrived in Spain we were very tired. On arrival in the hotel, we all went to bed. We got up the following morning and had our breakfast. While we had breakfast, I could see through the hotel window that there was a mountain not far from the hotel. We decided to climb the mountain. At the reception we got directions of how to get there. It was quite chilly and it was getting more chilly as we climbed the mountain. But the exercise was good and the wind and atmosphere was very fresh and invigorating. We were very pleased with ourselves, especially I was very happy that our children managed to climb without much difficulty. We lingered on top for a short while and decided to go down. We knew that coming down was not as difficult as climbing. I told my wife and children to climb down carefully, as one may slip and sprain an ankle. We were very careful where we stepped. Around half way, I looked back. I didn't see my son. We waited and called his name. No answer. We shouted his name. The only thing we could hear was the echo of our shout. I climbed up to see if I could spot him. I couldn't see him anywhere. We were at our wits end, didn't know what to do. Nothing else was moving on the mountain. We again scanned the mountain but could not see any movement. Again after shouting his name a few times, we felt that perhaps he had gone down from the other side.

We were very stressed and distressed and we didn't know where we were going or what we were stepping on. My wife stepped on a bee's nest. Thousands of bees surrounded us and stung us. We came running down at the double. Still there was no sign of our son. Again we scanned the mountain from below and tried to spot him, not a single movement anywhere. We climbed half way, we gazed, we shouted but nowhere could we see any movement at all. My wife wept and cried, "I want my son, where is he? It is your fault you brought us to climb the mountain." I had no answers to her questions. We then felt that we should go to the hotel and phone the police who would help us find our son. We got to the hotel and explained the situation to reception. Reception phoned the police who asked questions about his height, age, name, colour, etc so that they could try to locate him. On the phone I told them I should go along with them so that I could show them which way we went and which way we came down. They kept on saying that they were coming, but they never came for at least two hours. We kept telling the reception to phone the police again so that they would come quickly. I dare not sit near my wife, all the time she was blaming me and crying. I sat outside near the hotel main gate, holding my head in my hands, confused and thinking what else could I do apart from calling the police. I sat there holding my bowed head, I don't remember how long for. Suddenly I heard, "Dad, why are you sitting outside, where is Mum?" I looked up. It was my son standing there as if nothing had happened. Here our world was falling apart, and he came out of nowhere. I thought I was dreaming. I didn't expect him to appear like that. A thought occurred to me that perhaps he was a ghost. One reads so many ghost stories. I hugged him and took him inside the hotel where my wife and daughter were sitting near the hotel reception. For a while I couldn't speak, couldn't think clearly, just sat there in a daze. Finally I recovered and asked him what had happened and why we couldn't see him. "Dad, we were coming down together then suddenly I didn't see any of you. I then came down and waited for a while when I arrived at the base of the mountain. Still I couldn't see any of you, so I made my way to the hotel." He told us in such a matter of fact way, as if nothing had happened. Strangely enough he was not scared at all in the foreign country where we had just arrived and where he did not know the lay of the land. He was about eight years old then. I was very thankful to God who had been so kind and merciful to me.

On the subject of losing and gaining my son, a similar thing happened to our daughter many years ago. We went to the seaside, I believe it was Brighton. We were sitting on the beach, it was very hot and there were huge crowds of people everywhere. My wife and I were sunbathing and the children were building a castle in the sand, not very far from where we were sitting. I got a shock of a lifetime when I saw only my son building the castle, our daughter was nowhere to be seen. I went and asked my son, "Where is Nina?"

"I don't know, she was here."

"Where did she go?" I asked sharply.

"I don't know, I was busy building this castle. Look Dad, it is good isn't it?"

I looked around, I couldn't see her. I was very upset with my son, not looking after his younger sister. Since I couldn't see her nearby, I thought perhaps she had gone further along the beach. I told my wife, "I am going in this direction, in the meantime, you look around, she may be nearby."

I was very upset with her, she was only three years old, she shouldn't move away on her own, she could have at least told her brother where she was going, she may have gone to the toilet or somewhere else. I had remembered that she was wearing a flowery swimming costume. While I was looking around, I was paying attention to any child in a swimming costume. I don't remember how far I went, but suddenly I noticed a child building a sandcastle on the edge of the sea. Her back was towards me. When I looked hard, I could hardly believe it. Nina was building a sandcastle here, away from her brother and away from us. I was very pleased, I didn't want to be upset with her. I was so thankful that I found her. When I asked her, "Why were you building sandcastles away from all of us and not where we were?"

"I wanted to build my own."

"Why not where we were?"

"Sand was dry. I wanted the soft and moist one."

I was very glad that I found her and didn't want to point out that there was soft and moist sand over there as well. We were very scared because there were rumours then that children were being stolen and kidnapped and sold off to Arab countries.

Chapter Thirteen

How I Raised Myself from Failure to Success

It was 1970. We had just moved to our first house in Buntingford. It was a very small sleepy village. It was easy for me to go by car to my job with ICI in Welwyn Garden City. My income was good. That was how I managed to secure a mortgage to buy the property. We had a son of just a year old. My wife was expecting another child. We had agreed and arranged the second child soon after the first one. I had read that two children would be company to each other. They would demand less of their mother's attention. My eldest brother, Motiram, who had been in Nairobi was staying with us. He had no choice but to leave Kenya in a hurry. The Kenyans were insisting on him to either accept Kenyan citizenship, denounce British citizenship or leave the country. Around that time my mother had written to me to visit her. I arranged my passage and went to India. When I came back, I found a letter waiting for me. It was from ICI. The letter had said that due to an economic downturn they had no choice but to reduce staff. The news was like a bolt from the blue. Before I had left for India three weeks ago I was riding high. I had a good job and a very good income. Now I had no job and no steady income to support my family.

I tried to get another job. All the engineering companies had the same reply for me; there was a downturn in the economy. The only jobs available were for salesmen. I thought that I should try those to support my family. I came across an advertisement which caught my eye. It said 'Is the atmosphere in your office electric? Are you happy with the income you are getting? Are you satisfied with your job? If the answer is no, rush to the phone and call this phone number'. I was desperate to try any job. When I contacted them, I found out that it was a life assurance company called Abbey Life. They needed agents to work on commission only. There was no guaranteed salary. I was not happy but I thought that I could carry on with them till I got a job in engineering. I started with them. I was still searching for an engineering job and not paying 100% attention to the life assurance industry. Due to that I was not getting anywhere. My commission earning was very low. After three months came Christmas and the New Year holidays. One day on television I watched a programme. They were discussing New Year resolutions. I asked myself, what should be my New Year's resolution? I couldn't sleep that night. I was also very worried about my very low income which was not sufficient to provide a decent life for the family. In the middle of the night I had a thought; perhaps my attention is diverted and I am not paying full attention to the job in hand. There and then I convinced myself that the following should be my resolution:

I am a life assurance agent

Abbey Life is my company

life assurance is my industry

AND I AM GOING TO MAKE A SUCCESS OF MY PROFESSION.

Then I went to sleep. I had such a beautiful and sound sleep. Before that I had not slept soundly. My mind was always disturbed. Now with this resolution I had released the pressure from my mind. My mind was free to do and think what was best for me. I was waiting for the holidays to finish so that I could start the constructive work and earn some decent dollars.

I remember it was Wednesday the 4th January I went to the office. I had six names and phone numbers to work on and hopefully get appointments from. I had a terrible headache, but I had dragged myself to go to the office. I was not successful with the first five names. I got lucky with the sixth one. I arranged an appointment with a businessman in East London for Friday at six in the evening. He had mentioned that at that time he would have finished work for the day and would be relaxed. On Friday I visited his office. I still had a terrible headache. I never believed in taking tablets, therefore I was pressing my hand onto my head to relieve the pain.

I met the businessman. He looked at me and asked, "Have you got a headache?"

"Yes." He opened his drawer and gave me two pills to swallow. I thanked him. After that I did some 'fact finding'. I found out that he had three daughters. In Indian society parents are very concerned about their daughters. Parents always want to save aside a fund for their marriages. He wanted to do the same for his three daughters. I showed him an investment plan in which he could save monthly for future accumulation. At that time the tax man would give an incentive of tax relief on those savings. He liked the idea and immediately started three savings plans. His partner who was watching us came near to us after we had finished our business. He asked me, "Can I have similar plans? I have two daughters as well. I would like to invest similar amounts."

"Of course you can." Deep down I was very excited to get five saving applications of a substantial monthly amount. After I had finished with them I came out of their office. I couldn't walk; I had to run. I wanted to shout as well. I was so excited about getting so much business in a matter of two hours.

The next day I went to my office to submit my business. My manager, Clive Holmes, had a look at what business I had brought. He also couldn't control himself and uttered, "You bastard!" Even though he used abusive language he said it in such a loving way that I loved it and grinned. Looking back I could confidently say that he knew how to infuse confidence in me and in other agents. All because of him I progressed in the life insurance industry. He made me aware of the Million Dollar Round Table (MDRT). He also gave me a book by Frank Bettgar to read. Can you guess what was the title of that book? It was *How I Raised Myself From Failure To Success*.

I was very much influenced by that book. I used to read it while travelling by train from home to the office. The book was full of wise words. I was reading it very slowly and understood what message the writer was passing onto the readers. Halfway in the book I came across a chapter, 'How I sold $250,000 life assurance policy in fifteen minutes'. When I finished the chapter I felt as if a bombshell had exploded in front of my eyes. I read it again. I was very excited and decided that I should try it on someone as soon as I could. Luck would have it that I didn't have long to wait. The next day I had ten names to phone for appointments. The first nine were not interested in life assurances. The tenth one agreed to meet me in his office on the following day around eleven in the morning. His office was near to Old Street Station. I tried the method that the book had suggested. It worked like a charm. I had sold him not $250,000 but £250,000 life assurance policy. Everything happened so smoothly that when we finished he was very surprised and exclaimed, "Is that all? Is it done?"

"Yes. It is done. If your medical report is normal, in a few weeks time I shall bring the policy document for you."

"Thank you, Vasu. I have been thinking of it for a long time. Now you have arranged it very efficiently." He was very grateful.

"Thank you for the business and your hospitality."

I qualified for membership of MDRT in that year. Clive advised me that I should qualify every year and at least for six years. "You will be a life member of MDRT if you qualify consecutively for six years." I became a life member of MDRT. That was nearly thirty years ago. Clive also highly recommended to me that I must attend the MDRT annual meetings.

My clients were nice to me. Gradually my clients became my friends. I would arrange life assurances for their family and friends. In addition they had suggested to me to go to Spain and Africa and arrange life assurances for their business contacts.

In West Africa I came across my uncle Kishinchand. As mentioned in my chapter on Partition, every family found their own way to save themselves from the killings. My uncle and his family had gone to Ghana, West Africa, where his sister's husband had a business. Now they were well settled in Accra, Ghana. My uncle showed a great interest in starting an import and export business in

London. During those days, a British company had to have at least one director who was British.

"Vasu, can you be my British director?"

"Of course."

We opened an office in Regent Street, London, W1. My Abbey Life office was also in London W1. It was quite convenient for me to visit both offices without much trouble. At that time my uncle was looking for an efficient manager for his business.

One day I went to a businessman to sell life assurance. While we were discussing, his assistant came in the room. I looked at him, he looked at me. After he left the room I asked the businessman, "I have seen him somewhere. What is his name?"

"Harry."

"Harry Jagasia?"

"Yes."

I thought that this was definitely a stroke of luck. I had been looking for Harry since I had arrived in London in 1963. Harry was the person who had suggested and recommended to me in Bombay to apply for the British Employment Voucher. He had left for the UK in 1963 without giving me his address in the UK. After the meeting with the businessman I requested that, "I would like to meet Harry."

He called Harry. I met Harry and suggested that we meet after he finished his work. We went to a nearby pub. Last time we had met was in 1963. We had so much to talk about. After a few days we arranged our family gathering and got very close to each other.

"Harry, would you like to work with us? My uncle has an import and export business. He is looking for an experienced manager. I believe you are working in the import and export department of your company."

"Of course, I shall work with you. I would be delighted."

Harry gave the required notice period to his existing employer and started working for my uncle. I also had a room in that office. Harry and I would meet every day and more often than not had a pub lunch. Everything went fine for my uncle. After three years my uncle decided to close the London office. Harry got a job with another businessman from Ghana, who had an office near Piccadilly Circus, London.

During those three years I was in contact with many more businessmen from Africa. My business also shot up. My bank balance was very healthy. I was very upset when the office was closed. I had to bring all my business files to my house and work from home. I had a brainwave; why don't I buy a property in central London, use part of it as my office and use the rest to let. It was December 1983 when I bought a block of ten flats in Bayswater. I used the ground floor flat as my office and the rest for short let holiday flats. Bayswater is a tourist area. I never had any problem getting customers. My business clients and friends also helped me in getting customers for the flats. I used to hire a couple who would manage the flats' business while I continued with my life assurance business. Because I was on the premises, managing the flats business went extremely well. Harry used to visit me regularly and would have afternoon tea with me.

One day Harry came to my office. He was very depressed and thoughtful.

"What is the matter, Harry?"

"My boss is not a very nice person. He refused to give me any raise this year. I would like to leave him." After a thought he said, "Did you know that restaurant businesses have a very big margin of profit? My wife, Nimmi, and I would like to start a restaurant business. We haven't got that much capital. Can you be our partner?" I had a natural hatred for partnerships. In my first chapter you must have read how bad partnership was for my father.

"Harry, are you serious about starting a restaurant business?"

"Yes."

"I shall tell you what I will do. I shall buy a restaurant property. You be my manager and run the restaurant as your own. How does this idea sound to you?" Harry was delighted.

"From now on you look around for a property. I shall also look around. Since my office is in Bayswater, London W2, I would like the restaurant to be nearby to my office." I could see that he was very happy to hear that. He couldn't wait to tell this to his wife.

Shortly I bought a freehold property with a restaurant on the ground floor and a two bedroom flat above it. My bank manager was very happy with me. Immediately he lent me the required amount to buy the property. The property was just opposite to St Mary's Hospital, London W2. As soon as I exchanged the contract to buy the property Harry had an attack of flu. I went ahead thinking that Harry would come shortly and join me. He was supposed to manage the restaurant right from the start. I carried on with refurbishment. The time was passing by and Harry was still down with flu. In the meantime I hired restaurant staff. With the help of staff I ordered the required furniture, arranged fixing, fitting and anything needed for the restaurant business. Finally Harry came to my office. He was very weak. It seemed his energy had been drained away by prolonged flu.

"Vasu, I am very weak now. I don't think I can manage the restaurant. The restaurant working hours are long and unearthly. I don't think I shall be able to manage it. I am sorry, Vasu."

I was very disappointed when I heard that. I was already busy with my life assurance business and short let flats.

"Would you join me after you have regained your energy?"

"No. I don't think I will be able to." I could see that having flu had taken not only his physical energy but his mental courage as well.

"Harry, don't worry. I shall hire another manager. You go home and have a rest. You look very tired."

For the next six months I was very busy bringing the restaurant into shipshape condition. From the beginning we got very good business from St Mary's Hospital, Paddington Green Police Station staff, as well as from many small surrounding hotels. We named the restaurant Paddington Tandoori Restaurant, in short it was called PTR. The restaurant industry is inter-connected. The industry came to know that a newcomer had come into the market and was doing extremely well. I would get lots of offers from various restaurant staff as well as from owners of restaurants. Owners wanted to offload their restaurants onto me. I was lucky that I had good staff, not only in my flat letting business but also in the restaurant business. It was 1987. Property values had gone down. Restaurant businesses in general were not doing well either. I came across an offer of a good freehold restaurant property on Westbourne Grove, London, W2. It looked a bargain to me. I approached my bankers. The bankers sent their surveyor. The surveyor was so excited about the property that he said, "Vasu, this is a gold mine to you. As and when you happen to sell it, please give me the first preference. I will have a cash buyer for you." He sent the report to my bankers. The bankers were again happy to lend whatever loan I needed. I was very pleased and bought the property.

At that time a couple, Gary and Pam Parsons, were looking after my flat business. They had come from New Zealand to the UK for a couple of years to look around, earn some money, buy an XJ6 Jaguar car and then take the car with them to New Zealand. Gary and Pam had helped me quite a lot. They had looked after my flat business very well; as well as if it were their own business. I had no worries about that business. I was concentrating more on my two restaurant businesses. I thought that I should be physically fit to sustain all the pressure from the various businesses. Gary, Pam and I would go to a nearby tennis court and play tennis as and when time permitted. I would arrange my time in such a way that by 6.30pm I would leave my office and go home to be with my family. But sadly my family life was going from bad to worse. I was getting stress at work as well as at home. I never realised how bad it was till one afternoon when I was playing tennis with Gary and Pam. I fainted on the tennis court.

I still clearly visualise the scene. I was lying on my back on the tennis court. The darkness was all around me. I could hear very far away two people talking.

A woman's voice said, "Is he dead?"
A man replied, "I don't know."
"What shall we do, Gary?"

"I shall go and feel his pulse."

Gary came and felt my pulse. He was not sure about it. He said, "Pam, I shall call the ambulance."

In the meantime I had regained a bit of energy. I raised my hand.

"Yes, Vasu."

"Water," I replied very faintly.

They gave me a few drops of water. After a few minutes I told them to lift me up to a sitting position. I looked at Gary and Pam and faintly smiled.

"Can I bring the car around?"

"Not yet. Please sit down and talk to me."

They talked and I listened with my eyes closed.

After a while Gary brought the car around and said, "We shall take you to the office."

"No. Take me to my house."

"We don't know your house."

"I shall guide you where to go. I am now awake."

While they were taking me to my house, I promised myself; from now on I shall reduce my workload, stop playing tennis and relax a bit more. Another thought came into my mind. I asked myself, have I got sufficient life assurance so that my family is adequately provided for in the event of my death? I knew that I had covered all my loans. I had a few days rest and started my routine, but not as strenuously as before. I had an authority from Abbey Life to take my clients for medical examinations in Harley Street, London, W1, as and when needed. I applied for additional life assurance and took myself for a medical. I wanted to know if my health was back to normal. The doctor completed a general examination and couldn't find anything wrong with me.

"Doctor, why not take my ECG?"

"It is not necessary."

"I would like to see the result of it. Please perform an ECG on me."

He had a look at the ECG graph and sat down in deep thought.

"Doctor, is anything wrong?"

"No. There is nothing wrong. But I can see that sometimes the needle on the graph is jumping."

What does it indicate?" I did not tell him anything about me fainting on the tennis court few days before.

"It looks like you had a silent heart attack."

"I haven't heard of that before. What does it mean?"

"It seems you had a heart attack. Since you are physically fit, you withstood the knock. Now there is no harm done." I then realised that I should take it easy for some time. Even Gary and Pam had mentioned that I looked pale and weak.

After a few months my second restaurant, which I had just bought, was ready to start business. We had a very lavish opening night. We had invited three members of Parliament. John Watts, who was also a MP, my auditor, and Mr Wheeler who was MP for the City of Westminster. This restaurant was in the City of Westminster area. Mr Brooke was a MP from Paddington. I had another restaurant in the Paddington area. We all had a great time. I had invited my brother Jaik and his wife Haru from India to honour the occasion. Jaik had, and still has, two restaurants in Kolkata, both are called 'Oasis Restaurant'. I had opened this restaurant under the same name and used the same logo he had used for his restaurants in India.

The business was brisk from day one. Both my restaurants were doing extremely well. My flat letting was also very good. I had very efficient and sincere staff working with me. Every now and then my wife would come with her sister or a friend, to have a good meal in one of our restaurants. My son and daughter also would come individually with their friends. Everything was very rosy for me and for my family.

It is said, 'Success of a businessman takes it toll. A businessman either loses his health or family life or both', It so happened that without me knowing about it, I had a bit of a health problem. Luckily there was no permanent damage and I recovered. But my family life suffered quite a lot. My wife's Jehovah's Witness meetings did not help at all. I felt they were the main obstacle to our family life. Due to that I spent more and more time in my businesses. Immediately after that inflation went haywire and rose to 17%. The Chancellor of the Exchequer had no option but to raise the bank interest rate to 15%. That made a joke of my loan interest payments and of the equity in my properties. My bankers demanded not only extra capital to cover their loan but demanded higher interest payments. I tried to manage but another thought occurred to me; why am I struggling? Why am I working so hard and for whom? The blunt realisation and the solution to my problems came to me. It was, sell properties, pay back all the loans and get out of the mess immediately'. That was what I did in January 1990.

I brought home the files of all my life assurance businesses and started working from home. I was not happy. I was used to going out to work early in the morning and coming home in the evening. Similarly my wife was not happy either. I spent more time in the house than I used to do. It was interfering with her Jehovah's Witness activities.

Let me be a bit philosophical now. When a couple decide to go for a divorce, there is never one reason for the divorce. Every couple is different. Human nature is also very complicated. Also there is always change in the world. People's nature changes, situations change, health changes, needs change and so on. The list of 'changes' came to be quite a long one. In our case, we reached the point where it was futile to be together. Our children had grown and gone away and had joined universities. We had been on so many holidays and I thought that perhaps a good holiday might mend our relationship. Some time ago my wife and I wanted to go to the North Cape. I went to a travel agent and got a brochure for holidays to Scandinavian countries and the North Cape. My wife and I went on the holiday. It was a very good and enjoyable holiday. It was amazing that we were in shirt sleeves while we were in the North Cape. North Cape is the northern most point of Europe. One would imagine it would be cold and freezing. We enjoyed it as much as we could, but all the time there was an undercurrent between us.

When we went to the museum in the North Cape I noticed a notice saying that King Ram VIII of Thailand had visited the place some time ago. I was excited. In our Hindu literature King Ram is one of the reincarnations of our God Vishnu. I never realised that Thailand was ruled by a Hindu King. I wanted to know a bit more about it. I decided that once I reached London I would go to the Thai Embassy and enquire about it and perhaps try to visit Thailand. That was exactly what I did. I found out that Thomas Cook had a very good package tour which covered Thailand, Hong Kong and Singapore. I showed it to my wife and children. The children and I were very keen to go but my wife didn't want to go with us. We were very disappointed, especially the children were very disheartened. The next day I asked my children, "Would you like to go on this holiday even if your mum doesn't come?"

"Yes," Both said in unison and were very excited about it. I booked the holiday. The three of us went on that holiday between December 91-January 92. We had a fabulous time.

When we came back, my wife was very depressed. She didn't like the idea that we three had gone on the holiday and enjoyed ourselves and she was sitting at home and brooding. She also complained that I had purposely taken the children away and arranged their absence at Jehovah's Witness meetings. Shortly my wife filed for divorce. I had no option but to go along with the divorce. Finally, on Christmas Eve of 1994 we were divorced.

Chapter Fourteen

Start of the New Life

I am amazed at myself when I recall those days when my wife and I were facing each other in a court to sort out our divorce settlement. We were still living in the same house but in separate rooms. Initially I thought that divorce proceedings would be straightforward. I had read a book on 'Divorce'. It said that the court would make sure that both parties were reasonably comfortable. Also that children are to be looked after and provided for in all respects including education. Both our children were over 21 years old. There was no need to worry about them. I had to worry and provide for my wife. The judge had to make sure that she had a place to live and sufficient income for a decent living. The judge would make allowances for her capability of earning. The best solution I could see was that I should buy a flat for her. The flat would be fully paid and no loan outstanding on it. Her regular income would suffice to cover all other expenses and give her a decent living. I mentioned it to my wife and asked her where she wanted a flat. She said that I shouldn't talk to her; her solicitors would send me forms to complete. I waited for the forms. I found out that it didn't work that way. Her solicitors sent me lots of forms to be completed. These forms wanted all the details of my savings, investments and pensions. I thought that I should hire a solicitor who would handle them professionally.

Since I had three businesses, (the flat, two restaurants, and my life assurance business), my solicitor wanted to know everything about them in detail. He wanted everything in triplicate. He retained one copy for himself, one copy for my wife's solicitors and one copy for the court. Initially I went along with him. After two months I realised that it was a long procedure. One question from my wife's solicitors would promote lots of paperwork for me. Also he would call me for meetings. The more time he spent the more expensive he was getting and the more and more complicated. I discharged my solicitors and handled my divorce case on my own. It was a bit easier and less paperwork. Anything which was not clear to me, I would phone my wife's solicitors to clarify. I appeared in the court on my own without any barrister. My wife had hired a female solicitor in Ilford. The court we appeared was also in Ilford. We used to live in Enfield.

During the divorce proceedings my wife and I lived in the same house. It was difficult for her to travel to Ilford on the court day. My brother, Motiram, had retired and had given her a VW Beetle car. She was using it during those days. I thought that since I was visiting the same court I could give her a lift. We appeared three times in the court and three times I had brought her in my car to the court. On our first appearance, the judge wanted additional information. The next hearing was fixed on a day about four months hence. Again the same thing happened and the hearing was fixed on a day six months hence. The divorce case dragged on for quite a while. Due to my few businesses, the court as well as my wife's solicitors, asked lots of questions and wanted evidence of what I had said. I was glad that the divorce case dragged on for a while. I was getting wiser as well and knew what was happening and what the court was looking for. During those court appearances I had provided to the court what my wife's earning were and what she was capable of earning. That made a good impact on the court. The judge made allowances for her income and finally passed the judgement. The judge's final comment to my wife's solicitors was, 'You have been saying all along that this person is very wealthy. You haven't shown me any proof of it." I was delighted that finally it was all over on Christmas Eve of 1994. The court decided that the four bedroom house we had lived in should be given to my wife. I had to be out of it as soon as I could. Once, I remember I gave a curt reply to the judge. He got very angry with me and warned me, "Mr Daryanani, behave yourself. Otherwise we will hold you responsible for contempt of the court. We will not allow you to represent yourself." I realised that it would be a disaster for me not to represent myself.

I cooled down and said, "Sorry your highness." (Instead of Lordship). He smiled.

I brought my wife back home in the car. I rushed to the Abbey National Building Society office, I already had a mortgage with them. I thought that they should be able to quickly give me a new mortgage. I had to buy another property for myself. It was Christmas Eve and offices closed early. I just got in the office and completed a form for a new mortgage. The adviser gave me an indication of how much mortgage they would give me. Immediately I went to Lipton Housing Estate in Southgate, London, N14. I found out what was available and what I could afford. I booked a flat on the spot. I had requested the Abbey National adviser that she should arrange this very quickly and had explained to her the situation I was in. Everyone concerned did not waste any time at all. I moved into my flat by the middle of January 1995.

During that time a film called *War of the Roses* was shown on television. It had Michael Douglas and Kathleen Turner as Mr and Mrs Rose. I found the film very educational. It showed a couple who were fighting a divorce case. In the process they not only destroyed their assets but destroyed each other as well. I thought to myself, 'I shall not argue about anything with my wife, I will agree to give to her whatever articles in the house she wants'. When I was ready to move out, we both went around the house. I would point at an article and ask her, "Do you want it? If she said, 'Yes', then I left it alone. Whatever article she didn't want, I took away.

While I was going through the divorce I had plenty of time. I would regularly go to the local library and read not only about divorce but also about philosophy. One day I came across an article on divorce/relationship/marriage. It said, 'When a person is divorced, he/she lives on their own, thinking that they will get married to the right person. The person is on their own for a while. The time passes. The right person may not have come. In the meantime the person is so used to living on their own, that when the right person shows an interest, they asks themselves, why should I get married? I am happy as I am. The person takes shelter in the saying; Once bitten, twice shy'. I didn't want that to happen to me. I thought that I should get married as soon as possible, before I got used to being on my own. I grew in confidence and convinced myself saying, 'I can handle any woman I marry. I am not bothered about any caste, creed, colour, religion etc'.

I had just changed my residence and had come to a new place to live. Now I was on my own, ready to lead a new and different life. A wild thought came to me, 'Why not change my appearance as well?' I used to have a beard. On the first Saturday after I came to my new flat, I went to a local barber and got rid of not only my facial hair but hair from my crown. When I came home and looked in the mirror, I couldn't recognise myself. I was really tickled to see my bald and clean shaven face. I decided to wear a baseball cap. The next day was Sunday. Every Sunday I went for a walk with ramblers. I remember the walk on that Sunday was from Great Missenden in Buckinghamshire, England. Many ramblers had already arrived before I had. I was wearing my baseball cap. They had never seen me in a baseball cap. I wished them a very loud and happy 'good morning' and removed my cap to show them my curly top. There was silence for a while, then all of us burst into laughter. We laughed quite a lot on that morning. One rambler said, "Vasu, you look great in your new hairstyle."

I am generally in good health. I had a wild idea, 'Why don't I raise another family. My new wife should be child bearing age. Her own child would give her a new and full life'. Keeping these thoughts in my mind, I started looking around wherever I went. My first wife was a Protestant Christian. I didn't mind any religion but felt that Muslims were very different from people like us. Moreover Muslims were the people who were killing and murdering us in Pakistan. It was a long time ago. Our wounds had been healed by this time. It was 1947 then, now it was 1995. Times also had changed. But I thought that I should tread a bit more carefully if involved with a Muslim girl.

During my trips to the library, I came across a very interesting article in a magazine. It said, 'Many people wait for the right person to come along to get married. It is a fallacy that there is a right person. There is no such person. If there is, it is you. You have to be the right person. In addition, even if there was one, the person would be the wrong person in a while. Everything is changing in this world; the person's nature changes, the situation changes, job changes; residence changes, health changes, thinking changes. The list can go on and on. There is one solution for your predicament. Do not look for a 100% right person, look for about a 70% right person. Then by due love and care and also by 'give and take', both of you together can strive to attain the 100% compatibility'. Then the article added, "Make a list of twenty qualities you would like to see in the other person. Assign five points to each quality. When you meet a person, give him/her certain points out of five. Then add up the points the person has earned. If the points are 70% or higher, you take interest in him/her. If the points are less, you should reject them unless you have your own reasons for not rejecting'.

Now it was more of a game for me. I carried pen and paper wherever I went and started assessing the opposite sex. I also wrote to my brother Jaik in India and made him aware that I was looking for a wife of child bearing age. Jaik wrote back, 'Vasu, come to India as soon as you can. Here in India we have a system of "matchmaking". While you are in India, a matchmaker would meet you and advise and help you. Matchmakers keep an extensive portfolio of eligible girls. You could meet the girls and decide for yourself'. I immediately booked my ticket and went to India.

One of the best ways of meeting the opposite sex is attending a wedding reception. In Indian society, not only in India, but wherever they are held in the world, an Indian wedding reception is a huge social event. After I got to India I attended quite a few wedding receptions and was introduced to eligible girls. I would invite them for a buffet lunch in a five star restaurant. In Mumbai there is a Sheraton restaurant on the seafront. They did a very good buffet lunch. We would exchange news and views and get to know more about each other. It was a very nice way of finding my future partner. It is not easy to find a partner. Is it like finding a needle in a hay stack. Deep down I was determined to find the needle. The time passed by, still I didn't find my needle. I had gone to India for five weeks. Four weeks had passed. One day the neighbour of my brother, Jaik, visited Jaik and his wife Haru. I also was present there. Jaik introduced me to her and said, "He is my brother, Vasu. He has come from London. He would like to marry a good woman." The neighbour looked at me very hard and smiled. After a while she called Jaik in the other room and said to him, "My younger sister has just come from Bangalore. She is a widow with a fifteen year old daughter. She is child bearing age and she is beautiful. Perhaps your brother should meet her."

It was the month of March that I met her. Her name was Sujatha. We liked each other. It was now time for me to go back to London. I had no option but to say to her, "I shall contact you as soon as I arrive in London." We exchanged necessary details; photographs as well as address/phone/fax numbers. We were lucky that we liked each other. We were in constant touch with each other by phone calls and by faxes. It was a daily affair that I would get a fax from her early morning around 7.30am. Due to the time difference, it was lunchtime in Bangalore. She used to work in a large IT company. Lunchtime was the best time she could send a fax. Immediately I would reply to her by fax. I was very busy in my life assurance business because I had been away for five weeks. For a while I couldn't leave for India. We were very anxious to meet each other again. Finally the time came when I could again go for five weeks. It happened in the month of August.

I booked my ticket and told Sujatha which flight I was on and when I was arriving in Bangalore. On the day I got to the airport and presented my ticket and passport at the airline counter.

"Where is your visa?"

As soon as he asked me the question, I realised that I had forgotten to apply for a visa. I was so excited that I did everything else except get a visa to go to India.

"I am sorry, I have forgotten to apply for it. Why not allow me to travel by this flight? My people are waiting for me at the other end. I should be able to get the visa on arrival in Bombay. Originally I am from India."

"No, Sir. We can't allow you to travel without a visa."

"What happens to my ticket?"

"We will allow you to travel by the next flight, which is tomorrow at the same time."

"What happens if I don't get a visa by then?"

"If you make a request to them and explain, they should give you one."

I left my luggage in the 'left luggage office' at the airport and went straight to the Indian Embassy. I explained to them what had happened. I requested of them, "Can you please issue a visa for me today? I can then travel by tomorrow's flight. The airline are very kindly allowing me to travel by the same ticket."

The Indian visa office were very considerate. I got the visa, came home and phoned Sujatha to tell her what had happened. I was very unhappy and angry at myself that due to my mistake and inefficiency our meeting was delayed by another 24 hours.

We decided that we should get married. It didn't make any sense to us that we should be away from each other. She was a Hindu girl, having the same customs, eating the same food, praying to the same God, performing the same rituals and celebrating religious festivals, which made it easier for us to be closer. On 9th August 1995 we got married in Arya Samaj, in Bangalore, India. Arya Samaj is a purely Hindu institution. They have their own centres all around the world, especially wherever there are Hindus. In Ealing, London, they have a centre. There is another in the Midlands of England. One of their main functions is to arrange marriages in a very simple way. They perform marriages in an orthodox Hindu way. Fire is the eternal witness to the wedding of the couple. Perhaps we can compare a Hindu marriage performed in Arya Samaj to a Christian wedding in a church. During the wedding the priest helped us to take seven steps together as a couple. He chanted a few stanzas in the Sanskrit language. We didn't know

Sanskrit at all. It is an ancient Hindu language. After the wedding ceremony I asked the priest about the meaning of the seven steps and marriage vows we took. He explained as follows:

> Let us take the first step to provide a nourishing and pure diet.
> Let us take the second step to develop physical, mental and spiritual powers.
> Let us take the third step to increase our wealth by a righteous means.
> Let us take the fourth step to acquire knowledge, happiness and harmony by mutual love and trust.
> Let us take the fifth step to be blessed with strong, heroic and virtuous children.
> Let us take the sixth step to accomplish self-restraint and longevity.
> Let us take the seventh step with a vow that we shall always be true to each other, have mutual understanding, work together for prosperity and happiness and enjoy the world as life-long ideal partners.

I was delighted to know the meaning of these Sanskrit verses he pronounced during our wedding. I was very happy with the priest that he explained our vows in such a simple and lucid way. I thanked him profusely.

As you all know, Bangalore is the silicon city of India. Lately, due to IT industries and the establishment of many call centres the city has grown very fast. With that kind of speed of growth, we wouldn't be surprised if Bangalore, in the near future, becomes in India the third largest city after Mumbai and New Delhi.

Immediately after our wedding Sujatha and I came to London. Her daughter, Shalini, was studying for GCSE in India. We didn't want her education to be disturbed. As soon as Shalini completed her GCSE we arranged for her immigration papers and brought her to London. Shalini continued with her studies in London. She studied very hard and passed various examinations. She found her husband, Neeraj, and got married in March 2004. Now Shalini is working with the NHS. The couple are very happy, but very busy with work and further studies.

This was the first time Sujatha had been to the UK. Everything was new for her. I love travelling and visiting new places and countries. We didn't waste any time. Not only did we visit many places in the UK, but visited many other countries as well. We still do. This year we are booked to go to Morocco and then to Ireland. I have been to 54 countries. I intend to, if I can, make it to 100 countries. Let us hope for the best.

Chapter Fifteen

From North London to North India

It was the Easter holidays in the year 2007. We had received a few holiday brochures by then. Glancing through them, I noticed a holiday in Mexico. Now, since the year 2001 we had been thinking of visiting South American countries. Our first attempt didn't materialise even though we had booked and fully paid. Due to the 9/11 terrorist attack in the USA, our trip was cancelled a few days before we were supposed to leave.

Our second attempt was in the year 2003. We were ready to book our holiday to Mexico. Before we could book, we changed our minds and went to India instead. We suddenly had an urge to visit our families in India.

Our third attempt was in the year 2005. We thought that this time we should be able to go. My wife, Sujatha, had requested a holiday period from her employer. Again, before we could think seriously and book our trip to Mexico, my eldest brother, Motiram, who lived in Ilford, England, suddenly died.

Our fourth attempt was in the year 2007. We went through the holiday brochure and selected the appropriate package holiday from the brochure. When we phoned the tour operator, they said that the holiday dates were fully booked. Looking at our diaries we found out that we didn't have any other convenient days for the holiday. In the same brochure they had a few tours in North India. They looked very interesting. The only problem was that these tours covered few cities. Suddenly we had a brainwave. Why not cover the important cities in North India, make the tour a bit longer, say, four weeks. My wife and I had a good discussion about it to see which cities we should visit. When we phoned the tour operator about visiting the cities in one go, they were not happy. They said that it was very difficult to cover those cities in four to five weeks.

We contacted another independent travel agent – Southall

Travel. We had used them before. They were very efficient. We told them what we wanted. They were very happy to arrange a trip to cover all those cities within a period of four weeks. They used airlines, trains and private cars. The final route was designed as follows:

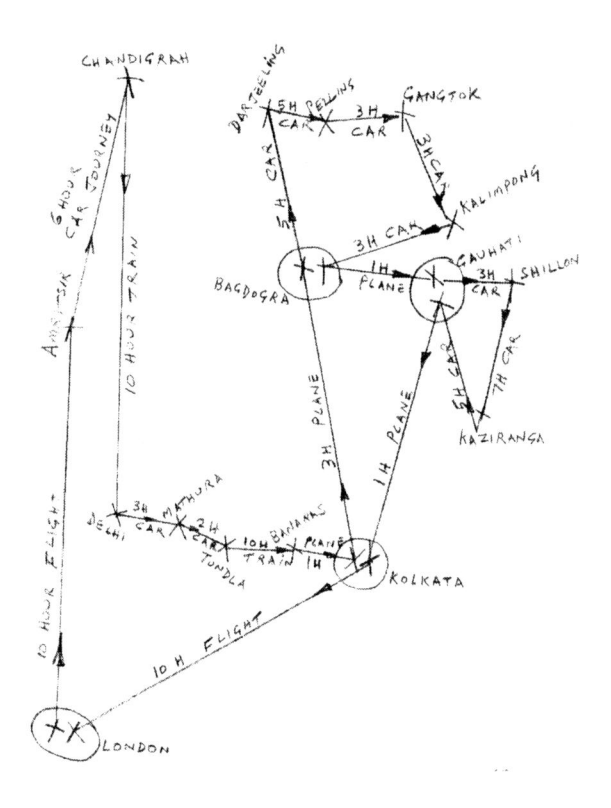

Hand-drawn map of travel in India

During our North India tour we had selected either four or five star hotels. The hotel in Amritsir was four star and had been recently built in the outskirts of the city. The first thing we did was to visit the Golden Temple. It is a world famous temple. Recently it was mentioned in the British press as one of the top twenty places to visit. The sight we saw was amazing. Not only was the temple built beautifully, having a lake all around it, but everything was very orderly. Most of the people working were volunteers. We saw families and their children all working as volunteers. It had a 24-hour open kitchen. Anyone can go; irrespective of caste, creed, religion, gender, and can have a meal. The service was courteous, very orderly and very clean. All the volunteers were busy with cleaning, cooking, washing vegetables, making dough etc. It was a sight to be seen. One has to see it to believe it. It seemed the main object of the temple was 'How best to serve the public'.

In every city we stayed for two days. We had a chance to have a city tour in every city we visited. After Amritsir our next city was Chandigrah. It is the newest city in India, well designed by a French architect, and built about fifty years ago. The whole city was very well planned. Here we had selected a five star hotel. We checked in and came to know that the Indian as well as the Pakistan Cricket Team were staying in the hotel. The Pakistan team were in India and were playing 20/20 cricket matches. In Chandigrah they were playing the second of the five matches. We generally watch it on TV, but this time we thought that we should go to the stadium and watch the game. We didn't have tickets. We found out that it was fully booked. No one would give us any tickets. We even requested the players who were also staying in the same hotel. We talked to the hotel manager. He could not help us either. We thought we should go to the stadium and try to get tickets from the ticket office. We had no luck at all. Suddenly we came across a person who had just come from Kashmir to watch the Pakistan team play. He mentioned that he got a ticket from a man standing under a nearby tree. We told our driver to get three tickets as we felt that he should watch with us as well. He was in luck. He brought three tickets; he paid only 20% more than the face value, since it was nearly the time to start the game.

Our next stop was Delhi. We went to Delhi by train. The train journey was very comfortable. In India they have special inter-city trains called Shadabdi. These train coaches are similar to airline coaches; seats can be reclined, compartments are air conditioned and seats reserved in advance. In addition, meals and water are included in the ticket price. All in all, the journey was very comfortable.

Very recently an underground train service had started in Delhi. We thought we should have a ride. The ride was very comfortable, the stations and trains were clean. It was a good experience. We had been to Delhi before and visited the usual tourist spots. We didn't want to waste any time in Delhi. After a city tour and a bit of shopping we went ahead to our next destination. Our driver drove us for three hours to Mathura, the birthplace of Lord Krishna. Luckily the road was quite good and we covered the distance very comfortably. In Mathura our hotel was not far from the highway, so we were not involved in any city traffic jams.

Whenever I visit India, initially I eat quite a lot, the food is so tasty. As usual, I suddenly suffered from loose motions. On the day we were supposed to leave Mathura, I went for a walk after breakfast. It was a mile and a half to the city centre. Since I was still suffering from loose motions, I went to a local doctor who gave me medicine to relieve me of my misery. One the way back I saw a barber who had no customers. I thought I should give him my custom. He was very happy to get an easy customer. As soon as I got back to the hotel, it was time to go to our next destination, which was Banaras. It seemed there was no direct link either by train or plane to Banaras from Mathura. Our driver drove for two hours to a station called Tundla to catch the train for Banaras.

Our train was ten hours late. The train was supposed to come from Kolkata to Delhi and the same train would come back to Tundla and take us to Banaras. For the last few days, there had been riots in Nandigram, West Bengal. The train was held up for ten hours at Kolkata station. Due to that, instead of arriving at Banaras at 5.20am, we arrived 5.20pm. We lost a whole day of sightseeing in Banaras. It is said that Banaras is the oldest living city in the world. It is on the bank of the Holy River Ganges. It is a very vibrant city. It is one of the holy cities for all Hindus. We had a Holy dip in the

Holy Ganges. Our guide took us around for a city tour. After the partition in 1947, I had lived in Banaras for two years. When the guide took us around the city I was looking at places to see if I could remember and recollect anything. During sixty years the city had changed so much that I couldn't recognise much except the river, its eighty Ghats (stairs down to the River Ganges) and Banaras University.

We caught a flight to Kolkata. As usual a driver was waiting for us at Kolkata airport. Throughout our tour, wherever we went, there was someone waiting for us to receive us and take us to the hotel and then to sightseeing etc. My elder brother Ramchand lives in Kolkata. After a quick wash in our hotel, we went to his house and met him and his joint family. Since we never told them that we were visiting, they were very surprised and equally glad to see us. The surprise meeting was absolutely fantastic. We were so excited and glad as if we had just come across a long lost treasure. We were extremely sorry to leave them as we were already booked for a flight to our next destination.

We went ahead to visit our next destination, Darjeeling. We were anxiously waiting for the moment to visit Darjeeling. Since there is no direct link by train or plane, first we went by plane to Bagdogra and then had a drive of five hours to Darjeeling. Darjeeling is about 5,000 feet above sea level. The car was now constantly climbing the mountains. We saw clouds above us. After some time when we climbed quite high, the clouds were under us. It was a sight worth seeing. The road was very narrow like a snake. Our driver had to be careful and make sure that at every curve he hooted to warn the oncoming traffic, which you couldn't see till you turned the corner. A few years ago, Mark Tully, the famous BBC reporter, had shown a programme on Darjeeling and its slow train passing through a high street. Since then my wife and I had wanted to visit and experience the same experience.

We had a very good hotel. We opened the window in our hotel room and were very surprised and tickled to view the peak of Kanchangenga, the third highest peak in the world. It was snow capped and shining in the rays of the sun. The next day, early morning around 4.30am, our guide took us to Tiger Hill. Lots of people had gathered to witness the sunrise and see the first rays of sun hitting Kanchangenga and its snowy peak. It was a sight worth beholding. People in Darjeeling were very nice. They were poor, but very proud. There were no beggars at all. No one hassled us for any business or forced us to buy souvenirs etc.

From then on we proceeded to Sikkim, Sikkim is also very beautiful. People there are also very nice and proud. I came to know that Nepal had ruled over Sikkim for some time. The Nepalese are very good fighters and very obedient to their commander. During the Second World War, their British commander took his Nepalese unit in a plane. The commander told the unit, "When the plane is about 1,000 feet above the ground, you jump." One person hesitantly requested and said, "Sir, can we jump when it is 500 feet above the ground?"

"What difference does it make if it is 500 or 1,000 feet, you will be wearing a parachute." The Nepalese never realised that they would be jumping with a parachute on.

People in Sikkim, as well as in Darjeeling were from Nepal. When we arrived in Pelling, Sikkim, again luckily we had a hotel room window facing Kanchangenga. They said this was the last time we would view the peak, after that we would be moving away from the peak.

After a five hour drive we arrived in Gangtok, the capital of Sikkim. The city was very vibrant. In Sikkim we noticed that they had proper footpaths. Most of the footpaths had a sheer drop of thousands of feet on one side. Due to that all the footpaths had strong metal barriers. In addition the footpaths had similar barriers on the road side as well to protect the public from the traffic. It was the first time we had seen footpaths like this. They looked strange, but then we found out that it was normal in Sikkim.

From then on, we were supposed to go to Kalimpong. Protest marches were being held all over the place. Due to that traffic was held up. Our guide suggested that we should go to Siliguri and not to Kalimpong. Also to avoid protesters, we should start at three in the morning when the protesters would be sleeping. That was what we did and arrived safely in Silliguri during breakfast time. Our driver drove us to Bagdogra to catch our flight to Guahati. From Guahari we arrived in Shillong after a three hour drive. Shillong was a hill station during British time. There were quite a few churches and Catholic schools. It also is about 5,000 feet above sea level. The climate and scenery was beautiful. The next day our guide took us to Cheerapunji. Cheerapunji is very famous for its rainfall. It gets about 500 inches of rain in a year which is the maximum rainfall in the world. Just imagine that much rain. London may be hardly getting 50 inches, or not even that. Cheerapunji is a mountainous area. Due to that rain doesn't accumulate at one place and create floods.

From Shillong our next destination was Kaziranga, the home of the 'one horn Rhino' and a safari park. When we started from Shillong, we did not come across any traffic at all. So we covered a good distance in no time. Suddenly we came across a police barrier. The police explained that there had been a public strike and rioters may harm vehicles on the road. They said that they would give us a police escort. We were in a hurry to reach Kaziranga and then to Kolkata and finally to London. The Police said that it would be at least two hours before an escort could be organised. We had a word with the chief in the police station and explained that we were in a hurry to go to Kaziranga, then to Gauhati, Kolkata and then to London. He was a very nice person and understood our urgency. He gave us his own personal escort. It seemed about every ten kilometres there was a police station who were in charge of their patch. He asked, "What hotel are you staying at in Kaziranga?"

"Wild Grass," I replied. That hotel is the best in the area. He was very impressed. He not only gave his personal escort to us, but phoned those three police stations ahead to tell them that they should escort us to the hotel 'Wild Grass'. He even offered us a cup of tea to refresh us. He organised the escorts in such a way that we had no problem and arrived in our hotel safely and without any hassle. He was a very nice person and very helpful. As soon as we arrived in London I wrote a letter to him thanking him for his kind assistance and consideration.

As soon as we arrived in Kaziranga, we had our lunch and went on a Jeep safari. We saw one horn Rhinos, lots of them, elephants, monkeys, various kinds of deer and a leopard. The next day around five in the morning we had an elephant safari. Sitting high on the elephant we could spot animals from a distance.

After that we had a five hour car ride to Gauhati. From Gauhati we got our flight to Kolkata. At Kolkata airport our driver was waiting for us. He drove us to the same hotel we had stayed in a few days before. It was luck that my brother and his family lived about 200 yards from the hotel where we stayed. After a quick wash we again went to my brother's house. This time it was not a surprise visit. Two weeks ago when we had met them we told them that on what day we came back from our tour and we would visit them before we left for London.

We finally left for London. We arrived in London after nearly five weeks away. The North India tour was very tiring but absolutely fantastic.

Chapter Sixteen

How I Became a Volunteer for Charity Shops

In 1984 I had bought a block of ten flats. I used them as a 'Holiday Flat business'. The business was good. I had a good manager to look after the business. I had continued running my life assurance business from the same premises. The block of flats was freehold property. Luckily I had bought them at the right time. Immediately property values started increasing. In two years its value doubled.

I have mentioned in my previous chapters that I wanted to help my good friend, Mr Harry Jagasia. I had bought a restaurant property in Paddington, London, W2. It was very near to St Mary's Hospital in Paddington. The plan was that Harry would run the business, but due to illness he couldn't. I had no choice but to run it myself. My hands were full with running the 'Holiday Flats' business in addition to my life assurance business.

Luckily I had good staff and a reliable manager. I had a 'husband and wife' team as my flat business managers. They were Gary and Pam Parsons. They had come from New Zealand. They had seen my advertisement in the *Evening Standard* for a job. When I hired them they told me, "Vasu, we saw the name of your business was Oasis Holiday Flats. We thought it was owned by an Arab company. We were reluctant to enter the house. We thought that perhaps this business was for exporting white women to Saudi Arabia." Pam smiled and continued, "Then we decided that we should find out more about the business."

I replied, "Perhaps it is. You don't know. Do you?" We laughed it off. They had been my best managers I ever had.

Because of a massive equity in the flats, I didn't have to put down any of my money. I could borrow the whole amount from my bankers and had then bought the restaurant property. Even this was increasing in value. The timing of my purchasing both properties was very good. I was riding high. A few of my businessmen clients wanted to have a partnership with me to do similar businesses. I have mentioned previously that my father had a very tough time due to his dishonest partners. I was very reluctant to do business in partnership.

In the restaurant business there is a lot of turnover in the staff. The staff always looking around and wanting to better their prospects. Many people would visit me and ask for employment in my business. Shortly restaurant owners would visit me as well and wanted to sell their restaurant to me. I could easily meet all these people and have meetings with them. I had good staff who could carry on with business without much help from me. I had no intention of buying additional property, neither start another business. My office was in the Oasis Holiday Flats. Luck would have it that one agent approached me and gave me details of a very good restaurant property not far from my office. It was just 200 yards away from my office. I went and met the owner as well. The owner was in financial difficulty. Commercial properties were not doing very well at that time. In a way he begged me to buy the property from him. I was not keen to buy any additional property. He persuaded me to give him an offer. I gave him a very low offer thinking that he would not accept it. He went away and did not accept my offer.

After a week he came to me, "Vasu, I accept your offer. You will not regret it if you buy the property." I believed him and bought the property. I borrowed from my bankers the whole amount against equity from all three properties. I did not have to put down any additional money. My bankers were very happy with my properties and my business. I didn't know how good this property was. The bank's surveyor who came to survey this property was very pleased with the freehold restaurant property and the price. He said, "Vasu, this property is like gold dust. If at any time you want to sell it, please give me the first option. I have a cash buyer." I was very pleased with this purchase. I realised that God was very pleased with me and had favoured me. Luckily the staff I had hired for this restaurant were also very good. All three businesses were running smoothly. I was busy attending to these three businesses. I did not pay much attention to my life assurance business. I stopped contacting my clients for life assurance business. It seemed that my businessmen clients knew what I was doing. They would contact me enquiring about my business activities. During that time I would talk to them about life assurances. To keep me healthy, my 'holiday flat' managers Gary and Pam Parsons and I would play tennis during our lunchtime.

One afternoon I was walking on Goodge Street, London, W1. I came across an empty shop with a notice displayed in the window: 'charity shop is to be opened soon. Volunteers required. Contact phone no…' I thought, my staff are good, they are handling everything efficiently. My life assurance business is also ticking over. Perhaps I could spare a few hours a week and devote it towards good charitable work. I went to my office and phoned to find out a bit more about the volunteering. I gathered that it was a charity shop to be managed by the YMCA. They sent me a form to be completed. I sent to them my completed form. As soon as the charity shop started, I started working with them. Every Friday afternoon I would help them in the shop. Mainly I would man the till. I would work till around 5pm, then go to my office and meet my manager. I would go to one restaurant and then to another, have dinner at one of the restaurants and then go home around 8pm. I was very pleased with myself that I could manage all my varied activities.

When I sold all three business properties I started working from home. Life became very dull. I used to have three properties, three businesses. I would rush around. But now the only thing I was doing was selling life assurance and allied products. I lived and still live in Southgate, London, N14. In Southgate I spotted a charity shop with a notice in their window: 'Volunteers needed, any day, any hours. Please meet the manager or phone…' This was a Church of England Children's Society charity shop, the manager let me start immediately with them. They did not have any volunteer for Monday afternoon. I agreed to work every Monday afternoon. It seemed the shop was empty. It was in the process of being sold. Till then with the owners permission, the shop would be used as a charity shop. After a year or so, it was sold and the charity shop was closed. Now it is occupied by a 'Pound Shop'.

While I was working in this charity shop, we used to have a regular visit from a lady customer. One day she said to me, "There is a sign "Sold" on this property. It seems you have to vacate it. If you want you could work with us."

"Who is us?" I asked.

"I am the manager of the Cancer Research shop just a few doors away from here." Then she added, "Whenever you are ready, just come and meet me." I thanked her.

I did not go to the Cancer Research shop when I stopped working with the Children's Society Charity Shop. After a few months I met her in the High Street. "Are you still volunteering?"

"No. Lately I have been quite busy."

"Whenever you are ready, you can come and meet me."

"I can come right now, if you are going to your shop," I replied. We went together to her shop. She gave me an application form. I gave back to her the completed application form and started working with them. I am pleased to say that I am still working with them every Monday afternoon. It is quite enjoyable work. Lots of people know me. Most of them are pensioners. Some of them would like to talk to someone, so they come to our shop, look around and always have a few words with me. Luckily I have a good knowledge of books, videos and music. I also have a very keen interest in health and yoga. I can engage in a healthy discussion with them.

Suddenly I had an idea, Why don't I learn about 'Counselling' and help pensioners more. I went to the local library and found out which universities hold these courses. I thought that I would pass first stage, then I could study more and work as a volunteer in institutions like MIND, Relate and any other similar organisations. These organisations specialise to work and help old age pensioners and people needing support. I finished the first stage and the second stage. Now I thought I was ready to do volunteering as well as study for the third stage and possibly for the diploma. But it seemed I was wrong. In the meantime the rules had changed. You couldn't work as a volunteer in 'counselling' unless you finished the Diploma in counselling. I tried my best but these organisations would not budge. I enquired about the Diploma course. It was a two year course after the third stage I just had completed. Not only had one to attend college but also go to a counsellor and get counselling for twenty hours. Then, and then only, I would get a Diploma certificate and would be allowed to be a volunteer counsellor. In addition to this, you had to be a member of BACP. BACP is a governing body who would supervise you and make sure that you were doing your job ethically. I also noticed that the rules were very stringent. I thought that all because of stringent rules and regulations, I came out of the life assurance business. Their governing body is the FAS. The FSA rules and supervision were very strict. Small deviation and one gets penalised. I wanted to be a counsellor so that I could help the community. I didn't want to be involved again in rules and regulations. I dropped the idea of being a counsellor. All the time I was on the look out for more varied volunteering.

I came across an advertisement for 'Volunteers for Victim Support'. I went for training. I was glad that I was selected for it. So now I have additional work of volunteering for 'Victim Support'. I started work with them. The work was interesting. I felt that I was helping the community and being useful to the old and infirm. As the time passed I noticed that most of the victims were either asylum seekers or illegal immigrants. I could see that they were looking for 'something for free'. I remember in one case, I went to visit a family who had reported to us. I went to them. The husband had gone to work. The wife showed me the main door of the flat and said, "Look, it is not shutting properly."

I pushed it and it closed shut.

"The door is shutting properly, it needs a bit of a push."

"Sometimes it doesn't."

I tried many times and every time I could shut it.

"What so you suggest we do?"

"I want a new lock on the door," she replied.

"There is nothing wrong with the door lock. The door is just a bit stiff. If you tell your husband to file away the wood from the edge, there should be no problem after that."

There was another incident. I visited a person who had complained about a thief stealing some money from his flat.

"Do you know who did it?"

"Yes. I had a person staying with me. I am sure he has stolen it."

"Do you know the person?"

"Yes. He is my cousin."

"How much has he stolen?"

"£500."

"Where is he now?"

"He has gone away out of the country."

"Do you know where he is now?"

"Yes. Cairo, Egypt."

"The police here can't recover that money for you. You have to collect yourself since he is your cousin and you know where he is."

"I want to claim £500 from the council. This is a council flat."

I wrote the report and sent it to the 'Victim Support' office. I could see that he was looking for something for nothing. I realised that most of my time was being spent on listening to similar stories and felt that I was not helping much. On the contrary, I was getting upset to notice that these people were taking advantage of the system.

Recently I saw an advertisement for 'Family & Friends'. The concept here is that a volunteer was to give at least two hours per week to a one parent family. The volunteer's job was to guide the family in every possible way. It was more like advisory work and you had to be with the same family, at least for a year. During that time, the volunteer would guide the family as an adviser. Mostly the family would have a child who would need a fatherly figure. Generally these families are one parent families. There is a danger that the volunteer may become attached to the family emotionally. After a year the volunteer would have to be careful to detach himself from the family without any heartbreak. A year is quite long time. Meeting the same family week after week may create a strong bond which may create emotional problems, not only for the family but for the volunteer as well. I went for the training and finished the course and got a certificate for it. It seemed that they had to match the volunteer to a family. They mentioned that as soon as they have a family for me they would let me know. But they haven't yet found a family. I am still awaiting their call, this may come any time. When the call comes, I shall keep in mind that I do not get involved emotionally with the family. If any time I feel that I am getting involved, I shall immediately come out of it before hurting anyone. WE SHALL SEE.

I feel that I have a lot of life experience. I have a lot to talk about and can perhaps impart information to other people. About a year ago there was a new series of *Big Brother* on Channel 4. A few days before the programme was to start, it said in the news, 'There is an Indian actress taking part in it, her name is Ms Shilpa Shetty. The betting shops are predicting that she will be the winner'. I had never seen the *Big Brother* programme before. I was curious. My wife and I watched the whole programme of 26 days religiously. We really enjoyed it. Do you know what was the result and who won? Shilpa Shetty, the Indian actress. Of course she had a very tough time from three women in the show. There was an outcry saying that Shilpa Shetty was being victimised and there was a lot of racial discrimination.

I thought by joining *Big Brother* I could impart my life experiences to a bigger audience. I applied for it. They wrote to me, 'We shall contact you as and when you are needed'. But they never did. I would like to appear in their *Big Brother* programme. I hope they call me for their next programme.

Big Brother 2008 has just started. I watched the first programme. I was very disappointed with the housemates they had selected. Now I have a second thought. Perhaps I would be a misfit in the crowd *Big Brother* are selecting. I don't think I shall apply to be a housemate. Unless they call me out of the blue. Then I would go along with them. Anytime I feel that I am not enjoying myself, I shall request for an early release.

Chapter Seventeen

How I Located Long Lost Friends

1. Lakhi Hassaram:

It was 1941. I was 7 years old. Every evening I used to call on my classmate, Lakhi Hassaram. We would go to a playground and play games in a group. It was a good life with nothing to worry about except go to school, study and then in the evening play games with boys. We used to hear riots and commotion in other parts of India against the British who had ruled the country. We were too young to understand what was going on around the world and in India. Our playground was in a fort where quite a few groups would play various games.

Within a year the situation changed quite a lot. In 1942, while we were playing, we were attacked by a Muslim group. I used to live in Hyderabad in the province of Sind. Sind had a Muslim majority. While Britain and India were negotiating freedom, it was decided that Muslim majority provinces would go to the Muslims who would form their own country called Pakistan. Muslims wanted Hindus to go away from Sind immediately. Their direct action was creating disturbances and riots and they started ethnic cleansing as and when they could. During the attack on the playing field, one person died, three were seriously injured and about 100 people injured with minor cuts and bruises. We had a British collector of that area. He very efficiently sorted out issues and everything was peaceful. Then came 1947, when India was physically divided into Pakistan and India. The situation throughout India became so explosive that millions were injured, killed and displaced. We Hindus just left all our possessions behind and arrived penniless in India. That was the time I lost contact with all my friends, including my classmate Lakhi.

It was 1977 I went to Las Palmas, Canary Islands to sell life assurance. During my visit I came across an import-export company called R. Hassaram. I went in and met Mr Pishu Hassaram, the director of the company. After the initial introduction I asked Pishu, "Pishu, I had a classmate in Hyderabad Sind, called Lakhi Hassaram. Is he one of your relations?"

"Yes. He is my brother."

"Where is he now?"

"He is in Hong Kong. He is in charge of that office and I am in charge of this office."

"I would like to meet him. Does he come to Las Palmas?"

"No. If you want to meet him, go to Hong Kong." He gave me his address, office phone number and telex number. I did not have any chance to go to Hong Kong for quite a while.

In 1991 my children, Kris and Nina and I went on a holiday covering Hong Kong, Singapore, Bangkok and Phuket Island in Thailand. In the meantime R. Hassaram company had closed the office in Las Palmas. I did not know if the company was still operational and if Lakhi was still in Hong Kong. To be on the safe side, when we started our holiday, I had taken the details on Lakhi given to me by his brother way back in 1977. As soon as we arrived in a hotel in Hong Kong, I flicked through the telephone directory. I was very happy to note that the R. Hassaram company was mentioned. They had the same address and phone number. I made contact with him. Luckily he was in town. I met him in his office initially. Oh, we were so happy and excited to meet each other after fifty years. That evening he took my children and I to his house, where we met his wife. We spent quite a few hours exchanging news about our past history. A lot had happened during those fifty years. Our visit to Hong Kong was only for two days. Lakhi and I made the best use of it and spent time together as much as we could.

2.   Gope Kundnani:

It was 1951 when I the passed matriculation examination. This is equivalent to the UK's GCSE. I joined a college to start the intermediate course. Intermediate course is equivalent to an 'O' level. It is a two year course. My college was walking distance from where I lived. I had found a short-cut but it was a dirt road. During the rainy season the road used to be very muddy. Gope also used to live not far from where I lived. We would use the same dirt road to go to college. His family used to live in a town about 1,000 miles from Bombay. He had come to Bombay for studies. He had no choice but to stay in a room in Ramkrishna Mission. I had mentioned Ramkrishna Mission where I used to go and consult a homeopathy doctor. Ramkrishna Mission is a non-profitable charitable organisation who try to do good for the community. Their main aim is to teach religious practice, hold yoga classes, arrange free medicines and consultations with a medical doctor and give residential rooms to students. They would not charge any rent to the needy students. Gope was not needy so he paid a full rent for his room.

Gope and I were together for two years in that college. During that time we walked together many times to and from college. On the way we would discuss many topics of the world and find out various ways by which the world's ills could be minimised. After two years we both applied for the engineering course. I went to engineering college in Bombay and studied mechanical engineering and Gope went to another city for civil engineering. After that we lost contact with each other.

It was now 1971, I was in London. I had started with Abbey Life Assurance Co Ltd as an insurance consultant. It was common practice to ask for the names of family and friends from our clients. I would then contact these people to sell life assurance products to them. One day one of my clients gave me six names to contact. One of the six names was Gope Kundnani. I never knew that Gope was in London. I thought that it may be that this Gope was not the one

I was thinking about. That evening I phoned him.

"Is that Mr Gope Kundnani?"

"Yes," he replied.

"I am Vasu. Do you remember me?"

"Vasu Daryanani? Were you in the National College, Bombay?"

"Yes." Now I got excited. He was the Gope I had studied with during 1951-53, in Bombay. I immediately made an appointment to meet him. I met his wife Mieke. Gope and I had a very good time talking about the 'good old days'. I found out that he was working in greater London Council (GLC). The GLC was afterwards broken up into small London councils. He has two sons. One son was educated in Oxford and the other in Cambridge. Gope and I are still in touch with each other. He is retired now. His wife is from Holland. They pass half the time in Holland and the other half in England/India. We try to meet each other and have family gatherings as and when we can.

3. Satu Daryanani:

I shall go back to the year 1944, when I was ten years old. I had just finished primary education. We had three schools in Hyderabad, Sind, where you could be admitted for secondary education. One of them was just five minutes walk from where we lived. The second was about a mile away. The third was about a mile and a half from where I had lived. Do you know which school I chose? Your guess would be wrong if you think I chose the school nearer to where I had lived. I chose the one which was the longest distance away. The reason was that all my elder brothers were educated in that school. I also wanted to go to that school. It didn't bother me to walk a mile and a half each way. That school was called Vidyalaya, which means 'a place of learning'. It was a very impressive building with a huge clock tower. You could see the clock from a mile away. Perhaps it was modelled on Big Ben in London. I did not understand the difference between school and college. I was too young at that time.

That school was called Vidyalaya College.

In our class there were two other Daryanani students called Satu and Kishin. They were cousins to each other. They had the same surname as mine, but they were not related to me. I had asked my mother and they had asked their parents. We couldn't find any close link between our families. Both of them were very famous in our school. All the students used to walk to the school; they would come in a Victoria carriage pulled by two hefty horses. From day one we three became good friends. The common surname helped in fostering friendship between the three of us. I found out that their fathers were partners in a business in Curacao, one of the Caribbean Islands. Their business was thriving. They also had a huge house where both families had lived. It was not a house, it was a huge mansion. The partition of India in 1947 dispersed all Hindu families. I lost contact with them. We had heard that their fathers had come from overseas and taken the families away before the real trouble had started. They had gone to Bombay and bought a good sized flat facing the sea. Long after that I read in the *Guinness Book of Records* that the building in which they had a flat had housed mostly very rich families. The wealth per square inch in the building was the maximum in the whole world according to the *Guinness Book of Records*.

It was 1951, I had just started my intermediate studies. During the first week in the canteen I couldn't believe my eyes. There they were, both cousins eating their lunch. After that the three of us would eat our lunch together. Whatever food we brought from our homes, we shared. They always had Kraft cheese to eat. That was the first time I had tried cheese. I didn't like it. It tasted and looked like a piece of soap. In a short while I got used to the taste. After six months of studies Satu's cousin Kishin had to go to Curacao. The reason was that Kishin's dad had died suddenly. Kishin was the only son who could look after the business. A few months after that, without finishing a year of study, Satu also left for Curacao. We had no contact after that.

Now we were in the year 1981. I had attended a wedding

reception in London. In Hindu society, wedding receptions are huge social events. During partition in 1947, most Hindus had lost practically everything. Many families had contact with foreign countries. Many had businesses in other countries. Slowly our community; with sheer hard work, picked up the pieces and became quite prosperous. Now our community has businesses in various parts of the world. Whenever there is a wedding in our community, lots of family and friends are invited. They come from all over the world to bless the couple. I met many people during that wedding reception. I came across a businessman from Curacao.

"Do you know Satu Daryanani?"

"Yes. He is one of my best friends."

"He was my classmate in Hyderabad and then in Bombay," I replied. "Why didn't he come to the reception?" I asked him.

"He is very busy with his business."

"I would like to meet him. Can you give me his address and phone number, please?"

He didn't have it handy. I gave him my business card to hand over to Satu.

A week later I had a phone call from Satu. The call was so clear I thought that Satu was in London.

"No, I am not in London. I am in Curacao."

"When are you coming to London?" I asked him.

"I have no plans. When are you coming to Curacao?"

"I don't know. As soon as I make plans I shall let you know." We had a very long chat on the phone. He gave me his office address and phone number.

We are now in 1996. I got married a year before. My wife and I had been on holidays to a few places.

"I would like to go for a cruise," my wife stated one morning.

"Where do you want to go?"

"Anywhere that is nice and warm. It is too cold in the UK."

I went to the travel agent and collected few holiday brochures. I flicked through them. I came across a two week holiday in the Caribbean Islands. It was an island hopping tour. The ship started from Barbados. Overnight it would sail to another island. After breakfast we would disembark and they would take us around the island. In the evening we would come to the ship, have our evening meal and have a good nights sleep, while the ship was sailing towards another island. I noticed that Curacao was one of the islands where we would land. I thought that perhaps I could meet Satu. I didn't want to miss him while we were in Curacao for a day. Before I booked the cruise I had phoned Satu to let him know what day we would be arriving and if he would be available on that day. Satu confirmed that he would be in town and was very anxious to meet me and my wife. Everything went according to the plan. It was 45 years ago that we had met in Bombay Intermediate College. We had a lot to talk about. He invited us to his house. We met his wife. We had high tea together. I couldn't meet his cousin Kishin. He had died a few years ago. We were very excited to meet each other after so many years.

4. Balwant Tamane:

Now we are in 1963. I had arrived in London in September 1963. My friend, Mr Khedekar, had booked a room for me with an Indian family in Golders Green, London, NW11. The house was quite large with five bedrooms. The family used the big house for a 'paying guest business'. When I arrived there were five of us as paying guests in the house. The rent included breakfast and evening dinner. In the evening we guests and the landlord's family would sit down together for a meal. The food was very tasty. We were all very happy to get an Indian meal in London. Some of you may remember that in 1963 Indian food was not popular at all. On the contrary, the British used to complain about the strong smell of burning spice. It was very difficult and expensive to eat out and have an Indian meal. Now, of course, we have in the UK lots of Indian restaurants, perhaps 30,000 of them throughout the British Isles. Even Indian spices are freely available now from supermarkets. At that time one had to go very far away to buy spices. I remember

Southall was the only place we knew where you could get Indian spices and an Indian meal at a reasonable price. This house was like a halfway house for guests. The other four guests were architects. I was the only mechanical engineer. One by one guests left the house and found their new job and a new place to live. I did the same. We lost contact with each other.

We all used to overeat the delicious Indian food. It seemed that the digestion of one of our guests was not very strong. A few times he complained about stomach ache. Perhaps due to that, after so many years I did not remember any other guest's name. I remember his name only.

It was year 2006. There was an Indian festival being celebrated in one temple in London. My wife and I attended the festival. Each of us was given a programme brochure. I was flicking through the brochure. I was looking at a list of organisers of the function. I couldn't believe my eyes. Mr Tamane was one of the organisers. I was not sure that it was the same person I had met in 1963. That evening during the function I contacted the chief organiser and asked him:

"Is Mr B. Tamane in the hall this evening?"

"Yes."

"I would like to meet him."

The chief organiser went in the back room and brought Mr Tamane.

42 years is a long time. I couldn't recognise him. If I had seen him anywhere else, I don't think I would have recognised him. The same thing applied to him as well. We just stared at each other for a while.

"I am Vasu. Do you remember me?"

"No."

"In 1963 we used to live in Mr Bhusate's big house as paying guests."

Slowly he recollected. Suddenly he opened his eyes wide open and exclaimed, "Vasu!"

We had a short chat in the hall. He was very busy organising.

He invited me to his house during that weekend. I visited him and met his wife. We had a very long chat talking about the past 43 years. He is now retired. He spends half a year in London and the other half in his hometown in India.

5.   Mr and Mrs A M Patel

Now I have to go back to my ICI days. One day during lunchtime, I noticed an Indian in the ICI canteen. I had not seen any Indian people working in ICI till that day. In a new and foreign country a face from my country was a very welcome sight. I went to him and introduced myself to him. We became very good friends. He was married and he invited me a few times to his house and fed me with delicious Indian food. Mrs Patel was a very good cook. I got married in 1968 and had invited guests for the wedding reception.

I neither had any relations nor any friends in North East England. All my friends were from the ICI family. Mr and Mrs Patel were among guests for my wedding reception. On the second day my wife and I had loaded our car with all our possessions and had come to London. I had kept in touch with my close ICI friends including Mr and Mrs Patel.

After a few years, out of the blue I got a phone call from Mr Patel.

"Vasu. We are in London now."

"Have you left ICI?"

"Yes. I am now working on a contract with another petro-chemical company."

It was much easier to be in contact with him, as Mr and Mrs Patel were living in Harrow, about fifteen miles away from where I had lived.

It was now 1995, I was divorced. I married again in 1995. I invited Mr and Mrs Patel for my wedding reception, which we held in the Conference Suites on Tottenham Court Road, London, W1. Now that hall is being used as 'Spearmint Rhino'. It is a men only nightclub.

MR AND MRS PATEL ARE THE ONLY COUPLE WHO HAD ATTENDED RECEPTIONS FOR BOTH OF MY WEDDINGS.

I visited them in early 2008. Mr Patel now suffers from a stroke. He told me that doctors in a hospital where he was given minor surgery had given him an injection with a strong medicine. That had given him the stroke. Now, with difficulty, he moves about in his scooter.

6.   Mr John Simpson

He could have been my long lost friend, but he is not. It is March 2008. I was coming home by the Piccadilly line to Southgate, London. N14. I spotted a person sitting opposite to me. His face looked familiar. I went around to him and enquired, "Are you Harry Lucas?"

"No."

"Your face is familiar. I used to work in ICI in North East England. Harry Lucas used to work in our engineering section."

"Where about in North East England?"

"Billingham."

"I worked in Billingham, but I am not Harry Lucas. I worked in the ICI management offices."

I came back to my seat and when the train stopped at Southgate, I got down from the train. He got down as well.

"I live in Leigh Hunt Drive."

"So do I," he replied.

It was such a coincidence that he was not Harry Lucas but worked in the same place I had worked forty years ago. And now he lived in the same road where I now live.

"What is your name?"

"John Simpson."

"No. You are not John Simpson. I have seen John Simpson on TV. He is a BBC reporter. Are you BBC reporter?"

"No. I am the other John Simpson," he replied and smiled.

Chapter Eighteen

Walking with Ramblers and Long Distance Walkers

It was 1988. It had been nearly eleven years ago that we had moved from Hertford to Enfield, Middlesex. When we were in Hertford, I had been very busy with my life assurance business. I visited West Africa, East Africa, Spain and the Middle East to arrange life assurances. I used to get recommendations from my clients in the UK who would encourage me to visit these places and arrange life assurance for their family and friends. The recommendations used to be so effective that family and friends of my clients would welcome me with open arms. Within limits they would take up whatever life assurance plans I used to recommend to them. Of course, at that time they never could get these plans in their countries. I had been to many Million Dollar Round Table annual meetings where I had listened to the world famous life assurance salespersons and soaked in many good ideas on selling life assurances. One of the best ideas which helped me not only in my business but in my life as well was 'Sell the product that you believe in and give to the other person, imagining the other person is you'. During thirty years of me selling life assurance, I had three complaints of mis-selling. I have a habit of keeping my files up to date and not discarding any paperwork. I am happy to write that all three complaints were rejected by the FSA, our regulators. I had justified my actions with documentary proof. Recently the FSA have brought out a rule whereby all independent financial advisers are to practice 'Treat Customer Fairly', (TCF). I am very glad to say that I had been doing it all along.

It is mentioned somewhere in my book that one afternoon I came back from my overseas trip and found my wife with two men reading and doing Bible studies. It seemed my wife was lonely and these two boys had knocked on the door. They were from Jehovah's Witness Society. At that time I didn't think much of it. Also I never knew what this society was or what they did. My wife started going every Sunday for their meeting in a nearby Kingdom Hall. I thought that it was just a fad, my wife was Christian. The fad would wear off, I thought. If I tell her not to go to these meetings, she would defy me and would make sure she goes. But her involvement grew. In addition to Sunday meetings, she would go to Thursday meetings as well. We were in the process of moving to Enfield. I felt that she would be away from these members. A week before we moved, she told me, "These boys have given me the address of the place in Enfield where their meetings are held. Also they have contacted their member in Enfield who will contact me and arrange Bible studies at home."

I went deathly pale and asked, "Do you have to attend these meetings and be a Jehovah's Witness member?"

"Oh yes, I want to be their member. They are very nice people." I couldn't say anything.

As soon as we occupied the house in Enfield, a family from the society visited us. "Since you are new here, we will come every Sunday and take you to the Hall for Sunday meetings."

As the time passed by my wife got more and more involved with them. In addition to Thursdays and Sunday meetings she would go on Tuesdays and Thursday afternoons. She would knock on houses in the locality and try to convince them to come for the Sunday meetings. To top it all, she would now take our two children for these meetings. Her behaviour changed considerably. They had told her that now she must convince me to join them and go to these meetings. I refused. That really upset her. Also, their teaching was that there was no husband and wife, only brother and sister relationships. They neither allowed her to celebrate any festivals like Christmas or Diwali nor celebrate birthdays. The children used to look forward to their birthdays when they would invite their friends and celebrate it in style. Now they could not. It seemed a lot of fun from life was gone.

We were very busy for the first five years in Enfield. It was a four bedroom house. We got the kitchen and sitting room extended.

We had a shower room added. The front garden was paved to park our car, as the garage was full of useless stuff. We organised it in such a way that we could garage our car. Also we modified the back garden. A patio was added and garden walls were built. We all loved our house. It was very spacious. But I couldn't get rid of the influence of Jehovah's Witness on my wife. Looking back I would say that it was the main cause of the break up in our family life. As a family we used to go for a walk after Sunday lunch. With these Sunday meetings we as a family could not go together. I used to go on my own.

In the meantime I devoted more time towards my life assurance business. I became quite good at it. My earning increased substantially. I was thinking of sending my children to private school. I had a good income and decided to invest money in properties. My property as well as restaurant ventures are mentioned in a separate chapter. In 1987 I had a terrible back pain. A few months later I had a 'silent heart attack'. These are described in a separate chapter. I became more and more philosophical and had plenty of time on my hands, specially during weekends. My wife and children would be very busy with Jehovah's Witness activities. I would spend my Saturdays in the local library and read books on various religions. Due to my constant back pain I was reading more on health as well. Sunday afternoons I would go for a walk after we had our lunch.

One day in the library I came across a leaflet about the Rambler Association. I thought that instead of me walking on my own I could walk with ramblers. Their head office sent me phone numbers and names of the secretary's of three nearby Ramblers branches. There were Bishops Stortford, Royston and Enfield branches. I contacted the secretary of the Royston branch. They told me where on that Sunday the walk would start from. I walked with them. I had a very good walk. The group was very welcoming. I felt that Royston was too far away. I should try the secretary at Enfield. After a few attempts I could not contact her, as she was on holidays. Later she sent me their walk programme. The first one I could walk with them was from Richmond Station. Brenda Sutton was our leader.

Initially I was a bit doubtful as to what kind of welcome I would get and whether I would fit in their system. But I am very pleased to write that after twenty years I still walk with them every Sunday and Brenda Sutton is still our member. I shall be finishing twenty years in September 2008. Perhaps I should celebrate by doing the walk that I did nearly twenty years ago.

During that walk, apart from the leader, I remembered three members: Vic Brownjohn, Alf Marshall and Edgar Nyman. Sadly Alf Marshall died a few years ago. Vic Brownjohn and Edgar Nyman have now stopped walking. When I arrived at the meeting point, I was given a very happy and smiling welcome. I got an impression that this group was very nice and welcoming. All these years my opinion hasn't changed. The group members are very nice and friendly. The walk was mainly in Richmond Park. Most of the time while walking I found myself talking to Edgar Nyman. He just had an operation on his nail which was growing inward in his big toe. He had a knack of describing all the details of what had happened and how they had happened. Since then Edgar became my good friend.

It was a ten mile walk. When I came home I just slumped in a chair. I felt very tired. I was so tired that I dozed off. Suddenly I woke up. For a while I was very confused asking myself, where am I? Slowly everything came to me. Even though I was very tired I had enjoyed the walk. Also I had enjoyed the day out with nice people. I decided that every Sunday I should walk with them. I am glad to write that I still walk with them every Sunday. Ramblers come from all sections of the British society, and from various professions. None of them have any 'axe to grind'. I feel that they are genuine people. This group fitted in my original plan. As you know my original plan was to know the British society and to mix with them. In a way I have become one of them. I feel that the feeling is mutual. Every Sunday when we meet, we generally talk about what we did during the last week, or where we went on holidays, etc. Most of the walks are about ten to twelve miles. Leaders organise it in such a way that half way we pass through a village. We all go to a village pub and have beer and something to eat. Most of us take our own sandwiches; we just order drinks. My favourite drink is a pint of Guinness.

I was quite happy with ten to twelve mile walks every Sunday with the ramblers. One Sunday in 1993, while walking, a rambler called Sheila Wills was walking with me. I asked her, "Are you walking next Sunday?"

"No. I am going to Eastbourne. My friend Wendy has invited me to walk with her. It is twenty mile walk."

"Do ramblers walk twenty miles?"

"No, ramblers don't. Wendy is a long distance walker."

"I would like to try a twenty mile walk," I said.

"Long distance groups are everywhere. There is one in Bedford in Bedfordshire, not very far from here."

After a while she produced a sheet of paper and read out a phone number of the secretary of the Bedford group. "Phone him, there may be a walk next Sunday." I thanked her. As soon as I arrived home, I phoned the secretary. His name was Roy Presland. He told me where the meeting point was. It was in Milton Keynes.

The day came. All the time I was thinking, can I do a twenty mile walk? It is said that one doesn't know till one tries. The start time was 9am. Ramblers generally start at 10.30am. I got up early, made a cheese and pickle sandwich, filled a flask with tea and started quite early, around 7.15am. It was a new area for me to go to. I allowed good time so that I did not miss them. Roy had given me good directions. I didn't miss any turning and arrived there around 8.45am. I introduced myself to Roy and his wife Jeanette. I found this group equally welcoming. It was a very enjoyable walk. At the end of the walk I felt quite tired. I noticed that other members were not as tired as I was. I thought that they were very fit walkers and possibly had been doing it for many years. Roy suggested that for future walks I should join the Essex & Herts group, which is nearer to me. He gave me the phone number of their secretary to contact. I joined the Essex and Herts section of LDWA. I am very pleased to write that I still am a member of E & H and walk regularly with them.

Even though I was tired after walking twenty miles, I felt that it was more satisfying than walking ten miles. Every four months, the LDWA publish a magazine called *Strider*. The magazine gives a lot of information about different walks in different parts of the country as well as different parts of the world where group members have walked. It is a very interesting magazine. The magazine also gives the details of walks in the whole country. I found out that in addition to the Beds-Bucks and Essex-Herts sections, I could walk with the Thames Valley and London section of LDWA. Actually I could walk with any LDWA group in the country. As soon as I get *Strider* I find out which walks and with which group I would like to walk and note them down.

There are a few ramblers who are very regular. I see most of them on Sundays, unless they are on holidays or I am on holidays. I have become quite close to two ramblers. One of them is Peter Mellows and the other is Philip Greswell. They are like my brothers. I feel that feeling is mutual. It is said, 'Treat brother like a friend and friend like a brother'. On that basis I treat my brother Jaik as my friend.

A few months before I had joined the ramblers, I had a terrible back pain. I had borrowed from the library a book on yoga. I wanted to help myself and get rid of the terrible back pain. I was very successful getting rid of the back pain. Since then I have been performing yoga positions. During walks I would impart information on yoga and what yoga positions were good for back pain, I would get such a pleasure out of rambling and meeting my friends that I would forget my break up in the family life. Every now and then I would become moody and would walk alone. The British have a very good habit of leaving you alone if you want to be alone. I found myself walking alone and brooding. I felt it was not healthy to brood. I told a few of the ramblers, "Whenever you see me walking alone and brooding, please talk to me." They understood and after that they never left me alone to brood. Always I felt that I was among friends while walking with the ramblers and LDWA members.

I had an idea, 'why don't I invite selected ramblers for dinner at my house?' I selected eight ramblers for the dinner. They gladly accepted my invitation. My son Kris had gone to study in Nottingham University and my daughter Nina had gone to Maidstone University. My wife and I were alone in the house. I wanted to have a bit of colour in our lives. I thought socialising may improve my wife's mood. I am quite a good cook. I cooked an Indian meal for all of them. I told my wife about the invitation and then planned my cooking programme accordingly. I made sure that the food was mild and not very hot. I was very pleased with my cooking and the whole set-up. The evening went extremely well. During that evening I told them, "I shall be sixty in two months time." It was a harmless comment, as far as everyone was concerned. After a few days I thought 'I never celebrate my birthdays. Why don't I celebrate my 60th birthday and invite a few more ramblers for that evening in my house?' I was just toying with the idea. Slowly my idea became a confirmed plan. I felt that if I could manage dinner for eight people, perhaps I could manage for more than that. I made a list of people whom I would like to invite. My list had eighteen members. I was confident that eighteen members could also be managed. On the following Sunday while walking, I told the selected members that they were invited for a dinner in my house to celebrate my 60th birthday. All of them gladly accepted. I was delighted with the response. When I arranged for eight people, I was a bit anxious. But now I was not anxious at all. I felt that I had done it before. It shouldn't be difficult. I went ahead. I am very glad to write that it was a great success. My food preparation had improved. The whole set up was pleasant and enjoyable. By the end of the evening everyone had thoroughly enjoyed themselves. I would say that I enjoyed it more than anyone else. I could see that the evening was a great success.

Now I was spending more time on my own. My wife and children would be busy with Jehovah's Witness meetings and Bible studies. Whatever spare time I had I would either spend walking or in the local library. I was on the look out for a new way of making myself busy. It is said 'Busy person is happy person'. I got myself very busy indeed. One Sunday while I was rambling with the ramblers, I was talking to an elderly couple named Bert and Barbara Bonner. They were in their eighties but quite fit to do a ten mile walk. Bert was a very knowledgeable person. He knew walks and countryside throughout the country. They had done many walking holidays. Bert was a good walk leader as well. Barbara said, "Vasu, our group don't have any social activities at all. Other walking groups generally meet regularly for a drink in the evening. We also should have some kind of social evening."

"What kind of activity do you have in mind?"

"We should have once a month meetings where we can have tea/coffee/drinks and snacks and socialise."

"Barbara, it is a good idea, but where can this be held? Surely not in someone's house?"

"No, it can be held in, say, a church hall where all of us meet once a month."

"Perhaps I could have a word with our chairman and see what he says," I suggested.

Luckily next Sunday the chairman, Alan Ashley, was also walking with us.

"Alan, what do you think if we were to have a monthly social evening?"

"It is a good idea. But who is going to organise it?"

"I don't mind organising it."

"Vasu, would you? That would be great." Then he added, "I will talk with our committee and see what they say."

"Have you any idea where this monthly social evening is going to be held?"

"I shall hire a hall for the evening. I shall find out from Enfield Council offices to see what hall is available."

"In the meantime I shall let our committee know about this exciting news," Alan replied. He was very pleased with this new activity in our group.

I thought that before I find out about availability of a hall, I should find out what evening and what time the majority of ramblers would prefer. After that, for a few Sundays while rambling I would enquire about it from walkers. It came out that the majority of them preferred Wednesdays around 7.30pm. Everyone mentioned that about two hours should be sufficient. I enquired about the hall. I was very surprised that the price of hire varied between £30 and £100 for the night. Luckily I came across a church hall on Chaseside in Enfield. They had a large hall with a kitchen and the charge was only £20 for three hours. This charge included heating and the use of the kitchen. I was very delighted. I thought that if the need arises I could even do some cooking. I booked the hall for one Wednesday from 7.30 to 10.30pm. I passed the circular around to members about the date, time and place where the social evening was to be held. All of us were very excited about this new group activity.

The Sunday before that Wednesday our social evening was to start, the chairman said to me, Vasu, very sorry but the committee hasn't agreed to the social evening."

"Why, what is the reason?"

"You are not a committee member. According to a clause in our Association rules, you as a non-committee member can't organise it. Or to put it this way, you can organise it, but it will not be a Ramblers' Association activity. If you start, it would be your activity. But our blessings are with you."

I was very perplexed and surprised. I was disheartened as well. I thought that I had already booked the hall and had paid a deposit for it. After a due thought I said, "OK, Alan. You have no objection if I organise it on my own?"

"No," he replied.

"Can you promise me that all committee members with their partners would attend the event?" I thought that by that way I would have at least eight couples attending.

"That we would do. Our support and best wishes are with you."

The social evenings became a successful story. Everyone enjoyed those evenings. Most of all I enjoyed them. I could see that I had done something worthwhile for the ramblers. After the first evening I planned ahead and fixed the dates for the next six months. I started issuing my newsletter. The newsletter would mention what the programmes were in the future dates. To make the evenings interesting, I arranged lectures on various subjects like yoga, reflexology, homeopathy, Aromatherapy, good diet, and similar topics. In addition, I invited a local doctor to give us a lecture on 'Keeping Good Health'. As time went on I arranged lectures on very varied subjects. I was so busy and happy that I forgot all about my 'horrible family life'.

While walking on Sundays, I would hand over my newsletter to everyone. I would ask members about their comments and find out what else they would like to see during our evenings. Any new member would get special attention from me. I would brief the new member all about the social evenings. During the Sunday walk, I would rush around like a busy bee and would try to meet as many members as possible and make them aware about the next social evening. One day I overheard another rambler saying to other, 'Look at Vasu. He is very social. Look how he is welcoming the new member. We need more people like him in our group'. They never realised that I wanted my social evenings to be successful. We had thirty members who attended our first social evening. Near the door I had kept a desk. On the desk I had kept a register. Everyone would sign in their name, address and phone number. Nearby there was a bowl in which members would deposit £1 per person.

Two years passed happily and successfully. Some members indicated that these meetings should be more interesting. I had an idea. It was nearly the end of year, in 1994. Britain had become a multi-cultural society. Why not have a different cultural evening every month for 1995? I made a list of various groups and found out their important festivals. Welsh night was arranged in the month of St David. Irish night was held in the month of St Patrick. Scottish night coincided with the month of Robert Burns. Indian night was held in the month of Diwali, etc.

In addition, I would arrange block bookings for plays and concerts. I would get quite cheap tickets when I arranged block bookings. I would mention all these in my newsletter. My newsletter also would include a 'Thought Of The Day'.

I remember that I was very partial to Indian night. During that Indian night, I did all the cooking. We all of us had a full Indian meal, Indian beer and Indian sweets. Since it was Diwali (Deepavali) time, I had lit lots of deeps (earthenware candles) all around the hall. I also had decorated the hall with flowers, etc. There was a huge sign saying 'Happy Diwali' in the front of the hall.

A sample newsletter is shown on the next sheet.

About fourteen years ago, a rambler of German origin called Gerd Rogner joined our group. He was a lively character. He used to work as a chef with the Ritz Hotel, London. One Sunday during the walk he brought a bag full of croissants. He said, "The hotel management throw them out if not used by the end of the day. I have brought them so that we all can eat." There was nothing wrong with them. We all enjoyed them. It became a regular affair. Whenever Gerd would walk with us, he would bring a bag full of croissants for us.

One Sunday I was walking with Gerd. Gerd said, "I would like to organise a walking holiday in Germany for our group." I wanted to give him moral support. I said, "Put my name on the list." He was very happy and started asking more members about joining him. He said, "Next week I shall go to Germany and find out a bit more and let all of you know the price, dates, and how many we can cater for." His plans went very well. Finally sixteen of us went to Ardennes, Germany, in four cars. We stayed there for a week. He was a chef, he did all the cooking for all of us. Also he would lead the walk every day. We had a fantastic walking holiday in Ardennes. I am sorry to write that about three years ago, Gerd was involved in a car accident. He was admitted to a hospital. He had a stroke. Since then he has been in a nursing home.

The Ramblers Association used to publish a magazine called *Rambling Today*. Now it is called *Walk*. I came across an advertisement, 'Pembrokeshire, South Wales Ramblers are organising a walking holiday for a week. They are inviting members from all over the country to join them. Local hotels have agreed to give special rates to ramblers. Contact…' I wanted to go. I phoned and found out all the information. Next Sunday while walking I told my friend Peter Mellows, "I am going for this rambling week in south Wales, would you like to come?"

"Yes, I will come."

I thought that why not ask other members if anyone would like to join. Finally six of us in two cars went for the walking holiday in South Wales. It was a very enjoyable holiday we had. Local hotels had given us such a good deal that it was too good to be true. We paid only £195 for the whole week in a three-star hotel with four course breakfast, five course dinner and a packed lunch every day.

It was drizzling on most days. But one day we had so much rain that we all got soaking wet. Around 1pm, our leader said, "The pubs close at 2pm, it is still four miles away. We have to walk very fast to reach there before it closes." All of us were soaking wet. We desperately needed our drink. We walked very fast. We just made it. I was the first one to go in the pub. Generally I would have a pint of Guinness. But I was shivering and feeling very cold, I said, "Double whiskey, please." I gulped it down. It was very satisfying. I could feel warmth inside me.

One day our chairman, Mr Alan Ashley said, "Vasu, every year we have an annual dinner in a restaurant. I have an idea. Why don't you organise our annual dinner?"

"Perhaps I can incorporate it into my monthly social evening. You tell me in what month you would like to have the annual dinner. My monthly social evening for that month would be the annual dinner."

"It is a good idea, let us do it."

It was three months before the annual dinner date was due. During my Sunday walks I would talk with our walkers and find out what sort of dishes would be acceptable to the group. Everyone said that in the restaurant they generally have:

>
> Starter
> Wine/beer. Whiskey to drink. Soft drink
> Main meal consisting of meat/fish and 2/3 vegetables
> Dessert
> Tea/coffee
> Liquor (this is optional)

Finally I decided on:

>
> Beer/soft drink/whiskey/wine
> Vegetable soup with bread and butter
> Grilled salmon and peas, cauliflower
> Boiled potato
> Apple crumble with ice cream
> Tea/coffee
> Baileys

I knew that I would not be able to cook all these dishes on my own. So I delegated cooking to a few of the ramblers:

> Soup was cooked by Gerd
> Grilled salmon by Mr and Mrs Newman. (they had a special grilling dish for a large fish)
> Boiled potato was boiled by me in the hall
> Peas and cauliflower were also boiled by me in the hall
> Apple crumble was baked by another rambler
> Tea/coffee was brewed in the hall

Drinks, including Baileys, were left on the tables for ramblers to help themselves.

The dinner was a great success. I had only charged £10 per person. I had hired a part-time waitress who I found from an advertisement displayed in the newsagent's window. I had kept maximum numbers to thirty, I felt that I could not manage more than thirty. They were having a sit down dinner. We all thoroughly enjoyed it and the chairman mentioned that every year we should do it ourselves rather than go to a restaurant. I was very pleased that everything went well and I had managed it without any problem.

A few weeks later I got a phone call from the chairman. "Vasu. I would like to meet you."

"What about?"

"I shall tell you when we meet."

I met him.

"Two women ramblers have complained that you are making loads of money out of this annual dinner. You charged them £10 per head. They say they did all the work, you did nothing at all."

Why they had said that I didn't do any work was that when the ramblers had come at 7pm, I was wearing a suit and pacing up and down in the hall. The tables were set, and I had boiled the vegetables. So these two women thought that I hadn't done any work, just paced up and down and waited for the food to arrive which was cooked by others.

"They said that I should see your account of the money."

"Why should I show my accounts to you? My social evening has nothing to do with the ramblers. You and your committee had denied the support." I had started on my own. I then added, "I only charged them £10 per person for all the food, drinks, hall rent and salary for the part-time waitress. What a cheek to say that I made money out of my social evenings. On the contrary, I was spending more than I was getting from the ramblers."

"I can very well understand that. They complained, that is why I had to clarify with you."

"Sorry, I can't show my accounts to you. There is no reason to show my accounts."

After that I lost interest in the monthly social evenings. I had organised them for three years. For me it was sheer enjoyment arranging those monthly social evenings.

Chapter Nineteen

Discrimination? What Discrimination?

It was August 1963. I had boarded the luxury liner P&O's *Chusan*. It was not only the first time I had travelled by a luxury liner but also the first time I had travelled to a foreign land. The ship had started from Australia. The ship was full of Australians. They looked similar to the British. The colour, the features, the behaviour, the language, all looked similar to the British we knew in India. There were quite a few British still living in India at that time. Many British companies like Lloyds Bank, the Department store Whiteway, etc, had many employees who were British. We were ruled by the British for nearly three centuries. The general Indian attitude was respect for them and we kept a distance from them. We couldn't understand their accent anyhow. I had seen many films in English language. Half the time I couldn't understand what they were saying. There was an untold gap between us and them. The whole atmosphere was new to me. My first day passed in exploring and orienteering. On the second day after breakfast I thought that I should have a swim in the pool. I put on my swimming costume and went in the water. I didn't know how to swim. I just stood in a corner and watched Australians making so much noise and enjoying themselves. They would dive in the pool, throw each other in the pool and were having a lot of fun. After a while one of them approached me and said, "Come on, join us."

"I don't know how to swim."

"No problem. I shall teach you." He told me to lie on my tummy. I didn't know how, so he first showed me how. I still couldn't do it. He then put his two hands under my tummy and told me to lie on them. Once I did this, he told me to splash with my arms and legs. Slowly I gained some confidence in myself. He asked me to practice for a while. I practised it for a while. He again came to me and encouraged me and said, "You are doing fine. Practice every day. Within no time you will be able to swim." He was right. After a few day's practice I could swim. After that the same Australian taught me how to dive as well. One day he told me, "When you happen to be underwater, don't breathe, otherwise water will go in your nose." A few minutes later, he pushed me in the water. It was so sudden that I was stunned. I didn't expect him to take that kind of liberty with me. When I went down in the water, I remembered his warning, 'Don't breathe, otherwise water will go in your nose'. I held my breath till I came up. I was very pleased with myself. But it seemed he was more pleased with me than I was with myself. He expected me to gasp for air when I came up out of the water. I had followed his instructions. He was very pleased with that.

He became such a good and helpful friend that I didn't feel any discrimination at all.

The company I worked with was very considerate. They gave me six weeks sick leave. I was feeling very sorry for myself. I felt that I had come for a short time. My time was being wasted sitting around with my arm in the plaster. I decided not to waste any time. I thought that for at least four weeks I could tour around the country. During that time I visited Birmingham, Manchester, Nottingham, Liverpool and the Isle of Man. Everywhere I went I had a very good but sympathetic service. There was not a single incident where people took advantage of my injury. On the contrary, they were very helpful to me. In Birmingham I had an experience which really shook me.

In Birmingham I went to the YMCA hostel to stay. They were full. The receptionist suggested that I could try a nearby house. They said that the house owner sometimes had a spare room to rent. I went to the house and knocked on the door. An elderly gentleman opened the door.

"Have you got a room for two nights?"
"Yes. Come in."

He showed me the room. The rent was quite reasonable. It was a very hot day and I was sweating. I wanted to have a bath.

"Where is the bathroom?"

"It is common to all of us."

"How many people are staying here?"

"Just you and me."

He gave me a towel and some soap. I went into the bathroom. I closed the bathroom door and undressed with much difficulty. But I was used to using only one hand, the other one being in plaster. Without knocking he came in the bathroom.

"I shall help you wash your back," he said.

"It is OK. I can manage."

"No, no. I shall help you."

"I am now used to managing everything with one hand. Thank you for the offer. I am alright."

He stood there looking at me.

"Please go, I want to have my bath."

I didn't like the way he looked at me, gaping with wide open eyes. Inwardly I got a bit scared.

"Please go, I want to have my bath." I looked at him and waited. After a few moments he left. I closed the bathroom door.

The following morning after breakfast I went to the YMCA to see if they had a room for me. Luckily they had one vacant. I immediately booked in. I went back to the house. "I just got a nice room in the YMCA. I shall leave in an hour's time." I gave him one day's rent and left. I was so relieved when I left. After I left I was thinking about the incident. He may have been a genuine person. He may have had pity on me when he saw my hand in the plaster. Perhaps he was too keen to help me. But the way he looked at me scared me.

After that I visited Manchester and Liverpool. I stayed for two days in Liverpool and caught a night ferry for the Isle of Man.

I realised that I would know more about the British if I stayed with a British family rather than stay in a hotel. Douglas, the capital of the Isle of Man is always full of tourists. There were many families accepting tourists to stay with them. I came down from the ferry and walked towards the town centre. On the way I saw a notice displayed in a window of one house. The notice said, 'Rooms to let, apply within'.

I knocked on the door. A middle aged lady opened the door.

"Do you have a room for two days?"

"Yes, come in. I shall show you." I was very pleased with the room, it had a beautiful view of the sea. I immediately paid her two days rent. She mentioned that the rent included breakfast as well as dinner.

"Please make sure that there is no loud music or noise after 11.00pm. Also girls are not allowed to stay after 11.00pm."

I was ready for breakfast after I had a shower. After breakfast I went out to explore. I don't remember what I saw and visited, but I visited as many places as I could. Tourist information had given me a list of places of interest to visit. The information brochure mentioned that there was a casino.

I came home, had my dinner, put on my suit and went out to visit the casino. I had a crazy idea. Why don't I put on my black cap and go out? I put on my black cap as well. I looked in the mirror. I had my nice shirt, tie, suit and my black cap. And of course my left arm was still in plaster supported by a sling over my neck. I realised that it was a very strange combination. But I wanted people to comment and talk to me. Perhaps this strange attire would promote some talk and discussion. Now I was ready for the new town in the new country.

I had never gambled. I didn't know much about gambling either. I just went there to pass my time and to see how others were gambling. As soon as I entered I spotted the drinking bar. I made my way towards it and ordered a half pint of beer. I looked round to see if I could talk to anyone. While I was surveying the area, a person came to the bar and ordered a drink. He looked at me, I smiled. He smiled back and asked me, "Where are you from?"

"I am from India."

"What do you think you are? An Indian prince?" he said jokingly.

"Of course. Do you have any doubt?" I said it curtly.

He got his pint of beer, turned around and surveyed the casino area.

"Where are you from?" I asked.

"I am from Wigan."

"Are you on holidays?"

"No. We are here to play rugby."

From then on we just talked about this and that. He was quite a nice and reasonable person. He mentioned that he had never come across a person from India. He wanted to know a bit more about India. I don't remember what we talked about. We talked and talked quite a lot. I offered him a drink. He gladly accepted it. After that he had quite a few pints of beer. I paced with him by drinking half pints for his one pint. As the time went on, I became light-headed and talked on various subjects on India and Indians. He was full of questions. He was asking questions in a joking way and I would reply in a very serious way, as if I was teaching him all about India. I didn't know how the time passed. I looked at the clock, it was past midnight. We felt hungry. We both of us had bar food while we were engrossed in our talk. After the bar meal, I offered him a drink, thinking that he would refuse as we both had quite a lot. His drinking capacity was great. He gladly accepted it. Our drinking session started again. Due to so many drinks, he couldn't stand still, he was slightly swinging backward and forward. I was also feeling the effect of drink. I continued, thinking that I wouldn't get such a chance of meeting and socialising with people like him. Now the bar area was full with people. Not far away from us there was a group of six people drinking. One of them approached me and said, "I have noticed that you have been offering drinks to my friend. Please don't give him any more. He has to play rugby tomorrow. I am the captain of the team. He should stop drinking now."

"Okay, I shall stop offering him any more drinks." After a quick thought I asked him, "Can I offer you a drink?"

"I shall buy a drink for you," he replied.

"I offered you first." He accepted my offer. I ordered a pint for him and a half for me. I raised my glass and said, "I wish you a win tomorrow in your game."

"Thank you."

The captain was also very hungry for information about India and Indians. He found this an opportunity not to be missed. I also felt that I was getting a kind of insight into British society. He then introduced me to his team. I didn't know how the time went. We just talked and drank. I was horrified when I had a look at the clock. It was showing 4.45am. I felt that it was time to go home. The captain and his team were thinking the same. I wished all of them goodnight/good morning and walked towards my room. When I entered the main door of the house, one person was going out.

"Good morning," I said.

"Good morning," he replied.

"I am just coming back from the casino."

"Did you win?"

"I was not playing. I was socialising with rugby players."

"Did you know them?"

"No, just met them last night. They were nice people. They had come from Wigan to play rugby."

"I am from Wigan as well."

"Where are you going now?"

"I am going for my morning walk."

I was too tired to talk more, so I said, "See you," and went to my room. I didn't want to miss my breakfast, so I had a bath, got ready and went down for breakfast. In the meantime the person who had gone for a morning walk, came back to have breakfast.

I came to know that he was working in a small factory. The factory had closed down. He was now out of a job. He felt that he should have a short break and then go back and search for another job. This was his first visit to the Isle of Man. We both spent the whole day visiting various places. At the end of the day we came back to the house. We had dinner in the house. I was happy that the landlady had made an apple crumble for the dessert. I love apple crumble.

"I love apple crumble. Can I have an extra portion, if you have any?" I asked the landlady greedily.

"Yes, I will give you an extra portion," the landlady replied.

"You can have my portion. I am not too fussy about it," the man from Wigan said.

"Shall I give you fresh fruit to eat?" the landlady asked him.

"Yes please."

I had to catch an early morning ferry to Liverpool. I wished both of them a good night and went to my room. By that time I was very tired and was ready for bed. I was pleased with myself. My trip to the Isle of Man had been very successful. I had met real British society and socialised with them. I also had a chance to impart a lot of information about India and Indians. I looked back and realised that I had been a very good 'self-appointed ambassador'. I had given a very good impression to all of the people I had met in the Isle of Man. With those kinds of pleasant thoughts I dozed off.

It was 1966. I had now moved from London to Middlesborough. I had finally landed a very good job with Imperial Chemical Industries (ICI). I was working as a design engineer, designing pressure vessels for the petro-chemical industry. My house was just 200 yards away from the football ground. At least once a week we would hear excited shouting from the spectators. During the football matches, I had to move my car away from being parked near my house. During football matches the atmosphere was always noisy but happy. That was the time the World Cup was being played. This football ground was selected for a few World Cup games to be played. The most exciting one was when South Korea played against Russia. The whole city was taken over by football frenzy. The atmosphere was electric. Everyone in the city was involved in one way or the other. Finally England won the World Cup. The city never slept on that night.

I used to work in the 'Vessel Design Division' in ICI. There were about ten engineers working in the division. After a couple of months, we all ten of us became like a big joint family. We would play various games during lunchtime; football, green bowling, swimming, table tennis, etc, whatever we fancied. Then we would go to the canteen to have our lunch. They were really good times. I didn't feel in anyway different from other British boys. Slowly and gradually, we had an in invisible bond among us. We would do most activities together.

We had one person in the group called Ken Hornby. He was a lively character. He was always looking for new activities. One day he declared, "This Friday night we should all go for a drink in the pub." It sounded a very good idea. Six of us agreed. The other four of us had prior engagements. It was decided which pub we should meet at for the drink. We had a very good time. By this time I knew how to keep up with people in a drinking session. They would order a pint of beer, I would order a half pint. In that way I was sober enough to drive back home. Sometimes one of us would have too much to drink and was not fit enough to drive home. I would then offer to take them home. I would knock on their door. Their wives would open the door. When I took Lenny home I would say, "Joan, I have brought Lenny safely home. He was sober enough to drive, but I felt that it was safer for me to bring him home." Their wives would be very thankful to me. Sometimes they would ask me to stay for supper. I would gladly accept. I could see that I was well mixed with the British community. I didn't want to miss the opportunity.

We all had a very good time. Ken commented, "We are having a good time. Why don't we do it every Friday?" We all agreed. After that we started meeting in a different pub for a few drinks. After some months, it was boring to go to a pub and have a few drinks. It was suggested that we should go to different pubs and have one drink in each of them. This started our so-called 'pub crawling'. After pub crawling we would all be very hungry. We would go to a fish and chip shop and would have fish and chip supper. We wanted to have a change. Ken Hornby suggested that we should go to a Chinese restaurant. He knew a very nice one. We all in our cars followed his car and went to the restaurant. I didn't know much about Chinese food. When the waiter came I told Lenny who was sitting opposite me, "Lenny, I don't know much about Chinese food. Whatever you are having, I shall have the same. As long as it is not beef, I am alright. As you know we Hindus do not eat beef."

We were very hungry. Whatever was given to us, we polished it off very quickly. Lenny finished first. I noticed that there were a few morsels on Lenny's plate. I remarked, "Lenny, you haven't finished your food."

"Yes I have."

"No, you haven't. Look there are a few pieces of food on your plate."

We both were still drunk. Lenny asked me, "What shall I do?"

"You should clean it in such a way that they don't have to wash the plate."

"How?"

"Lick the bloody thing, Lenny."

Do you know what Lenny did? Surprise, surprise. He took the plate in both hands, licked it and asked me, "Is it clean enough?"

"Yes, it is clean now."

The following Monday in the office I commented to Lenny, "Lenny, do you know that you licked the plate in the Chinese restaurant?"

"No, I did not."

"Yes, you did," I replied.

Kenny Hornby was sitting beside us. He said, "Yes you did you silly sod."

Lenny giggled. We all laughed.

We found out that not all the pubs did supper. Only one of them we came across did supper. It was time consuming as well as expensive to go to a restaurant. So our Friday night pub crawling was arranged in such a way that our last pub would be the pub who gave us supper. He would give us pie and mushy peas. That pub also had a gaming room. We would play darts, dominos and cards. Playing cards became our favourite game. We started spending more time in that pub. We would have a few drinks, play cards and then have our pie and mushy peas supper. Generally we would play 'flush'.

One evening we were playing 'flush' as usual. We had quite a few drinks. I was unaware that a few local people were also watching us. I was winning. I was intoxicated, not only by alcohol but winning as well. Suddenly I heard an argument between one of our group called Douglas Macdonald and one local person. I didn't know what was happening. I just kept on playing. The argument stopped and both of them shook hands. I only heard Douglas saying, "Do you know he is whiter than white, whiter than you are." We finished our drink. I asked my friend Lenny Pope, "What was Douglas arguing about?"

"He was arguing about you."

"What about me?"

"The local man commented and said that this darkie from East of Suez had all the luck, etc, etc. Douglas got very upset with him and said to him 'Do you know he is whiter than a white. He is whiter than you are, you bloody Arab'. I know him very well." (At that time in North England, the swearing was not as bad as it is now. If one wanted to abuse someone, he would be called an Arab).

"What did the local man say?"

"He kept quiet. Then he apologised and both of them shook hands."

At that time I was fairly drunk. My reactions were a bit slow. I didn't say anything to either of them. But the next day when I recollected what had happened, I was very touched. I didn't know what to say to Douglas. On Monday morning when I met Douglas in the office I jokingly commented to him, "Douglas, last Friday the man in the pub was giving you a hard time, was he?"

Douglas retorted, "It was your bloody fault. It was all because of you I had an argument. He didn't realise that I was joking. Once he realised that I was joking he laughed."

While we are talking about Douglas, let me give you a very important episode on him. He had become quite friendly. He was closer to me than any other in the group.

Once he said, "Vasu, you are quite slim, even though you eat quite a lot – more than I do. I wish I was as slim as you are. I would then play football again. What is your secret?"

"I watch what I eat."

"What do you mean?"

"You can reduce your weight naturally, you know."

"How?"

"For example, every day in the morning as well as in the afternoon, during tea break you have a cup of tea and a Penguin chocolate biscuit. Don't you?"

"Yes."

"You just cut down on that. In a few months time you will lose a few pounds."

"A dietician has given me a diet to follow. It is very boring. I don't follow it."

"Can you stop eating chocolate biscuits?"

"Yes. At home I also have a creamy dessert. I shall stop that as well."

He followed my advice. After a month or so, he commented showing me his loose trousers. "It seems I have lost weight."

"Good. Carry on. You will be able to play football in a few months time."

"I used to play with our local team. At the moment they are not doing very well. I would like to play with them and help them. The players are all youngsters. The season starts in a month's time. I should go and meet the manager."

Douglas was determined to play football with the local team. He was so excited and told me after a few days, "Vasu, I met the manager. He has selected me and has appointed me team captain. I am the most senior." He was very happy and grinning from ear to ear.

The season started. Every now and then he would give me an update on the progress of his team. Once I watched him playing. He was playing to win. He was everywhere on the pitch. He would shout at his team and encourage them. The manager and I were sitting together and watching the game. The manager commented,

"Douglas is a very good player. He has infused a new life into the team. The whole team love him. If he continues playing like this, we will definitely win the cup." Do you know what happened when the season finished? HIS TEAM WON THE CUP!

Douglas was very grateful to me. My advice and encouragement had given him one of the best trophies in his life. During the presentation of the cup, he went to the stage and delivered a very short speech. Tears were rolling from his eyes when he said, "I am here with this cup and it is all due to my good friend and his encouragement." He couldn't continue; he was very emotional. He came down from the stage and sat down. He wiped his tearful eyes. I was very touched with that scene.

I got married in November 1968. He was my best man during my wedding. He was really my best man and a very good friend while I was living in North East England.

It was mid 1968. In our ICI office, six of us had attempted to walk a 42 mile walk across the Yorkshire Moors. It was called Lyke Wake Walk. It was quite a tough walk. None of us could finish it. It seemed all of us needed special training before we could attempt it again. I decided that my training would be a good walk every day. I used to live far away from my office. I decided that I should live a bit nearer to my office. I could then walk every day from home to work and back. At that time I was courting. My fiancée, who became my wife, and I, looked around the area about two or three miles away from my office. We came across an advertisement in a paper shop advertising a room for rent. I thought that if I phoned for the room, the landlord would recognise my Indian accent and would say, 'It is gone'. I told my fiancée to phone for the room. The following Saturday we both went to visit the house. The landlord opened the door. When he saw me he hesitated. My fiancée said, "My boyfriend Vasu works in ICI as a mechanical engineer. He would like to rent a room. Can we see it?"

"Oh, you work in ICI?"

"Yes."

"Which section?"
"Pressure vessel division."
"I work in ICI as well."
"Which section?"
"I am in the administration office."

Obviously his mind was working. He realised that I was a mechanical engineer in ICI. He also worked in ICI. ICI was kind of a common bond between us. Also I was a mechanical engineer. He was just an ordinary clerk. It seemed these factors overweighed my colour and ethnic origin. He showed us the room. It was spacious and had big windows. There was plenty of light in the room. It was a lovely room. Also the window was facing the road. We both liked it. I took the room. I retained the room till I got married in November 1968. After marriage we moved to London.

My wife was a Geordie. Her accent was very difficult to understand. Initially when we met, I couldn't understand her accent, nor could she understand my accent. When we came to London, her accent was modified. Also we both got used to each other's accent. We have two children. When they were about eight and ten years old, we used to see a series called *When The Boat Comes In* on television. The location of these stories was in Geordieland. All the characters would have the same accent as my wife used to have. Sometime after the programme, my wife would get a phone call from her family. It was very strange that my wife's accent would change when she would talk with her family. For a few minutes she would retain the same accent, and talk with us in that accent. I remember that my daughter would say, "Mum, we can't understand you. Please talk in English." My wife would smile and talk in a normal English accent.

I came across a book in two volumes: *A History Of India* written by Dr Percival Spear. It is a very interesting book. The book mentioned that India, in the time of Mughal rule, was very prosperous. It was so prosperous that many Europeans would visit it. At that time, the book mentioned that income per capita in India was higher than in European countries. One Sunday I was walking with the ramblers. One rambler, Bill Boyes, was walking with me. I had gathered that Bill was also fond of reading books on various topics.

"Bill, recently I read a book called *A History Of India*. I was very surprised to read that at the time of the Mughals, India was very prosperous country. Their income per capita was higher than Europe's at that time."

"You should read *White Mughals*; it is a very interesting book. You will like it."

I had never heard of that book. I knew that the English sense of humour was very subtle. I had come across some subtle humour. I felt that Bill was trying to be funny. For a moment I didn't say anything. I didn't know what reply to give. Finally I asked him, "Who is the author?"

"William Dalrymple."

I was not keen on reading that book, didn't sound right to me. The time passed. A few months later another rambler had visited India. He came back. His name was Philip Greswell.

"Philip, did you have a good time in India?"

"No."

"Why?"

"I had terrible loose motions. I was really ill with it."

After talking about this and that Philip said, "Vasu, I read a very nice little book, you will like it."

"What is it called?"

"*White Mughal.*"

Then I realised that Bill was right when he told me a few months ago that I would like the book.

The following week Bill happened to walk with us. I asked Bill, "Do you have that *White Mughal* book?"

"Yes. It is somewhere in the house. I shall find it and keep it for you."

"The local library is just across from where I live. I shall find out if they have got the book. If not I shall phone you and let you know so that you can bring the book next week."

Luckily the library had a copy. I borrowed it. I told Bill that I had a copy from the library and was then reading it. It is really a good book. The writer had done a very deep study and research to compile the facts in the book. I liked the book so much that one by one I have read most of Dalrymple's books.

Finally I would like to close this chapter by saying that discrimination is everywhere. It is the degree of discrimination and the reason for it which can be very damaging to society as well as to the country. We saw discrimination in Banaras, India, when our family went to Banaras from Pakistan in 1947. My brother Jaik was discriminated against when he joined the Indian Air Force. We all should realise that all people of the world can't have the same shade of colour, nor the same culture and upbringing. Even differences in income can divide people. Degrees of intelligence vary in people. As long as we all understand that every one of us are different in many ways; we all can't be the same, we should have less friction in the world.

Hindus believe that we all have a soul. The soul is a part of the super soul (God). Each one of us has a soul. From that point of view we all have the same father (God). We in this world are brothers and sisters. Then why there is so much friction and dispute between brothers and sisters in this wide world?

Chapter Twenty

Sickness/Illness/Accident/Hospitalisation/Homeopathy

Looking back over my seventy-odd years I would definitely say that God has been very kind to me. I have had quite a few narrow escapes and brushes with death. Right from the very day I was born, I had a narrow escape. My mother had left me for dead and was not interested if I lived or died. My dad had just died leaving my mother with children to look after and no asset to show. All my dad's assets had been swindled by his two partners as mentioned in chapter one.

It is said that a cat has nine lives. Perhaps I am a cat as well from that point of view. To see if I had nine escapes or not, let me describe and enumerate my escapes:

1. **It was 1934.** I was just born. I was born premature and was very weak. My mother had left me for dead. I have already described this fully in chapter one. I was told that it was a near thing – as near as you can get to death.

2. **It was 1964.** I was working as a draughtsman/designer in engineering. After saving £1 per week, I had at last saved sufficient money to buy my own scooter. Every weekend I would be away to visit nearby towns/cities. One day an advertisement for a holiday caught my eye. The holiday was in the Isle of Wight. During the holiday they taught us boating, sailing and canoeing. I had never done those activities. I should definitely enjoy them. I booked the holiday. I went on the holiday by my scooter. It was a wonderful and enjoyable holiday. Everything I learned over there was new to me. I had never been to the Isle of Wight either. It was a memorable experience. When the holiday finished I caught a ferry to Portsmouth. I was coming back from Portsmouth by scooter to my residence with the Khan family in East London.

I would carry my camera by hanging it from my neck. I found it easy to carry that way, as well as use it as and when I could. I was riding my scooter and was in a very happy mood. I was musing and saying to myself, 'What a wonderful holiday I had'. Suddenly it caught me unaware. I couldn't control my scooter. My scooter just stopped dead. I was thrown forward and fell on my face. It was just an instinct that I defended myself and broke the fall on my two hands and my chest. My camera had given its life to save my chest. I couldn't imagine how bad I might have been hurt, if the camera was not hanging from my neck. Luckily I was not hurt anywhere else except that my left wrist was aching. A few people came and helped me get up. One of them said, "You are very lucky that I did not hit you. I was just right behind you. To miss you I had to divert my car to the left and nearly hit a truck." I got up and noticed that the front of my scooter was all twisted up. The whole machine was out of shape now.

"I don't think you can drive the scooter. It is all messed up. Where do you want to go?"

"I live in East London."

"So do we. Where in East London?"

"Stratford."

"We are going that way, perhaps we can take you to your house. We live in Upton Park."

"What shall we do with the scooter?"

"It looks like it is no use to me. We should push it from the road and leave it beside the road."

We pushed the scooter and left it beside the road. I got in his car. His wife and a child also were in the car.

I thought that I was not hurt much. As the time went on, my wrist became very painful. It became so painful now that I felt like crying. After a while the pain became unbearable. I was in agony. I couldn't sit straight on the seat, I had to lie down. My wrist was now swollen. I felt like fainting due to extreme pain in my left wrist. Now I started groaning in agony.

"Perhaps we should take you to a hospital. Do you think?"

"Do you know any hospital nearby?"

"We know a hospital in Upton Park. We shall take you straight to the hospital." I was silent and closed my eyes. Now I was very concerned and was thinking whether I would reach hospital before I died.

I was immediately admitted into the hospital. The doctor said, "You have broken your wrist." My good Samaritan wished me good luck and went away. Before he left he asked me, "Can we inform your family?"

"Yes please." I gave him Mr and Mrs Khan's address and phone number. "Please tell them what has happened and tell them not to worry."

The hospital set my wrist and put a plaster on it and left it for six weeks. The next day Mrs Khan visited me in the hospital. When she saw me on the hospital bed with my arm in the plaster and my ashen face, she started crying. It was very strange that when I saw her crying I started crying as well. I realised that my plight was much worse than I thought.

After a few weeks they removed the plaster. I was amazed that the doctors started discussing my wrist. I didn't know what was going on. Finally the doctor said, "Mr Daryanani, we are sorry that we have not set your wrist right. It has to be set again. They again gave me an injection of anaesthetic to sleep. They set it again and put a new plaster on my wrist and arm. My arm was again restricted in the new plaster for another five weeks. If you look at my left wrist now, you will note that they did not set it right, it is still a bit twisted.

3.   It was 1967 I was working for ICI in Billingham, North East England. I had come to the UK only for two years. I stayed for four years thinking my job was not done. My mother wrote to me to go back to India. I felt that I should go to India, meet my mother and the family, then decide about my future plans. During that time it was not easy to get an airline ticket for India from North East England. Travel agents were not that advanced at that time. If they were, I couldn't find them anywhere. I decided to go to London in my car, and go direct to a travel agent I had contacted. He had agreed to hold a ticket to India for me. At that time I had a Renault Gordino car. Everyone told me that my car had a very high centre of gravity. My car would topple over even by hitting a kerb. I used to drive it carefully making sure that I did not hit the kerb. I was driving on the A1. The A1 is the road from Edinburgh to London. I had started quite early so that I could reach the travel agent well before his closing time. I was driving quite fast, possibly too fast for my little car. Near Doncaster I had a front wheel puncture. I was driving in the outside lane. At that time there was no central crash barrier on the A1. It was the first time it had happened to me. I didn't know what was happening. Suddenly my car rolled over, not once or twice but three times. I came to know afterwards that it rolled over three times. I was wearing a Longine watch given to me by my brother Jaik. The watch had a date display. It seemed that with every roll over, the date on my watch changed. I was driving on 8th September 1967, towards London, I landed on 11th September 1967, on other side of the carriageway facing Newcastle On Tyne. Then it wasn't compulsory to wear a seat belt. My car was fitted with it but I was not wearing one.

Finally my car stopped rolling over. Still I did not know what had happened. I was dazed and confused. My car door opened and a person said, "Are you alright?" I did not look at him. I was just gazing at the floor of the car and replied, "Yes, I am alright."

"Come out then."

"Yes, I am coming out." But I still sat there trying to figure out what had happened.

Again another person peeped in and said, "Are you hurt?"

"No, I am not hurt." He said, "Please come out."

I came out of my car. When I had a look at my car I nearly fainted. I could not believe that I had come out of that wreck of a car. The car was all smashed in. I couldn't recognise my car. I saw a very long queue of cars waiting for my car to be removed from the carriageway before they could drive towards Newcastle or wherever they wanted to go. A few people pushed my car away to clear the road. I suddenly saw blood on my left knee. I rolled up my trouser-leg and noticed that I had a minor scratch on my left knee.

I was a member of the RAC. One car owner phoned the RAC who came quickly. The police also did not take long to arrive. A policeman had a look at my car and then at me and said, "Do you know you are lucky to be alive. Were you wearing the safety belt?"

"No, I wasn't wearing it."

"Do you know that safety belt would have strangled you when your car rolled over?"

"What do you want to do with it?" the RAC man asked me.

"Has it got any scrap value?"

"No," the RAC man replied.

"Please scrap it."

At that time I was feeling feverish, maybe I had realised that I might have died. One car owner had a tea flask. He gave me a warm cup of tea. He could see that I was shivering. I thanked him. A policeman wrapped me in a blanket and asked me, "Where do you want to go?"

"I know a family in East London. I would like to go to them." The policeman took me to his police station in Doncaster. Suddenly I had an attack of intense hunger. He gave me something to eat and drink. After that he drove me direct to the house where my previous landlord Mr and Mrs Khan lived. Luckily they were at home. I thanked the policeman. Mr and Mrs Khan offered him a cup of tea but he refused saying he was in a hurry.

They were very surprised to see me. "Vasu, why didn't you tell us that you were coming," they enquired. I narrated what had happened. They were very glad that I had survived with the grace of God. Mr and Mrs Khan were just like my family. During August that year, they had visited me in Middlesborough. We all had gone in my car – the same car which was now a wreck – to Scotland. We had a very good time. It was during the Edinburgh Festival we had gone. There was so much activity. The city was really vibrating with excitement.

The next day I went to the travel agent, got my ticket and visited India. I met my mother and our joint family. We all were very happy to meet each other. Specially I was very glad that I survived and was able to meet them. I was very thankful to God that He allowed me to meet my family. If I am not mistaken, I never told them about this accident. When they read about it in this book, they will be very surprised to know about it.

4. Now it was 1968, I had been to India and met my family. During my stay of four years in the UK, my nature had unintentionally changed. Obviously it had changed so much that I couldn't identify myself with my family. I got the shock of a lifetime. I came back and decided to settle down in the UK. I wanted a car for me to use. Sometime ago, I had read that Alan Ladd, a famous Hollywood actor, owns a Jaguar car. I thought it would be out of my reach. While I was looking through a newspaper's car column, I came across a second-hand Jaguar car for sale. It was not expensive at all. It was the same model that Inspector Morse drives in the famous TV series of the same name. I was courting around that time. My fiancée and I decided to get married.

The marriage day was fixed. We decided to have a registry marriage. On the wedding day, I got up early in the morning. The silencer of my car had developed a crack in it. It was very noisy. I went to Halfords, and bought a bandage for the silencer. I jacked the car up and went underneath the car. Immediately I came out as I wanted a tool and stood beside my car, suddenly I heard a crash. The car jack socket had snapped and the jack had sliced the side of the car. The car came crashing down on the ground. When I saw it, I prayed to God that He had saved me. I could have been under the car when it crashed down on the ground. For a while I was shaking with a fright. After some time I gathered my wits. I realised that in a couple of hours time I was supposed to get married. Luckily my neighbour had a special jack which did not need the jack socket. It lifts the whole car and not just one side. He helped me put the bandage on the silencer. I had my shower and went and attended my wedding just in time. Did I mention this episode to anyone? I don't think so. It was so long ago that I don't remember if I did or did not.

5.   **Now we are in 1981**, I had been working with Abbey Life Assurance Co Ltd for quite a few years. I had been quite successful. By this time I had qualified for Million Dollar Round Table and had become a life member. I had had a chance to visit Africa, Spain and Dubai and sold a good number of life assurances to friends and families of my clients in the UK. One of the managers in Abbey Life, Mr Bill Oberoi, knew that I had been quite successful selling policies to non-residents. One day he approached me and said, "Vasu, have you been to Kenya?"

"No," I replied.

"My elder brother is in Nairobi. I was born and brought up in Nairobi. Let us both go to Nairobi and sell life assurances. We should do very well. Not only do I have good contacts in Kenya, but my brother has many business contacts. We shall stay with him."

"Yes, it is a good idea."

"My wife and my little daughter also will be with us."

I felt that it was a good opportunity to visit a new country. I love visiting different countries. I have so far visited 54 countries.

"Yes, I don't mind. Hope your brother doesn't mind," I replied.

"I shall phone him and find out. I shall let you know tomorrow."

The next day Bill came. He was all smiles and said, "My brother has a big house in Nairobi. He is quite happy to welcome you."

"When do you intend to go and how long for?"

"Next month. We should be there for two weeks." We immediately planned accordingly.

His brother really looked after us. He had a servant, a cook and a driver. Life was very easy for us. In the mornings we had a substantial breakfast of eggs and bacon, papaya, toast, marmalade and a cup of tea. His driver would take us to our clients for meetings. The car and the driver was at our disposal. He would bring us home for a substantial and very delicious lunch. We would have a beer with our lunch. Again our driver would take us to our clients after lunch and again bring us back home. Evening dinner used to be in a friends/family's house or in a restaurant. In the evening also we would have beer/whisky/etc. We really had a very enjoyable time. At that time I never realised that this kind of lifestyle could be very harmful to my health.

Nairobi is a beautiful city. The weather was very pleasant. I did not realise that I was in Africa. In the evenings it was quite chilly. A jacket was necessary in the evening. I liked the place. There was a huge Indian community. Most of them had their own businesses. They were really thriving. Someone suggested that we should go to Mombassa, which was the second largest city after Nairobi in Kenya. Mombassa is a seaside town. Many tourists visit Mombassa specially for sea/sand/sunshine and a good night life. Bill and I caught a flight and went to Mombassa. The city had many Indian businessmen. They also were thriving. We came back to Nairobi by a two engine plane. I was sitting near a window and was looking through it. Suddenly I noticed that one of the engines had stopped. I got really scared. 'What happens if the other one stops as well?' I thought.

"Bill, one of the engines has stopped. It has only two engines," I informed Bill.

"We are life assurance salesmen. You do one large life assurance on me, I shall do the same on you. We already have forms which we can complete and sign," Bill said jokingly. He was equally scared.

"How do the forms get to Abbey Life?"

"We shall address them to Abbey Life and throw the envelopes from the plane window."

We just laughed it off even though we were scared. After that we kept quiet. I closed my eyes and prayed silently. It seemed no other passenger had noticed it. No one made any comment at all. After a while, I do not remember how long, the engine started. A few minutes after that the pilot announced, "We had a bit of engine trouble. That was the reason the plane was leaning on one side. The engine is alright now."

The next day I went to my Abbey Life office. I would get off at Oxford Circus tube station and walk about half a mile to reach the Abbey Life office. On the second day I found it a bit difficult to walk as briskly as I used to. On the third day I was even slower. I couldn't understand why I was not able to walk briskly. There was no pain or any other indication except that my movements were slower. On the fourth day I had gone very slowly and I was sweating. I couldn't carry on. I stopped and leaned against a wall. I couldn't even stand. The energy was ebbing away from me. I felt like fainting. I felt that perhaps it was my end. While I was leaning against the wall, I asked myself, 'Have I got sufficient life assurance for my family? Have I made my Will?' The answers to both were 'Yes'.

I arrived at my office and phoned my GP to arrange an immediate appointment. Luckily I got an appointment for three in the afternoon on the same day. I had a rest in my office and went to meet my GP at the appointed time. He asked me a few questions and prescribed a milky colour solution to take with a spoon, with every meal for a week. After five days I could not feel any improvement. It was Saturday morning. I wanted to resume my work from Monday. I couldn't see how I could resume my work in my situation. I had got very slow and was very tired. During those days, GPs used to work on Saturdays as well. I did not phone for an appointment; I just went to the surgery to consult any doctor available in the practice. There was a doctor who was a replacement for Saturdays only.

"Doctor, I am not getting better with the medicine I have been taking. In addition I have a bit of tightness in my chest. I suggest that you take my ECG."

"Our ECG machine is not working. Take this medicine I am prescribing. If you don't get better within a week, I shall send you to a hospital for an ECG."

Again he prescribed a milky solution to be taken one spoon with each meal.

"Doctor, what is this medicine?"

"It is milk of Magnesia. You have excessive acidity in your system."

I am a great believer in homeopathy medicines. I came home, opened my book on homeopathy and read the 'acidity' section. They had prescribed a medicine. I took one dose of it in the morning and one before going to bed. I did the same on the next day, which was Sunday. I got up on Monday morning. I was very surprised and glad that I was feeling much better. I had a good sleep as well. I realised, and was very confident, that I was then cured, and could go to my office and carry on working as normal. I was so glad to be able to walk normally that I felt like shouting at the top of my voice and telling everyone, 'I am cured now'.

6. Now it was early 1986, By that time my holiday flats and my restaurant in Paddington, were both established. I called my restaurant in Paddington 'Paddington Tandoori Restaurant', PTR for short. I was working hard; facing banks, the Inland Revenue, staff, clients, in the best possible way. That was the time my family problem started. I realised that I could work hard in the business and manage everything without much stress. I was enjoying my work. For me it was not hard work – it was enjoyment. My family problem gave me a lot of stress. Due to that I developed a terrible back pain. I carried on with my life and suffered this back pain without any painkiller medicines. The pain became so bad that it was very difficult for me to stand up from my sitting position. I had to roll over and then could get up. The pain became unbearable. I went to my GP for consultation.

"You are getting old. Take it easy. It is wear and tear."

I was only 52 years old. I felt that I was not that old to have to take it easy.

"Doctor, can you please help me?"

He prescribed painkillers for me. I thanked him. I thought 'painkillers will not cure me, they will just relieve me for a while'. It seemed I had to rely on those pills once I started on them.

A few years ago while I had visited India, I had bought a yoga wall chart. This was hanging on my bedroom wall. I had a look at it. I thought that I should help myself, as the doctor was not helping me. I went to the nearby library and borrowed two good books on yoga. I read them and found out which yoga positions would be beneficial for my back pain. I selected a few positions and regularly performed them. In addition, I started swimming as and when I could. Within a week I could feel a considerable benefit. I did not try any homeopathy medicines thinking that my back pain was not a disease, it was a warning to me. The body was telling me, be careful, do not abuse me, otherwise I shall abuse you. I started playing tennis with my manager team, Gary and Pam Parsons. We three would play at a nearby tennis court during lunchtimes. I am glad to write that I do not suffer from back pain at all now.

7. It was early 1987, I was offered to buy a restaurant property just 200 yards away from my office. I couldn't refuse. The owner had accepted my offer. It was mid-March 1987 that I finalised the deal and bought the property. According to the surveyor from my bankers, the property was gold dust. I was very happy and delighted that I had got a very good deal. The following week, as usual, we three went to play tennis. At that time I had been very much under pressure from my expanded work and also from my home front. It is futile to explain why and how I had trouble from my home front. I shall therefore leave it at that and proceed with my story.

The day was pleasant and not very hot. There was a cool breeze blowing as well, but for no reason at all I was feeling hot and started sweating. In the middle of our play, I stopped playing. I felt dizzy and everything went black for me. I couldn't stand and just went down in a heap. While I was lying on the ground, I could hear voices from very far away.

"Gary, is he dead?"
"I don't know!"
"Why don't you feel his pulse?" Gary came and felt my pulse.
"I can't feel anything. Perhaps his pulse has stopped."

"Don't be ridiculous. Vasu can't die like that."

"Shall I call an ambulance?" Gary asked. At that time we did not have mobile phones. It wasn't easy to call for an ambulance from the middle of a public park.

When I heard it I raised my hand. My eyes were still closed. All this time I was barely conscious. I was thinking and saying to myself, 'If I survive from here, I shall stop playing tennis and I shall slow down'.

Gary and Pam came near to me. I just uttered one word, 'Water'.

They tried to give me some water. I could barely open my mouth. A few drops of water went into my mouth. I then indicated to them to raise me in a sitting position. They supported me with three tennis bags we had brought with us. I opened my eyes and faintly smiled at them.

"Vasu. You gave us a scare."

I just nodded. I didn't have any energy to do anything else.

"Vasu, I shall bring my car around and take you to the office."

"Take me to my house."

"We do not know where you live."

"I am conscious now, I shall guide you."

They took me home. I was then fully conscious of what was happening. My wife called the doctor. He had a look at me and said, "You will be alright. Just have plenty of rest."

After a few days I started visiting my office. I was quite weak, so I was taking it easy.

I had an authority from Abbey Life to take clients for medical examinations, if needed. I felt that I should apply for more life assurance and take myself to a doctor for a medical examination. The doctor in Harley Street did a general medical examination on me and said, "You are fine, Vasu."

"What about an ECG, doctor?"

"Don't need it."

"I would like you to do an ECG on me. The insurance company is going to pay your fees."

After he performed an ECG on me, he started staring at the ECG graph. He became thoughtful.

"Doctor, what is wrong?"

"There is nothing wrong. Just every now and then the needle is jumping. I don't understand it."

"What does it indicate?"

"It seems you had a silent heart attack."

"I don't understand it."

"It seems you had a silent attack, perhaps in your sleep. Since you are fairly healthy, your body could withstand the knock. No harm done. You are alright now."

I never told him what had transpired a week before on the tennis court.

I thanked him. I also thanked God that he had saved me. He just had given me a warning. I heeded the warning. I stopped playing tennis. I also slowed down very much in my business activities. I delegated more work to Gary and Pam Parsons. Both were very helpful to me. They helped me as much as they could.

My brother Jaik, and his wife Haru, had come from India to the opening of my new restaurant. Haru remarked and said, "Vasu, you don't look right. Are you alright?"

"Yes, I am alright, just tired due to so much work."

"You don't look healthy. You look pale."

I just kept quiet and didn't tell them about my 'silent heart attack'. I didn't want to worry them.

Before the opening celebration of the restaurant, Jaik, Haru, my wife and I went for a holiday. We toured around England and Scotland for a week and came back fairly refreshed.

8. After that I became very careful with my health. I was well aware of the stresses in my life. I understood why they happen and its effect on my health. It is said, 'Knowledge is power'. I knew and understood it. I felt powerful and faced the stressful conditions in a positive way. I passed through my divorce which had dragged on for a while. I was lucky to face it and made sure that it did not affect my health in any way. In September 1988 I had come across a leaflet on rambling. I started rambling with the ramblers. Every Sunday without fail I would walk with them. The regular walking also boosted my health. I enjoyed good health. In 1995 I remarried. Now my married life was, and still is, a very happy one.

My wife likes to go to India at least once a year, if not twice. It was the year 2004 that she went to India for two months. It seemed that I had neglected my health. It was difficult to look after myself when I was used to being looked after by my wife. Suddenly I developed sciatica. I don't know if you have heard of it. It is very painful. The base of the back right down into both legs is very painful. It was very difficult to go for my Sunday ramble. I am very disciplined and I continued with my walking. The pain became unbearable. I couldn't get a good night's sleep. I went to my GP for consultation. He prescribed a medicine, I have forgotten the name of it. I was to take two pills very day for fifteen days. I started taking them. I took only for two days and my legs went numb. There was no feeling in my legs. In addition, I was getting migraine every half an hour. I got scared and stopped taking the tablets, (six months after that it came out in a national newspaper that the medicine the doctor had given me is banned. They found out that the medicine promotes a heart attack). Again I thanked God that he had given me the sense not to continue with that medicine. I would have suffered a heart attack if I had continued with them for fifteen days as suggested by my doctor. As usual I went for a ramble. It was fifteen miles walk. I noticed that once I started walking, I could carry on walking, but once I had stopped, it was very painful to start again. I told the leader, "I shall carry on walking even though the group wants to stop. You just point out to me which way you are going. I shall continue. The group can catch up with me." It worked. We had finished about twelve miles when we came across Harlow Railway Station. I was in agony. I thought that I could catch the train and go home. I told the leader, "I shall catch a train and go home. I am in terrible pain. I shall see you next Sunday."

I carried on with my life, just dragging myself about very slowly. Next Sunday I went for a ramble as usual. It was only twelve miles. But that day for rambling was very bad. It rained the whole day. I finished the walk, but I got completely soaked in the rain. I came home. When I had a shower, I felt that the water was not hot at all. I increased the temperature of the water, but still the water was not hot enough. I realised then that I had a fever. In addition, I caught a terrible cold in my head. My body was aching as well.

I had heard and read about 'detox'. The theory of detoxing is that the body accumulates some kind of poison. One can get rid of this poison naturally by eating little and easily digestible food for a day or two. I thought that perhaps I should try it and get rid of my health problems. For two days I did not eat anything. Whenever I was thirsty, I would drink a glass of warm water. Whenever I was hungry; which was not often due to fever, I would drink very weak milk. My cold had turned into catarrh. I was regularly sniffing eucalyptus oil. I did not go out at all, just stayed in bed most of the time. After the third day, in the morning I couldn't believe it; my sciatica pain was gone, my fever was gone and the catarrh had nearly gone. I felt hungry as well. I had a bowl of porridge. It was Thursday. I thought that if my recovery continued in this way I should be able to go for my Sunday ramble. I am pleased to write that my recovery was permanent; the sciatica has not come back yet. I was able to go to the Sunday ramble.

9. My wife came back from India. She had had a very good time with her family. She had seen a few Bollywood movies. It seemed two movies she had seen had been shot in Sun City in South Africa.

"I would like to go to South Africa and visit Sun City," she stated.

The following year my wife and I booked a holiday in South Africa. Not only did we visit Sun City, but we joined three jeep safaris while we were in South Africa. We also visited Victoria Falls in Zimbabwe. Victoria Falls are the highest falls in the world. The sight was amazing, one has to see it to believe it. We had booked three jeep safaris with our tour through the tour operator. They had arranged one in South Africa, one in Namibia and one in Botswana. All three safaris were very enjoyable. They had a good system whereby about six jeeps would start for the safari. Each one had a driver and a guide. The guide would be on the lookout to spot an animal. As soon as he spotted one, he would guide the driver to that place. Each jeep had an intercom contact with the base office. Any jeep spots an animal, the guide would contact the base office to let them know. Base office would let all the other jeeps know about it. By this way no jeep missed the animal. In South Africa, jeeps have certain tracks to follow. You could see the animal from the track, but the animal may be far away from the track. But on the other two safaris, jeeps could leave the track and go into the bush and we could view the animal from a very short distance, as short as ten yards. Once we were just ten yards away from a lion family. Our guide told us that we must not make any noise and we must not get out of our jeep.

We had told our tour operator, "It is our wedding anniversary. Please make all the hotels aware of it." All the hotels had given us special treatment wherever we went. They had upgraded our room; some had left flowers in our room, some had left a bowl of fruit, and one hotel had left a bottle of champagne. We were very delighted with the attention we received. But the treatment in Botswana was the ultimate. They had upgraded our room to a semi-presidential suite. Our suite had a large bedroom and a reception. There was room for an assistant and a drinks bar near the door. We also had our own private garden facing the Chobe River. The hotel manager had also left a bowl of fruit and a champagne bottle in an ice bucket. We were just amazed at the attention they gave us. We thought that we should play our part as well. My wife and I dressed in the best way we could and went down to the dining room. We passed near the reception. The receptionist was very cordial and wished us a happy wedding anniversary. The waiter had also paid special attention to us. It seemed everyone in the hotel knew that we were celebrating our wedding anniversary. The president of Madagascar was staying with his family in the hotel. When he passed our table in the dining room he also congratulated us. We had noticed that previously Bill Clinton and Nelson Mandela also had stayed in the same hotel. They had displayed a few photos in the reception area. The service in the hotel was absolutely fantastic.

The next evening was our last evening in the hotel. We arrived in the dining room. We were very surprised when the head waiter brought a celebration cake and placed it on our table. There was a musician who played 'For he's a jolly good fellow'. We didn't know what to say or do, we just grinned and thanked everyone present. After that fantastic evening, we went to our suite and sat for a while in our private garden looking at the scene of the Chobe River. While we were sitting, we could hear mosquitoes buzzing. I couldn't feel any bites, so I thought that they were not biting us. In the night we slept under the mosquito net. The following morning I was feeling a bit lethargic. I didn't understand. I thought that perhaps I was tired due to a very busy holiday. During the flight I felt that I had a bit of a fever. In the evening the fever was gone. I was happy that I had got rid of the fever. We arrived in London early morning. Again the fever came back. We arrived home safely. While I had a shower in the morning I noticed three large spots full of pus. I thought, but was not sure if they were mosquito bites. I immediately went to a 'walk-in NHS' centre.

I showed the spots to a doctor. The doctor prescribed a course of antibiotics and said, "Take two tablets a day for a week."

"What about the fever?"

"Take Paracetemol."

"How long for?"

"As long as it takes."

"Doctor, are these mosquito bites?"

"Could be."

"Is my fever a malarial fever?"

"Maybe."

I was very disappointed with the doctor's replies. He was not committing to anything at all. I came home and opened a homeopathy book I keep with me. There were six medicines prescribed for an intermittent fever. Five of them gave an indication that cause of fever may be due to trouble from inside of the body. Only one mentioned trouble from an external source like insect bites. The name of that medicine was Arsenic Alb. I know that arsenic is a deadly poison. Perhaps poison may kill and neutralise the poison of an insect bite? It is said, 'poison kills poison'. I took one dose in the morning and one dose before going to bed. I had a pleasant surprise when I found out that my fever was gone. That day I had a good rest to make sure that I recovered soon. The following day those three bites with pus had shrunk.

On the fourth day the pus was gone from them. In the next few days I couldn't see any indication that I had had three large bites. I had been lucky that the medicine had worked on me. One of my ramblers mentioned, "Vasu, you are lucky. People die from malaria if they don't take proper medicine. You didn't even have a course of quinine tablets. I always have quinine tablets when I go to any tropical countries." He was amazed that my homeopathy medicine had worked for me. I feel that they work on me because I believe in them. It is said, 'with belief, you have won half the battle'.

10.   Now we are in June 2007. I have continued rambling with the ramblers every Sunday. I went for the Sunday ramble. It was a twenty mile walk starting from Welwyn in Hertfordshire. It had rained heavily the night before. The ground was muddy and slippery. The weather was quite warm. Everything was fine. We had arrived at a pub to have our lunch and a beer. I had a pint of Guinness and a cheese sandwich which I had brought with me. We all started off to finish the walk. Half an hour after we started, I felt a bit uncomfortable. I thought that I should rest for a while. I sat down in the middle of the muddy field and told the leader, "You all go ahead, I shall catch up with you."

"We shall wait for you, Vasu."

After a few minutes I got up and had to sit down, I couldn't stand. One of the ramblers had his mobile phone and called for an ambulance. The ambulance took me to the QE2 Hospital in Welwyn Garden City. They were very efficient. A bed was ready for me. The hospital staff quickly gave me an oxygen mask, wired me to an ECG machine, and a blood pressure machine and took my reading for fever. After two hours observation, they could not find anything wrong with me but remarked, "You have an attack of angina."

"But doctor, I have no pain in my chest."

"Surely you must have a pain in your left-hand side of your chest."

"I have a bit of tightness but no pain." I had to go along with the idea of 'angina'.

"You have to stay in hospital for further observation."

"Since you haven't found anything and I am also feeling better, I would like to go home."

"You have to discharge yourself, because you are leaving against our instructions."

I discharged myself and caught a taxi from hospital to Welwyn where my car was parked. I drove carefully. In hospital they had given me some pills which were making me lethargic. I arrived safely. As soon as I was in my house, I felt faint. My wife had gone to India. She was due back in three days time. There was no one in the house. I wanted to have a cup of tea. I felt that I had no energy left to even make a cup of tea for myself. I went to bed for a rest. I was very uncomfortable during the night as well. I felt as if my energy and my life was ebbing away from me. Suddenly a thought came to my mind, 'Suppose I die and there is no one to help me. My wife would come home in three days time and find a dead body in the house. That would be tragic, wouldn't it?' I really got scared. Around five in the morning I phoned for an ambulance and said, "Please help me, I am dying." They asked me for my name, address and phone number and said, "Please keep your main door open so that we can enter." I put on my jacket and slippers, got hold of my house keys, a small amount of money and my freedom pass and went down. I opened the door. What did I see outside? An ambulance was waiting for me. They had been very quick. I thought that many people complain about the ambulance service. They had been very efficient in my case.

The ambulance took me direct to Wittington Hospital. It seemed the ambulance had phoned and reserved a bed for me. I was very impressed with the service I was given. The hospital staff very quickly gave me an oxygen mask, and wired me to an ECG machine and blood pressure machine. Every half an hour they came to take my temperature. Also they regularly gave me various pills to swallow. I was very impressed with the service. After investigation they pronounced, "You had an attack of angina." They also mentioned a list of health troubles I had, they were:

> You have an attack of angina
> Your heart is enlarged
> You have a fever
> Your blood pressure is low
> You have water in your lungs
> Your blood has very low oxygen
> You have high cholesterol

When I heard that I nearly died. My first day in the hospital was very stressful. They would visit me every half hour. I couldn't get a good sleep. Perhaps I couldn't due to my poor health. The next day the same kind of attention from the staff continued. They had even booked a bed in a heart hospital in Harley Street so that I could be operated on for my angina problem. I know a bit about angina. I know that the angina patient has a chest pain. I had no chest pain at all. I had no pain anywhere except in my arms where hospital staff had jabbed me to take some blood for blood tests. At least twenty times they took my blood for blood tests. Perhaps medical students were practising on me. I soon realised that I was being used as an experiment. My friend from the ramblers, Mr Philip Greswell, who had visited me in the hospital on the second day, told me a few months later when we were rtambling, "Vasu, I thought you were a goner. When I visited you, you were all wired up and looked very pale and helpless. Even the male nurse who attended you told me, 'Mr Vasu has lots of health problems'." Philip mentioned, "The way he said it, as if you would not survive." So possibly students were experimenting on me thinking that I was nearly gone.

On the second day around five in the afternoon, I got really sick and tired of staff coming to me every half an hour and either doing something to me or giving me pills to swallow. I thought that they were killing me with kindness.

"I want to go home," I told them.

"You can't go."

"Why not?"

"Wait till the doctor comes."

"I want to see him."

"You can't see him now. You can see him tomorrow morning, when he is on duty."

I had no choice but to wait for him.

The next morning I had breakfast and got ready to meet the doctor and then go home.

The doctor came, I told him, "I want to go home."

"You can't go home in your state."

"I want to go home. I am alright now."

"You will die if you go out of the hospital," the doctor was emphatic.

"I would rather die in my house than in a hospital."

"No. You can't go."

"I shall discharge myself. Please give me a paper which I shall sign."

With very strong persuasion, I discharged myself. To be on the safe side, they gave me thirty days of medicine to take for cholesterol, blood pressure, water on the lungs and low oxygen in the blood. Before I left I told the doctor, "I shall come and see you in four weeks time for the final check-up." He looked at me as if saying to me, 'You fool, you will not survive that long'.

I came home, freshened up and opened my homeopathy book. I thought that I should get rid of the fever which they still had not got rid of. In the book they had mentioned five medicines for fever. I read the 'fever' section very carefully. My eyes popped out. For one medicine it indicated, 'the patient is very uncomfortable lying on his left side'. I couldn't believe it. For the last year and a half I have been very uncomfortable lying on my left side. I took one dose then and another dose of that medicine before going to bed. What a miracle it was. My fever was gone. I had a very peaceful sleep as well. I was feeling much better. I even felt hungry. As the day passed I was feeling much better. The next day I felt so much better, as if I never had any problem with my health. I was just a bit weak. My wife also came back from India. Her return completed my recovery. In a few days time I was back to normal.

I waited for another week and made an appointment with the doctor for a general check-up. I went to meet the doctor in the hospital. He couldn't believe it when he saw me. On the contrary, he was upset when he saw me alive. After examining me, he said, "You are fully recovered now."

"For your information, I did not take any of the medicine you gave me." Then I added, "Do you want to know what medicine I took?"

He was neither interested in the medicine I had taken nor what indicated me to take that medicine.

"Doctor, I feel you are very busy. I shall write to you and let you know about it."

He was silent.

I wrote down all details of the medicine as well as the indication which promoted me to take that medicine. I handed it over to his assistant to be given to the doctor, and left. I did not get any response to my letter.

I was very happy that with the grace of God I got rid of my health problem. Just imagine they had booked me in the heart hospital for an operation. That operation would not have helped me. My health troubles would still have persisted. My homeopathy book had prescribed the medicine for 'sluggish liver' and got rid of all my health problems.

Looking at that list above, I can see that I have survived not nine times but ten times. So perhaps I am a supercat. I don't know how many more lives I have. LET US HOPE FOR THE BEST.

Epilogue

Why did I write my autobiography? What is so special about me that I should write it and get it printed so that others can read about me? It is very simple. In 1991, the children and I were on holidays in Cornwall and Devon. It was a long drive coming back to London. While I was driving, my son, Kris, asked me lots of questions about where I originally came from and how had I come to the UK, what made me come to the UK? What did I do and how did I do? He was very impressed and fascinated by my travels. He was also amazed that I had left my country of origin, left my joint family and settled down in the UK. Finally he said, "Why don't you write all about it? It would be a fascinating story. I feel people would like it a lot." At that time I was not ready. Also, the idea of people looking into my private life didn't grab me. During the last sixteen years I have done quite a lot, had a good life experience. I suddenly felt that I was ready to write all about myself My life has been an open book anyhow. Sometimes I sound rude and maybe rude, but it is unintentional. I accept my faults and ask for forgiveness.

Even though I came to the UK for only two years, two years became four years. During those four years I had been behaving like a self-appointed ambassador from India. I was always on good behaviour and ready to impart good information about India, specially Hindus. In 1968 I got married, to an English girl. I had a good opportunity to integrate with British society and continued being an ambassador. I have visited many countries; seen a lot of the world, met all kinds of people, met the Pope and shook hands with him. I felt that I had a lot to tell about my life experiences. After watching *Big Brother* in 2005, I thought that I should be one of the housemates in *Big Brother* so that I could impart my knowledge to a wider audience. I wrote to *Big Brother* – I am still awaiting their call.

I have come from a happy and truthful family. In our family no one lied, specially to harm anyone. It was not done in our family. From childhood I had seen lots of American western movies and read many western books by Max Brand, Clarence E. Mulford, Zane Grey and many more writers. Heroes in western books and films are always very straightforward people. They had their principles. They would never divulge from them, even in the face of death. If a hero was called a liar, there was a showdown with the hero, unless the culprit took back his words.

I became a volunteer for Cancer Research shops. I still am, in addition I became a volunteer for the Victim Support organisation. To help society, I passed three examinations in counselling so that I could help the older generation by giving them counselling.

During my life assurance days I sold lots of life assurance and pensions. I have lots of clients. These clients and their families became my life-long friends. I have learned a lot from Million Dollar Round Table meetings. One of the best lessons is, 'Advise your client in such a way as if you were sitting opposite to yourself, instead of your client'. That lesson has helped me quite a lot. My client would look at me as a helper, a helper to help them solve their financial problems.

I have written my autobiography as it happened. I have had a good life. In addition, my God has been very good to me. He has bestowed on me his grace and led me to a straight narrow path.

Hope you had a good time reading my book. I definitely had a fabulous time narrating it.

INDEX

Abbey Life	158, 268
Anita	100, 154
Ashley, Alan	239
Bell, Martin	152
Bettgar, Frank	187
Bhagvat, Gita	48, 86
Boati, Luciana	121
Boati, Angelo	124
Bonner, Bert &Barbara	239
Bonny and Clyde	101
Borde, Chandu	143
Boyes, Bill	260
Brand, Max	74
Brownjohn, Vic	235
Brooke MP, Peter	194
Chawla, Mohan	81
Cellaram, K	68
Churchill Winston	93
Clinton, Bill	278
Cooper, Gary	127
Dalrymple, William	260
Dayaram	54
Duke of Edinburgh	81, 93
Engineer, Farouk	142
Gidoomal, R	49
Gogia, Shyam	81
Greswell, Philip	237, 260, 281
Grey, Zane	286
Hamilton, Neil	152
Haru	202, 274
Hassaram, Lakhi	223

Hassaram, Pishu	223
Hawkins, Bob	111
Hinduja, Amar	57
Hinduja brothers	49, 58
Hiranand	34, 35, 51, 52
Holmes, Clive	168
Homeopathy	76, 87
Hornby, Ken	121, 254
Howarth, Ron	145
Jagasia Harry & Nimmi	84, 189
Jaik	30, 52, 201, 274
Jamna	42
Kanal	59
Kell, Ron	112
Khedekar, Chan	228
Kishinchand	188
Krishna	154
Kundaram	143
Kundnani, Gope &Mieke	66 73, 224, 225
Ladd, Alan	267
Lambelle, George	152
Lord Shiva	48
Macdonald, Ian	111
Macdonald, Douglas	111, 256
Macdonald, Stewart	111
Mandela, Nelson	278
Marshall, Alf	235
Mason, Roger	112
MDRT	159, 187
Mellows, Peter	237
Mahatma, Gandhi	47
Mother Theresa	37
Motiram	55
Mr and Mrs Khan	264
Mr and Mrs Newman	245

Mr and Mrs Patel	230
Mulford, Clarence E	40
Neeraj	205
Nina	172
Nyman, Edgar	235
O'Sullivan, Dan	172
Oberoi, Bill	268
Parsons, Gary & Pam	170, 171, 192, 272, 274
Patuadi, Nawab of	143
Pearson, John & Leslie	111
Pope, Len	112, 255
Pope John	128
Presland, Roy & Jeanette	236
RSS	33, 42, 47
Raft, George	37
Ramchand	45
Ramkrishna Mission	75, 77, 224
Rankin, Ian	147
Roberta	103
Rogers, Bill	112
Rogner, Gerd	242
Shalini	205
Shareef, Omar	147
Shetty, Shilpa	220
Simpson, John	231
Sitaldas	23
Southall Travels	206
Surti, Rusi	142
Satu & Kashin	66
Sujatha	202, 203, 204, 205
Sutton, Brenda	235
Tamane, Balwant	228
Tully, Mark	210
Vishwanath	143
Wadekar, Ajit	142

Wallace, Edgar	74
Watt MP, John	194
Wendy	236
Wetherspoons	173
Wheeler MP, John	194
Wills, Sheila	236